THE MARSHALL CAVENDISH ILLUSTRATED ENCYCLOPEDIA OF
WORLD WAR II

Volume 6

An objective, chronological and comprehensive history of the Second World War.

Authoritative text by
Lt. Colonel Eddy Bauer.

Consultant Editor
Brigadier General James L. Collins, Jr., U.S.A., Chief of Military History, Department of the Army.

Editor-in-Chief
Brigadier Peter Young, D.S.O., M.C., M.A., F.S.A. Formerly head of Military History Department at the Royal Military Academy, Sandhurst.

Marshall Cavendish New York & London

Editor-in-Chief Brigadier Peter
   Young, D.S.O., M.C., M.A., F.S.A.
Reader's Guide Christopher Chant, M.A.
Index Richard Humble
Consultant Editor Correlli Barnett,
   Fellow of Churchill College, Cambridge
Editorial Director Brian Innes
Illustrators Malcolm McGregor
                Pierre Turner
Contributors Correlli Barnett, Brigadier Michael Calvert, Richard Humble,
   Henry Shaw, Lt.-Col. Alan Shepperd, Martin Blumenson, Stanley L. Falk,
   Jaques Nobécourt, Colonel Rémy, Brigadier General E. H. Simmons
   U.S.M.C. (ret'd), Captain Donald Macintyre, Jonathan Martin, William
   Fowler, Jenny Shaw, Dr. Frank Futrell, Lawson Nagel, Richard Storry,
   John Major, Andrew Mollo.
Cover Design Tony Pollicino
Production Consultant Robert Paulley
Production Controller Patrick Holloway
Cover illustration The end of war;
   Corporal C. Dunn, U.S.M.C., raises the U.S. Flag over Yokosuka Naval
   Base in Japan.

Reference Edition Published 1981

Published by Marshall Cavendish Corporation
147 West Merrick Road, Freeport, N.Y. 11520
©Orbis Publishing Ltd. 1980, 1979, 1978, 1972
©1966 Jaspard Polus, Monaco

Printed in Great Britain by Jarrold and Sons Ltd.

Bound in Great Britain by Cambridge University Press

Cataloguing in Publication Data

Marshall Cavendish Encyclopedia of World War II.
   1. World War, 1939-1945—Dictionaries
   I. Young, Peter, *1915-*
   940.53'03'21   D740

   ISBN 0-85685-948-6 (set)
   ISBN 0-85685-954-0 (volume 6)

Picture Acknowledgements
Page 1401: U.S. Army; 1402: Bundesarchiv, Koblenz; 1403: Keystone, H. Le Masson; 1404/1405: Keystone; 1406: Bundesarchiv, Koblenz; 1407: Orbis, 1408/1409: Imperial War Museum; 1410: Keystone; 1411: Keystone; 1412: Popperfoto; 1413: Popperfoto; 1414/1415: Orbis; 1416: Keystone, H. Le Masson; 1417: Bundesarchiv, Koblenz; 1418/1419: Keystone; 1420: Bundesarchiv, Koblenz; 1421: Bundesarchiv, Koblenz, *Simplicissimus;* 1422: Keystone; 1423: Orbis/Alan Rees; 1424: Keystone; 1425: Keystone; 1426: Bundesarchiv, Documentation Française; 1427: Fox Photos; 1428: Keystone, I.W.M./Camera Press; 1428/1429: Fox Photos; 1429: I.W.M./Camera Press; 1430: Orbis; 1431: Keystone, Fox Photos, Keystone; 1432: Fox Photos; 1432/1433: U.S. Air Force; 1433: Fox Photos; 1434: I.W.M./Camera Press; 1435: I.W.M./Camera Press, I.W.M./Camera Press, I.W.M./Camera Press, Keystone, I.W.M./Camera Press; 1436: Fox Photos, I.W.M./Camera Press, I.W.M./Camera Press; 1437: Fox Photos; 1438: Ullstein, Keystone; 1439: Keystone; 1440: Orbis; 1441: Imperial War Museum, Keystone; 1442: Imperial War Museum; 1442/1443: Fox Photos; 1443: Fox Photos; 1444: Imperial War Museum; 1445: Orbis; 1446: Conway Maritime Press; 1447: Keystone, I.W.M./Camera Press; 1448: U.S. Air Force; 1448/1449: Bibliothek für Zeitgeschichte, Konrad Adenauer/Foliot; 1449: Bibliothek für Zeitgeschichte, Konrad Adenauer/Foliot, *Signal*/Nicole Marchand; 1450: I.W.M./Camera Press, Keystone; 1451: Orbis; 1452: H. Le Masson, Imperial War Museum, Imperial War Museum; 1453: Süddeutscher Verlag; 1454: Conway Maritime Press; 1455: U.S. Army; 1456: I.W.M./U.P.I.; 1457: Imperial War Museum; 1458: Camera Press, Orbis; 1459: Orbis; 1460: Camera Press; 1461: U.P.I.; 1462: U.S. Army, Fox Photos; 1463: Camera Press; 1464: Keystone; 1465: Conway Maritime Press; 1466: Keystone, Fox Photos; 1467: Keystone, U.P.I.; 1468: Fox Photos; 1468/1469: Fox Photos; 1469: Fox Photos, U.S. Army; 1470: Imperial War Museum; 1471: Holmès-Lebel; 1472: Fox Photos, Imperial War Museum; 1473: Camera Press; 1474: U.S. Army, U.P.I.; 1475: Fox Photos; 1476: H. Le Masson; 1477: Imperial War Museum; 1478: Keystone, Camera Press, H. Le Masson; 1479: Documentation Française; 1480: Keystone, Musée de la Guerre, Vincennes/Dorka; 1481: Imperial War Museum; 1482: *New York News, Evening News;* 1483: *Daily Mirror;* 1484; Orbis; 1485: I.W.M./Camera Press; 1486: Orbis; 1487: Orbis; 1488: Keystone; 1489: Orbis/Alan Rees, Musée de la Guerre/Vincennes; 1490/1491: Imperial War Museum, I.W.M./Camera Press; 1492: I.W.M./Camera Press; 1493: Holmès–Lebel, I.W.M./Camera Press; 1494/1495: U.S. Army; 1496/1497: I.W.M./Camera Press; 1497: Imperial War Museum; 1498: Imperial War Museum, Keystone; 1499: H. Le Masson, I.W.M./Camera Press; 1500: Keystone; 1501: Keystone; 1502/1503: Keystone; 1503: Imperial War Museum; 1504: Keystone; 1505: U.S.I.S., Robert Hunt Library; 1506: I.W.M./Camera Press; 1507: H. Le Masson, H. Le Masson, I.W.M./Camera Press; 1508: Bibliothek für Zeitgeschichte, Konrad Adenauer/Foliot; 1509: United Press; 1510: Documentation Française, H. Le Masson; 1511: H. Le Masson, Keystone; 1512: Orbis; 1513: Orbis; 1514: Keystone; 1515: Camera Press, Imperial War Museum; 1516/1517: I.W.M./Camera Press; 1517: Keystone; 1518: Imperial War Museum, John Hillelson; 1519: U.S. Army; 1520: John Hillelson; 1521: Musée de la Guerre Vincennes/Dorka, Fox Photos; 1552: Keystone, Camera Press; 1523: Keystone, Camera Press; 1524: Camera Press, Keystone; 1525: Camera Press; 1526: I.W.M./E. Tweedy; 1527: New York Public Library/Nicole Marchand, Keystone; 1528: Black Star; 1529: New York Public Library/Nicole Marchand; 1530: Keystone; 1531: Black Star, Keystone; 1532: I.W.M./E. Tweedy; 1533: Keystone; 1534: Fox Photos; 1535: Fox Photos; 1536: Keystone; 1537: Keystone; 1538: Keystone; 1539: Keystone; 1540: Fox Photos; 1541: U.S. Army; 1542: Documentation Française; 1543: Keystone; 1544: Keystone; 1545: I.W.M.: 1546: Keystone; 1547: Keystone; 1548: Keystone; 1549: Orbis/Alan Rees, Musée de la Guerre Vincennes/Dorka; 1550: Keystone; 1551: Keystone; 1552: Orbis; 1553: I.W.M., I.W.M./Camera Press; 1554: U.S. Army; 1555: U.S. Army; 1556: I.W.M.; 1557: Orbis; 1558: U.S.I.S.; 1559: I.W.M., Bettmann Archive; 1560: Orbis/Alan Rees; 1561: I.W.M.; 1562: Associated Press, *Daily Express;* 1563: Documentation Française, I.W.M./Camera Press; 1564: Orbis; 1565: Orbis; 1566: I.W.M./Camera Press; 1567: Keystone, I.W.M.; 1568: U.S. Army; 1569: U.S. Army; 1570: Keystone, I.W.M.; 1571: U.S. Army; 1572: U.S.I.S., Keystone; 1573: Keystone, U.S.I.S.; 1574: Associated Press; 1575: U.S. Army; 1577: Süddeutscher Verlag; 1578: Orbis; 1579: Orbis; 1580: Barnaby's Picture Library; 1581: Ullstein; 1582: Bundesarchiv, Koblenz; 1583: Documentation Française; 1584: Popperfoto; 1586: Ullstein; 1587: Ullstein; 1588: Orbis; 1589: Orbis; 1590: Ullstein; 1591: U.P.I.; 1592: Ullstein; 1593: Ullstein; 1594: Ullstein; 1595: Popperfoto; 1596: Keystone; 1597: Ullstein, Popperfoto, Keystone; 1598: Süddeutscher Verlag; 1599: Documentation Française; 1600: Bibliothèque de Nanterre/Foliot; 1601: Musée de la Guerre Vincennes/Dorka; 1602: Associated Press; 1603: Popperfoto; 1604: *Sondagnisse Strix,* Stockholm, Kukryniksy, *New York Post;* 1605: Novosti; 1606: Kukryniksy/Nicole Marchand, Kukryniksy; 1607: Kukryniksy/Foliot; 1608: Kukryniksy; 1609: Kukryniksy; 1610: Camera Press; 1611: Camera Press; 1612: I.W.M./Tweedy; 1613: I.W.M./Tweedy; 1614: I.W.M./Tweedy; 1615: I.W.M./Tweedy; 1616: Snark International; 1617: Musée de la Guerre Vincennes/Dorka; 1618: Barnaby's Picture Library; 1619: Black Star; 1620: Psywar Society; 1621: Psywar Society, I.W.M./R. R. Raikes; 1626: *Signal*/Nicole Marchand; 1627: I.W.M./Camera Press; 1628: Novosti; 1629: Camera Press/Tass, Novosti; 1630: Novosti, U.S.I.S.; 1631: Novosti; 1632: Orbis; 1633: Novosti; 1634: Novosti; 1635: Novosti; 1636: Camera Press/Tass; 1637: Keystone, Camera Press/Tass; 1638: *Signal*/Nicole Marchand; 1639: Novosti; 1640: Ullstein/Dr. Paul Wolff und Tritschler; 1641: Staatsbibliothek, Berlin, Bundesarchiv, Koblenz; 1642: Kukryniksy/Nicole Marchand; 1643: Novosti, Keystone, Keystone; 1644: Novosti; 1644/1645: Novosti; 1645: Novosti; 1646: Bibliothek für Zeitgeschichte/Konrad Adenauer, I.W.M./Tweedy: 1647: Novosti; 1648/1649: Orbis; 1650: H. Le Masson; 1650/1651: Novosti; 1651: Novosti; 1652: Keystone, Novosti; 1653: Novosti, Pictorial Press; 1654: Orbis/Alan Rees; 1655: Bibliothek für Zeitgeschichte/Stuttgart; 1656: Novosti; 1657: Novosti; 1658: *Signal*/Nicole Marchand; 1659: Keystone; 1660: *Krokodil,* Moscow, *Göteborg Hand Tidning,* Gothenburg, *Detroit Star;* 1661: Novosti, H. Le Masson; 1662: Novosti, Robert Hunt Library; 1663: Camera Press; 1664: Orbis; 1665: Novosti; 1666: Bibliothek für Zeitgeschichte; 1667: Novosti; 1668: Novosti; 1669: Dr. Alexander Bernfes; 1670/1671: Polish Underground Movement (1939-1945) Study Trust (P.U.M.S.T.); 1671: P.U.M.S.T.; 1672: P.U.M.S.T.; 1672/1673: P.U.M.S.T.; 1674: I.W.M./Tweedy; 1675: P.U.M.S.T.; 1676: P.U.M.S.T.; 1677: Orbis/Alan Rees; 1678: P.U.M.S.T.; 1679: P.U.M.S.T.; 1680: Dr. A. Bernfes, P.U.M.S.T., P.U.M.S.T.

Contents of Volume Six

CHAPTER 107
Threadbare fortress

△ *Dusk watch on the Channel at a German flak post. Beach obstacles can be seen on the foreshore.*

Though it is now more than 30 years after they occurred, there is no difficulty in reconstructing the logical succession of events which in less than 11 months–from June 1944–would take the Western Allies from the Normandy beaches to the heart of the Third Reich. But does this mean that everything was already fore-ordained and that "History", as those who do not know it say, had already rendered its verdict?

Allied landings to be thrown back

On March 20, 1944, Adolf Hitler delivered an appreciation of the situation to the commanders-in-chief of his land, sea, and air forces in the Western theatre of operations. By and large, he was less pessimistic with regard to the immediate future than most of his generals, and the arguments he advanced were not without relevance. As he considered the threat assembling on the other side of the Channel, he no doubt remembered his own hesitation in autumn 1940 and the arguments he had put to Mussolini and Count Ciano in January 1941 to excuse his procrastination over Operation "See-löwe".

"We are", he had told them, "in the position of a man with only one cartridge in his rifle. If he misses the target, the situation becomes critical. If the landing fails, we cannot begin again because we would have lost too much *matériel* and the enemy could bring the bulk of his forces into whichever zone he wanted.

But so long as the attack has not come, he must always take into account that it may."

And so, according to Rommel, he declared to his generals, whom he summoned that day to the Berghof:

"It is evident that an Anglo-American landing in the West will and must come. How and where it will come no one knows. Equally, no kind of speculation on the subject is possible . . . The enemy's entire landing operation must under no circumstances be allowed to last longer than a matter of hours or, at the most, days, with the Dieppe attempt as a model. Once the landing has been defeated it will under no circumstances be repeated by the enemy. Quite apart from the heavy casualties he would suffer, months would be needed to prepare for a renewed attempt. Nor is this the only factor which would deter the Anglo-Americans from trying again. There would also be the crushing blow to their morale which a miscarried invasion would inflict. It would, for one thing, prevent the re-election of Roosevelt in America and with luck he would finish up somewhere in jail. In England, too, war-weariness would assert itself even more greatly than hitherto and Churchill, in view of his age and his illness, and with his influence now on the wane, would no longer be in a position to carry through a new landing operation. We could counter the numerical strength of the enemy— about 50 to 60 divisions—within a very short time, by forces of equal strength. The destruction of the enemy's landing attempt means more than a purely local decision on the Western front. It is the sole decisive factor in the whole conduct of the war and hence in its final result."

And so Hitler made the final issue of the conflict depend on the check that his enemies would receive during the first hours of the landing on the coasts of France. Hitler's vision was clear. There can be no doubt that a defeat of the nature of the one suffered by the 2nd Canadian Division at Dieppe, but five times as great, would have struck a terrible blow at the morale of the British and Americans. Nor can there be any doubt that long months, perhaps even a year, would have passed before the Allies could launch another attack.

By that time, O.K.H. would have received the necessary means from the West to stabilise the situation between the Black Sea and the Gulf of Finland,

△ *Too late for Dönitz. One of the superb new Type XXI U-boats with which Hitler, clutching at any straw, boasted that he would win the Battle of the Atlantic in 1944, lies impotently in dry dock with one of its smashed predecessors slumped against its flank.*
◁ *Genuine advantage for the U-boat arm: a boat fitted with an air-breathing Schnorkel.*

while the Luftwaffe and the Kriegsmarine would have once more challenged the British and Americans by bringing new arms of terrifying efficiency into use.

New weapons

1. V-1 and V-2
It is, in fact, well known that the strides forward taken by German science in the field of jet propulsion could have taken a heavy toll of the British and American bomber squadrons if they had been applied with priority to fighter interception. In addition to (and in spite of) the delays caused by the bombing of Peenemünde on the night of the August 17–18, 1943, the Wehrmacht was still getting ready its new attack on London with the help of its V-1 flying bomb and V-2 rocket. The former, flying at a maximum speed of 410 mph, was still within the capacity of

▽ and ▽ ▽ How the Atlantic Wall defences were portrayed in the German illustrated press: massive cliffs of concrete and guns frowning from their emplacements. But apart from the Pas-de-Calais and a few other sectors the Atlantic Wall had not even been started by the end of 1943.

fighter defence and anti-aircraft fire, but not so the V-2. This was a real missile in the sense in which we now use the word. It plunged on to its target at a speed close to 2,350 mph and was unstoppable. These missiles, carrying nearly a ton of explosive, had a range of between 190 and 250 miles. The V-1 was technically simple and could be mass-produced, unlike the V-2 which was more complex and suffered considerable teething troubles.

2. The 'Schnorkel'

At the time when Hitler was expressing the opinions just quoted, U-boats fitted with the *Schnorkel* (or more properly *Schnorchel*) device were first appearing in the Atlantic. This device had been invented in the Netherlands, and consisted of a retractable pipe through which, so long as it stayed at a depth of 20 to 25 feet under water, a U-boat could run its diesels and vent its exhaust. The U-boats could also recharge their batteries without surfacing for weeks on end.

It has been calculated that from summer 1944 the *Schnorkel* had become so common that the success rate of Allied

△ △ *A stepped concrete gun embrasure, designed to give maximum shelter from offshore bombardment and air bombing.*
△ *Anti-tank wall. Both sides learned from the Dieppe raid, where the sea wall had thwarted the attempt to push Churchill tanks off the beaches.*

destroyers in their battle against the submarines had fallen by half. But there is a bad side to everything and, some 15 years ago, Admiral Barjot wrote in this connection:

"On the other hand, the *Schnorkel* slowed down their strategic speed. From a surface speed of 17 knots (20 mph) the *Schnorkel*–equipped submarines found their rate reduced to six knots (6 or 7 mph). The unavoidable delays in reaching their targets were doubled or even tripled."

The consequences he drew can be illustrated by the following: of the 120 operational boats, 39 were in port and 81 at sea. Of the last, 64 were in transit and only 17 actually in their operational sectors.

"So," Barjot concludes, "in April 1942, though the number of operational submarines was similar, only 23 per cent of them were in transit, whereas after the *Schnorkel* had been fitted, half of the U-boats were in transit."

Therefore at best the *Schnorkel* was only a palliative for the problems faced by Dönitz, and there was even another disadvantage: it appeared on the screens of the new British and American radar

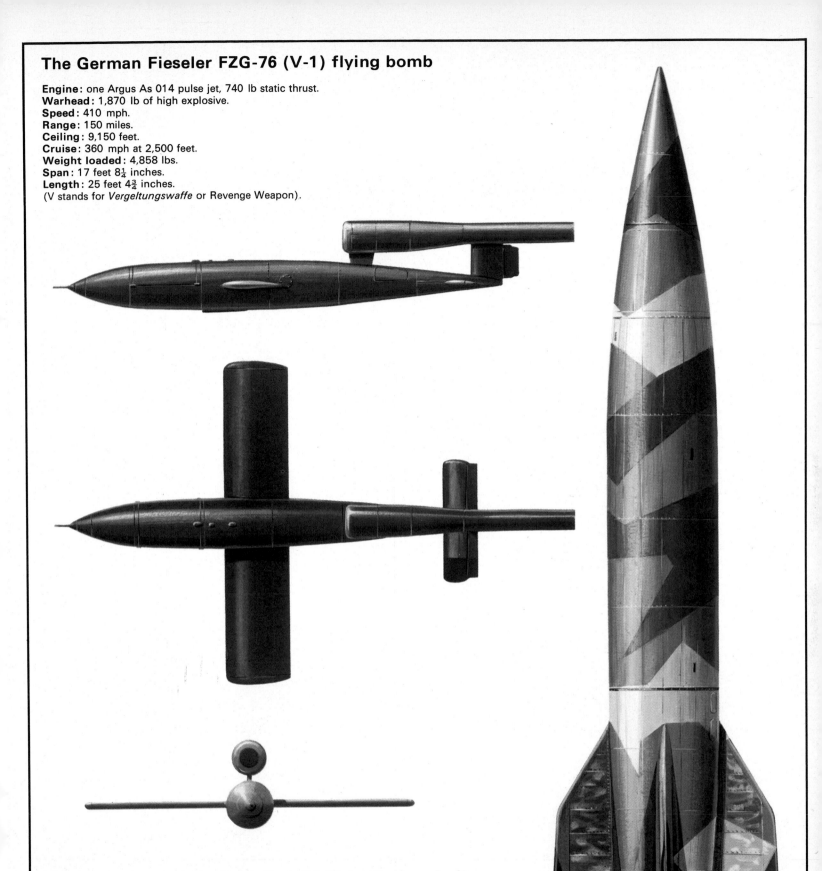

The German Fieseler FZG-76 (V-1) flying bomb

Engine: one Argus As 014 pulse jet, 740 lb static thrust.
Warhead: 1,870 lb of high explosive.
Speed: 410 mph.
Range: 150 miles.
Ceiling: 9,150 feet.
Cruise: 360 mph at 2,500 feet.
Weight loaded: 4,858 lbs.
Span: 17 feet $8\frac{1}{4}$ inches.
Length: 25 feet $4\frac{3}{4}$ inches.
(V stands for *Vergeltungswaffe* or Revenge Weapon).

The German Peenemünde A-4 (V-2) ballistic missile

Engine: one liquid oxygen- and ethyl alcohol-fuelled liquid propellant rocket, 70,000 lbs of thrust.
Warhead: 2,150 lbs of high explosive.
Speed: 3,440 miles per hour maximum.
Range: 185 miles.
Weight loaded: 28,500 lbs.
Diameter: 5 feet 5 inches.
Height: 46 feet 11 inches.
Span: 11 feet 8 inches (across fins).

sets operating on centrimetric wavelengths.

3. The Type XXI . . .

On the other hand, if the Type XXI and XXVI U-boats had come into service earlier, they might have been able to change the course of the submarine war.

The Type XXI U-boat, beautifully designed, was driven under water by two electric engines with a total of 500 horsepower. These enabled it to travel for an hour and a half at the up till then unheard of speed of 18 knots (21 mph) or for ten hours at a speed of between 12 and 14 knots (14 or 16 mph). It could, therefore, hunt convoys while submerged and then easily avoid the attack of the convoy escort. Furthermore, it was remarkably silent and could dive to a depth of more than 675 feet, an advantage not to be scorned in view of the limitations of the listening devices used by its enemies.

Dönitz intended to use prefabricated

◁ ◁ Above and below: *V-1s are prepared for launching, and one is shown taking off. About the size of a fighter aircraft the V-1 was powered by a pulse-jet which emitted a characteristic guttural drone, hence its other nickname "buzz-bomb". The pulse-jet cut out over the target and the missile plunged to earth. That was the theory; they were wildly erratic machines.*

◁ *Engineers prepare a V-2 rocket for launching. The V-2 was a much more formidable proposition than the V-1 as its approach could not be detected.*

△ *and* ▽ *How they looked in flight—the sinister dagger-shape of the V-1 with its stabbing pulse-jet exhaust flame, and the streamlined shape of a V-2 lifting off.*

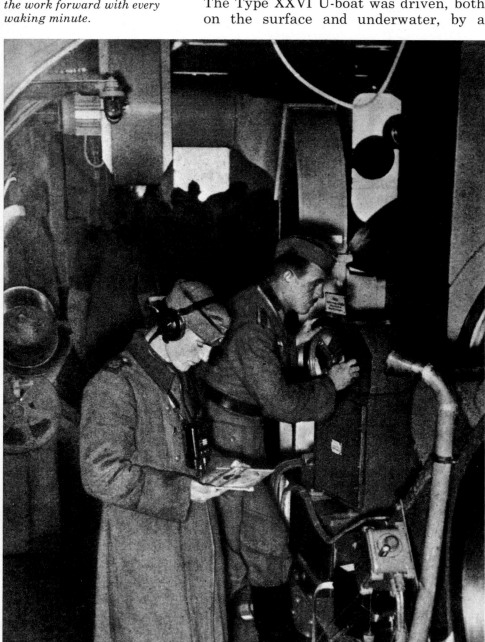

▽ *Fire-control centre in one of the big German coastal batteries.*

▷ ▷ Above and below: *The man who nearly made a myth into a terrifying reality for the Allies: Erwin Rommel. Within weeks of being appointed to inspect the defences of the West he had toured the entire coast from the Pyrenees to the Danish frontier and was horrified with how little he found. Rommel threw himself into his new task with characteristic energy. As in Africa in the old days he was everywhere, inspecting, exhorting, criticising, and urging the work forward with every waking minute.*

methods of production and thus hoped to see the new U-boats come off the slipways at a rate of 33 per month from autumn 1944 onwards. The parts would be assembled in three yards, in concrete shelters. But he had failed to take into account the destruction of the German railway system under the hammer blows of British and American strategic bombing, and so the pieces which had been prefabricated in the heart of the country reached the assembly shops at very irregular intervals.

And, in fact, of this class of ship, only *U-2511* (Lieutenant-Commander A. Schnee) actually went to sea on service. This was on April 30, 1945.

4. . . . and XXVI U-boats

The Type XXVI U-boat was driven, both on the surface and underwater, by a Walter turbine which used hydrogen peroxide and could reach, even while submerged, speeds of 24 knots (28 mph), that is four times the best performance claimed for its British or American rivals.

But neither type was operational by the time Germany capitulated. The fact is, however, that after the war, the Type XXVI U-boat was copied by all the navies of the world, and has sailed in particular under the Soviet flag, which calls to mind, inevitably, that imitation is the sincerest form of flattery.

Evidently then, the Führer had quite a number of good cards up his sleeve, but only – as he himself admitted – provided that his Western enemies could be wiped out on the beaches on the very day they landed, for the Wehrmacht could no longer fight a long holding battle between the rivers Orne and Vire. The situation demanded unquestionably that victory in the West should be swift, so that the victors could be sent with the minimum delay to the Eastern Front.

But the least that can be said is that on this front, considered decisive by Hitler, the German high command was as badly organised as it could possibly be, perhaps by virtue of the principle "divide and rule".

On the other side of the English Channel, General Eisenhower had absolute control not only over the land forces in his theatre of operations, but also over the naval forces under Admiral Sir Bertram Ramsey and over the Tactical Air Forces commanded by Air Chief-Marshal Sir Trafford Leigh-Mallory. He also retained overall command of Lieutenant-General Carl A. Spaatz's Strategic Air Force. The situation was quite different at Saint-Germain-en-Laye, headquarters of the Commander-in-Chief West or O.B.W. *(Oberbefehlshaber West)* and at la Roche-Guyon, headquarters of Army Group "B".

Lack of co-operation

The O.B.W., Field-Marshal von Rundstedt, was not entitled to give orders to Admiral Krancke, who commanded German naval forces in the West, to Field-Marshal Sperrle, head of *Luftflotte* III, to General Pickert, who commanded III Anti-Aircraft Corps. Krancke came directly under the command of Grand-Admiral Dönitz, and the two others were responsible to *Reichs-*

marschall Göring. Of course Krancke had only a small number of light ships and Sperrle found his forces reduced by June 6 to 419 aircraft, of which just 200 were operational. Nevertheless, considering that the aim was to destroy the enemy on the beaches, the lack of coordination between the three arms was to have catastrophic consequences for Germany.

In regard to the Navy it should be said that though Rommel, commanding Army Group "B", had a judiciously chosen naval attaché on his staff in the person of Vice-Admiral Ruge, he still could not manage to make Krancke lay down a sufficiently thick minefield in the estuary of the Seine. Yet the Germans possessed a mine triggered by the pressure wave of a ship passing over it, and this could have

△ Rommel, complete with his familiar desert goggles, holds a snap conference on Panzer tactics in the field. Thanks to Hitler's vacillation he failed to get complete control of all Panzer units in France, which was to have serious effects on the German defensive deployment.
▷ Intended to prevent French hopes from getting too high: the spectre of Dieppe is evoked by German propaganda.

INVASION

CIMETIÈRE DES ALLIÉS

proved a devastating weapon.

In addition to these already considerable failings, naval gunners and army men could not reach agreement on the question of coastal batteries, their location, and the fire control methods to be used. The ex-Commander-in-Chief in Norway, Colonel-General von Falkenhorst, later expressed his thoughts in terms which were rather critical of his naval colleagues, when he wrote:

"When I look back, I can see that responsibilities were badly apportioned, and that this brought several mistakes in its train. The results were severe overwork, difficulties, and conflict. Army artillery officers had received a totally different training from the naval gunners, a training which had developed under very different sets of circumstances. Moreover, the ideas of the older senior officers—the generals and the admirals—on the problems often differed greatly. The locations of covered or uncovered batteries, camouflage, the setting of obstacles, etc, were in general fields which were entirely new to the naval gunners, since these problems never arose on board their ships, and, consequently, did not appear in their training schedules. They used naval guns as they had been installed by the engineers and could not or would not change anything at all. The result of this was that, all along the coast, batteries were set in the open, near the beaches, so that they were at the mercy of the direct fire of every enemy landing ship but could not effectively contribute to the defence of the coast. There followed several most unhappy conflicts between generals and admirals."

Falkenhorst, who had installed 34 coastal defence batteries covering the approaches to Bergen, would seem competent to level these criticisms. Some of these guns, between Narvik and Harstad, were of 16-inch calibre. It is nonetheless true that the naval gunners also had some right on their side, because the army gunners thought they could hit moving targets like ships by using indirect fire methods.

Göring's malign influence

The deployment of anti-aircraft forces also created new tension between the arms. This time the disagreement arose between the commanders of the land and air forces, under whose joint command the anti-aircraft defences came. Rommel knew, better than anyone else, how efficient the 8.8-cm anti-aircraft gun could be when used as an anti-tank gun, and he would have liked to place a large number of such batteries between the Orne and the Vire. But Göring was obstinately opposed to any such redeployment and Rommel had to resign himself to not having his own way.

This tension lasted after the Allied landing, and brought these bitter words from Colonel-General Sepp Dietrich of the *Waffen*-S.S., commander of the 5th *Panzerarmee*:

"I constantly ordered these guns to stay forward and act in an anti-tank rôle against Allied armour. My orders were just as often countermanded by Pickert, who moved them back into the rear areas to protect administrative sites. I asked time and time again that these guns be put under my command, but I was always told by the High Command that it was

impossible."

On the other hand, Major-General Plocher, chief-of-staff of *Luftflotte* III at the time, has taken up the cudgels for Pickert:

"We had insisted on these guns being controlled by Luftwaffe officers because the army did not know how to handle such equipment. There was always a great deal of argument about who was to deploy the 88's but Field-Marshal von Rundstedt finally allowed us to chose our own localities." He adds, with a sting in the tail: "This was necessary in order to prevent the army from squandering both men and equipment. We used to say that the German infantryman would always fight until the last anti-aircraft man."

The least that can be said of these incoherent remarks is that, though Rommel and Rundstedt had received orders to wipe out the Allied landings in the shortest time possible, they were refused part of the means necessary to carry out their orders.

△ *The work goes forward. More concrete defences are piled up at Lorient. The Atlantic ports were the natural foci for the extension of the Atlantic Wall complex.*

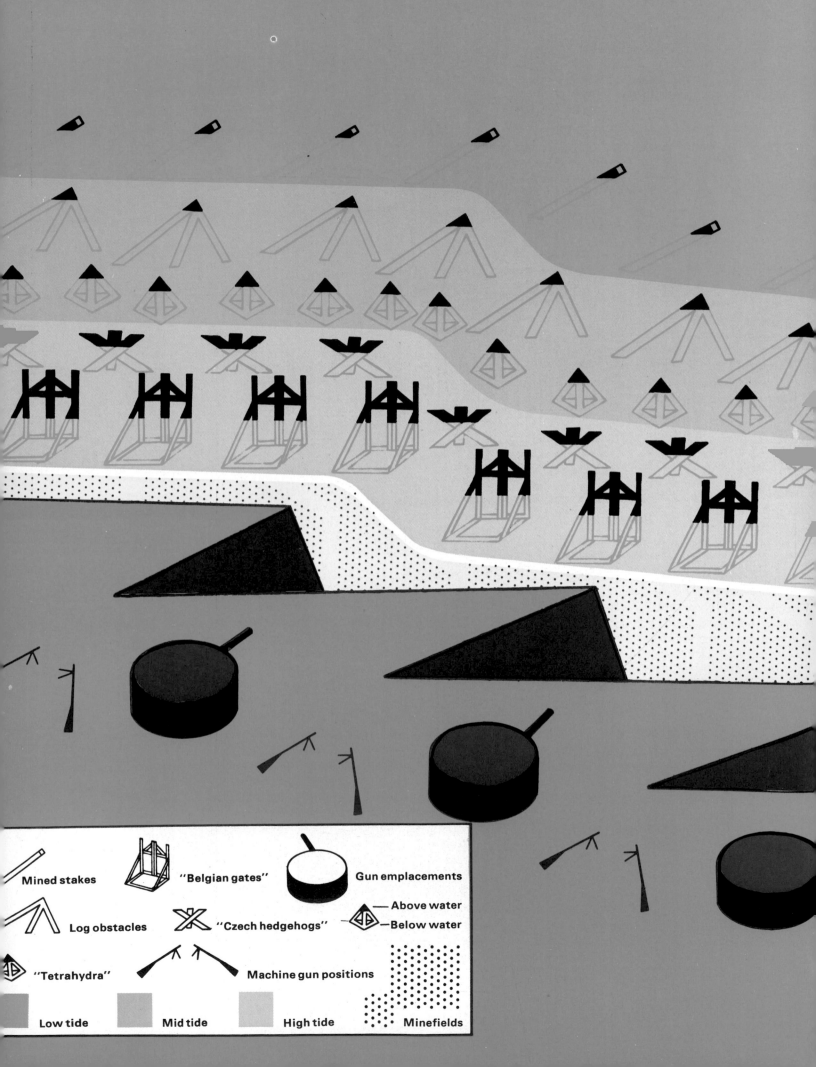

Mined stakes

"Belgian gates"

Gun emplacements

Log obstacles

"Czech hedgehogs"

— Above water

— Below water

"Tetrahydra"

Machine gun positions

Low tide

Mid tide

High tide

Minefields

ATLANTIC WALL: THE ROMMEL PLAN

How Rommel planned to win the "battle of the beaches"—with a sketch he made to show how the various elements of the foreshore defences should be integrated. Whatever the state of the tide when the Allies finally landed, he hoped to keep their assault troops floundering on the beaches under constant fire until they lost heart and re-embarked. This diagram shows all the main obstacles planted along the invasion beaches, in the form they would have taken if Rommel had been given a few more months to extend and complete the defences.

CHAPTER 108

Rommel's achievement

△ *Rommel (left) confers on the siting of a new battery with German Navy officers. His chief Navy liaison man, Admiral Ruge, found that Rommel's no-nonsense approach made him an easy man to work with over practicalities.*

▽ *German flak crew goes through gun-drill . . .*
▷ *. . . as do their comrades on a torpedo-boat.*

On D-Day, Rundstedt, as Commander-in-Chief in the West, had the following under his command: two army groups ("B" and "G"), comprising four armies (7th, 15th, 1st, and 19th). These in turn had 15 corps between them, totalling 40 infantry, four parachute, four Luftwaffe field, nine Panzer, and one *Panzergrenadier* divisions.

However, for all this it is by no means true that Rundstedt exercised over this force the authority normally given to a commander-in-chief. In the first place, the Luftwaffe units (one corps, eight divisions) were only under his tactical command; the same was true of his four *Waffen*-S.S. divisions and the I S.S. Panzer Corps. He had no authority over these units in the questions of training, promotions, the appointment of commanders or in the field of discipline. That is what Hitler cruelly reminded Rommel, who had requested that action be taken against the 2nd *"Das Reich"* Panzer Division of the *Waffen*-S.S., after the appalling massacre at Oradour-sur-Glâne.

Even more, O.B.W. had had it made quite clear that it could not, without the Führer's permission, move two of its best armoured divisions, the 12th *"Hitlerjugend"* *Waffen*-S.S. Panzer Division, stationed near Lisieux, and the 130th Panzer-*"Lehr"* Division, formed the previous winter from Panzer instructors and now stationed around Châteaudun. Moreover, O.K.W. did not cease interfering in Rundstedt's sphere of command, as the latter explained bitterly to the British officers who questioned him after his capture:

"I did not have my way. As Commander-in-Chief in the West my only authority was to change the guards in front of my gate."

As will be seen later, everything confirms the truth of this account. Therefore it appears that Hitler did not appreciate the complete incompatibility between despotic, arrogant, and meddling authority, and the need to make rapid decisions, the vital importance of which he soon came to recognise.

Where would the Allies land?

A major part of the success of the landings can be explained by the inefficiency of the German Intelligence services. Here the Nazis Kaltenbrunner and Schellenberg, who had ousted the professionals Canaris and Oster, could neither get a clear idea of the British and American plans nor escape being deceived by the Allies' diversionary manoeuvres. Therefore hypotheses were the order of the day

at O.K.W. as well as Saint-Germain-en-Laye, headquarters of Western Command (O.B.W.) and la Roche-Guyon, headquarters of Army Group "B".

Hitler had given a long analysis on the situation on March 20. Though he recognised that there was no way of being sure in which area the Allies would land, over the whole coastline from Norway to Greece, he nevertheless made his point:

"At no place along our long front is a landing impossible, except perhaps where the coast is broken by cliffs. The most suitable and hence the most threatened areas are the two west coast peninsulas, Cherbourg and Brest, which are very tempting and offer the best possibilities for the formation of a bridgehead, which would then be enlarged systematically by the use of air forces and heavy weapons of all kinds."

This hypothesis was perfectly logical and the order of battle of the German 7th Army (Colonel-General Dollmann), was correctly arranged to face this possibility. Of its 14 divisions, 12 were deployed between the Rivers Vire and Loire.

▽ *Wheeling a "Belgian Gate" into position on the foreshore—a massive construction of angle-iron designed to disembowel landing-craft. There were other unpleasant surprises, too—but never enough of them to satisfy Rommel.*
▷ ▽ *Like an outsize concrete bolster—a tank trap doubling as a parapet for the infantry behind.*

Rundstedt did not share Hitler's opinion, and considered that there were a great many more advantages from the Allied point of view for them to cross the Channel and land in the Pas-de-Calais. Later, in 1945, he supported his views by using these arguments, according to Milton Shulman:

"In the first place an attack from Dover against Calais would be using the shortest sea route to the Continent. Secondly, the V-1 and V-2 sites were located in this area. Thirdly this was the shortest route to the Ruhr and the heart of industrial Germany, and once a successful landing had been made it would take only four days to reach the Rhine. Fourthly, such an operation would sever the forces in Northern France from those along the Mediterranean coast. Against the Pas-de-Calais being chosen was the fact that this area had the strongest coastal defences, and was the only part of the Atlantic Wall that even remotely lived up to its reputation. I always used to tell my staff that if I was Montgomery I would attack the Pas-de-Calais."

But this would have meant coming up against the strongest part of the Atlantic Wall, whose concrete-housed batteries on either side of Cape Gris-Nez kept the English coast between Ramsgate and Dungeness under the fire of their 14 11-, 12-, 15-, and 16-inch guns; also Colonel-General von Salmuth's 15th Army was well deployed in the area, with 18 divisions between Antwerp and Cabourg. These troops were of good quality, and so it would seem that at O.K.W. Field-Marshal Keitel and Generals Jodl and Warlimont expected a landing between the mouths of the Rivers Somme and Seine, outside the range of the heavy artillery mentioned above but still within the 15th Army's sector, under the overall command of Field-Marshal Rommel.

Overleaf: *A foreshore sector, sown with defences in concentric belts, seen at low tide.*
Bottom left: *Gun emplacement under camouflage net.*
Bottom right: *Stone cairns– another simple landing-craft obstacle.*

Problems for Coastal Defence

Rommel commanded Army Group "B", which included the 7th and 15th Armies and LXXXVIII Corps, with three divisions for the defence of Holland. His main worry was the weakness of the defences on the beaches of the bay of the Seine, where three divisions were thinly stretched between Cabourg (exclusive) and the port of Cherbourg. More important, this weakness was not compensated for by the density or heavy calibre of the coastal artillery. Actually, on the 125-mile front between Le Havre and Cape Barfleur, the Swedish coastal artillery expert Colonel Stjernfelt has identified only 18 batteries, 12 of which could not reach the Calvados beaches or did not fire at all on D-Day.

Another concern of Rommel's was what form he should give to this defensive battle for which he was responsible and which might begin any day. But on this question, his point of view was almost exactly the same as the Führer's, detailed previously.

In his opinion, a sea-borne landing differs from a ground attack essentially in that the latter has its maximum force on the first day of the offensive. It then decreases in momentum because of the losses that are suffered and logistic difficulties. This allows the defending army to put off its counter-attack. On the other hand, the enemy who comes from the sea will be weak at the moment of landing, but will become steadily stronger within his bridgehead, so that any delay at all in the counter-attack will reduce in like proportion its chance of success.

The Panzers were indubitably the best means of counter-attack, and so the sensible thing was to deploy them in such a manner that they could be hurled against the enemy wherever he might appear (Low Countries, Pas-de-Calais, Normandy, or Brittany) on the actual day of the landing. This is what Rommel explained in a letter to Jodl on April 23, 1944:

"If, in spite of the enemy's air superiority, we succeed in getting a large part of our mobile force into action in the threatened coast defence sectors in the first few hours, I am convinced that the enemy attack on the coast will collapse completely on its first day."

But he added: "My only real anxiety concerns the mobile forces. Contrary to what was decided at the conference on the 21st March, they have so far not been placed under my command. Some of them are dispersed over a large area inland, which means they will arrive too late to play any part in the battle for the coast. With the heavy enemy air superiority we can expect, any large-scale movement of motorised forces to the coast will be exposed to air attacks of tremendous weight and long duration.

But without rapid assistance from the armoured divisions and mobile units, our coast divisions will be hard put to it to counter attacks coming simultaneously from the sea and from airborne troops inland. Their land front is too thinly held for that. The dispositions of both combat and reserve forces should be such as to ensure that the minimum possible movement will be required to counter an attack at any of most likely points . . . and to ensure that the greater part of the enemy troops, sea and airborne, will be destroyed by our fire during their approach."

This led him to conclude: "The most decisive battle of the war, and the fate of the German people itself, is at stake. Failing a tight command in one single hand of all the forces available for defence, failing the early engagement of all our mobile forces in the battle for the coast, victory will be in grave doubt. If I am to wait until the enemy landing has actually taken place, before I can demand, through normal channels, the command and dispatch of the mobile forces, delays will be inevitable. This will mean that they will probably arrive too late to

△ *Japan's military attaché, General Komatsu, chats with a Todt Organisation official on the Channel coast.*

▽ Simplicissimus *comments on Churchill and Roosevelt hesitating before taking the plunge in the "bath of blood".*

△△ *Dollmann, commander of 7th Army in Normandy.*
△ *Geyr von Schweppenburgh, of* Panzergruppe *"West".*
▽ *Bayerlein, commander of the* Panzer-*"Lehr" Division.*
▷ *Wehrmacht deployment in the West.*

intervene successfully in the battle for the coast and prevent the enemy landing. A second Nettuno, a highly undesirable situation for us, could result . . ."

The Generals in disagreement

And, in fact, after the conference of March 20, Rommel had received from the Führer the right to have *Panzergruppe* "West" put immediately under his direct command. This force, under General Geyr von Schweppenburg, constituted Rundstedt's armoured reserve and, on D-Day, consisted of:
1. I *Waffen* S.S. Panzer Corps;
2. 1st *"Leibstandarte Adolf Hitler"* S.S. Panzer Division (at Beverloo, 45 miles east of Antwerp);
3. 2nd Panzer Division (at Amiens);
4. 116th Panzer Division (in the Gisors–Beauvais region);
5. 12th *"Hitlerjugend"* S.S. Panzer Division (in the Evreux–Lisieux region);
6. 130th Panzer-*"Lehr"* Division (near Châteaudun); and
7. 21st Panzer Division (at Saint-Pierre-sur-Dives, 20 miles south-east of Caen).

But no order had come from O.K.W. to give executive force to Hitler's concession. And so Schweppenburg refused the rôle which Rommel allotted to him. His view was that the Western Front's armoured reserve should be concentrated in a central position downstream from Paris, so that it could intervene with all its strength in that sector where it looked as if the enemy was about to make his main push, after all tricks and feinting movements had been discounted. From this point of view, the way that Army Group "B" at la Roche-Guyon wanted to distribute the Panzers seemed to fit the verdict that Frederick the Great had proclaimed against all systems of wide-stretched defence: *"Wer alles defendieren will, defendiert gar nichts"* (He who tries to defend everything, defends nothing).

Rundstedt, and also Colonel-General Guderian, agreed with this point of view, which could clearly be defended on the principles of war. But were they applicable in those circumstances? Rommel denied that they were and cited as an example, as has been seen, his North African experience. His opponents had

not had this experience as they had all come from the Eastern Front, where the enemy's tactical air force was only just beginning to show its power to paralyse ground movement. Events showed that his reasoning was without doubt the more pertinent. However that may be and in spite of his attempt on April 23, Rommel received no satisfaction on this vital point. Better–or worse still–depending on one's point of view, the Führer was equally negative when Rommel suggested that he should advance the Panzer-*"Lehr"* Division to between the Orne and the Vire, deploy the *"Hitlerjugend"* Division in the region of Saint-Lô, and reinforce this sector, which seemed dangerously weak to Rommel, by a brigade of *Nebelwerfers* (976 15-, 21-, and 30-cm barrels) and a large number of heavy (8.8-cm) anti-aircraft batteries. Faced with silence from Hitler, Rommel left la Roche-Guyon at dawn on June 4 for Berchtesgaden, not without having consulted his barometer and obtained Rundstedt's leave.

Hitler's personality ensures failure

In spite of the documents published since 1945, Hitler's attitude when faced with the problems of the German high command remains incomprehensible, for it abounds in contradictions. The facts speak for themselves.

Though he did not believe the forecasts of his subordinates at O.K.W. and of Rundstedt, all of whom envisaged the British and the Americans approaching the French coast between Le Havre and the Pas-de-Calais, he accepted their forecast the day after the Allies landed in the bay of the Seine and stuck to it obstinately until a decisive hole was punched in the German line on the left bank of the Vire by the 1st American Army. In fact he was convinced, up to July 24, that the only purpose of the Battle of Normandy was to trick him into lowering his guard in the Pas-de-Calais. Here he too was deceived by the Allied cover plan, which continued to give the impression that there were powerful forces in south-east England about to attack directly across the Channel in the Pas-de-Calais.

However, though his hypothesis of March 20, concerning the first objec-

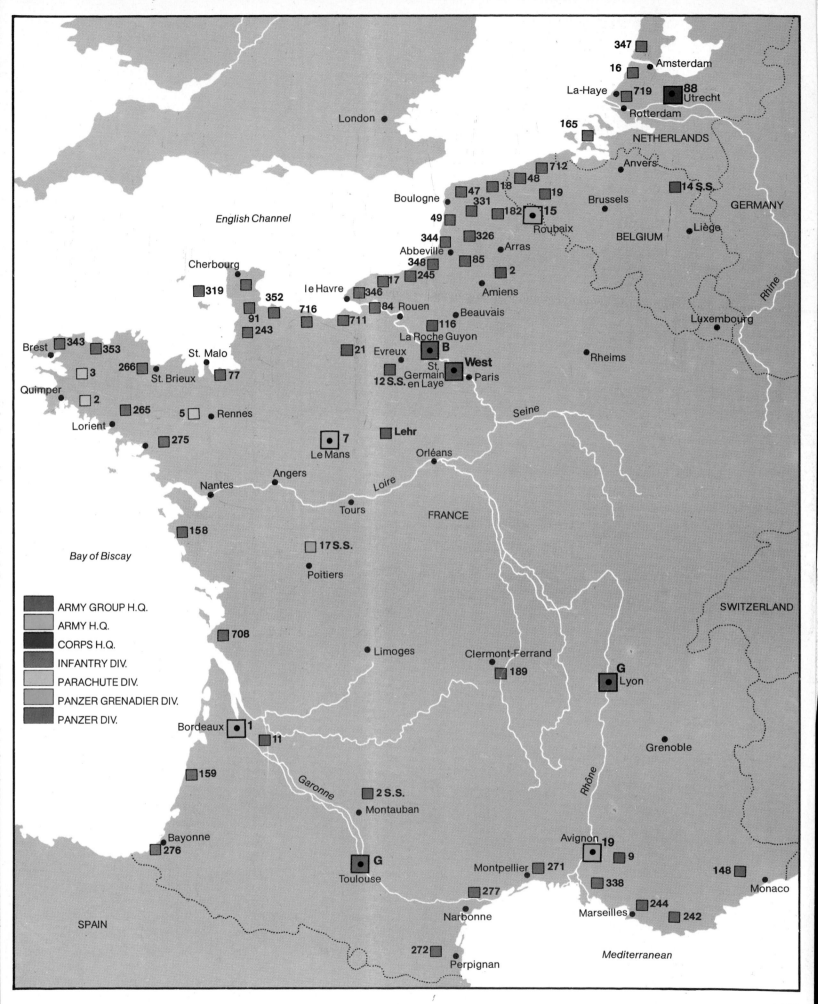

347

16 • Amsterdam

La-Haye 719 88
Utrecht

Rotterdam

165 NETHERLANDS

712 Anvers

48 14 S.S.

47 18 19 Brussels GERMANY

Boulogne 331 182 115

49 Roubaix BELGIUM

344 326 Liège

Abbeville Arras

348 85

245 2

English Channel 17

346 Amiens

Cherbourg 84 Rouen

319 le Havre Beauvais

352 716 711 116

91 La Roche Guyon Rheims

243 21 Evreux B Luxembourg

St. Malo St. West

343 266 77 12 S.S. Germain • Paris

Brest 353 en Laye

St. Brieux Seine

3

Quimper 2 265 5 • Rennes Lehr

Lorient 275 7 Orléans

Le Mans

Nantes Angers Loire

Tours FRANCE

158

17 S.S. SWITZERLAND

Bay of Biscay • Poitiers

ARMY GROUP H.Q.

ARMY H.Q.

CORPS H.Q.

INFANTRY DIV. 708 Limoges Clermont-Ferrand

PARACHUTE DIV. 189 G

PANZER GRENADIER DIV. Lyon

PANZER DIV.

Grenoble

Bordeaux 1

11

159

2 S.S. Rhône

Montauban Avignon 19

Bayonne G 9

276 Toulouse Montpellier 271

277 338

244

SPAIN Narbonne Marseilles 242

148 Monaco

272

Perpignan Mediterranean

London •

1423

tives of the Allied attack, only partially coincided with Rommel's views, in other respects there was perfect agreement between the two men concerning the way to repel it: an immediate counter-attack on the beaches so as to avoid a long battle of attrition, like the one the armies had fought at Anzio–Nettuno.

But here there came a further contradiction. If, for perfectly valid reasons, the Führer rejected the plans of deployment put forward by Geyr von Schweppenburg, he nevertheless refused Rommel the means to fight the battle according to the plans on which he had been in entire agreement with him. Though it is a risky business to try to rewrite history, it will be noted that if Hitler had drawn all the conclusions from the principles he had enunciated, and had agreed with the suggestions of his distinguished general, the following would have happened:

1. Rommel would have been at his head-quarters at la Roche-Guyon on June 6, and would have been alerted by British and American parachute drops, slightly after 0130 hours, while in the event he only knew of them five hours later while still at his private house in Herrlingen on the outskirts of Ulm.

2. The counter-attack launched in the afternoon of June 6 by just the 21st Panzer Division in only the British sector, could have been executed by the Panzer-"*Lehr*" Division and the 12th

Four views of Rommel, taken during the last months before D-Day. Behind the furious energy with which he urged on the laying of minefields and the construction of energy lay a carefully worked-out strategy, born of the painful lessons learned in Africa. These were the effectiveness of the minefield and the paramount need to deny the enemy freedom to manoeuvre – or to establish a foothold and make it too strong to eliminate. Rommel forecast – with complete accuracy – that the battle for Normandy would really be won on the beaches.

The men of the Atlantic Wall:
△ *Workers pressing on with the uncompleted defences . . .*
▷ *. . . the soldier who would have to defend them.*

"Hitlerjugend" S.S. Panzer Division. From the positions which Rommel wanted them to occupy, they could have simultaneously attacked the bridgeheads that the Americans were establishing. By reinforcing these two with 400 or 450 tanks and assault guns, the first would almost certainly have wiped out "Omaha" Beach before nightfall and the second was well-placed to attack the poorly placed parachute units around Saint-Mère-Eglise.

True enough, if this had in fact happened, the Panzer-"Lehr" would have found itself under the fire of the Allied naval forces, and the precedents of Gela and Salerno showed how redoubtable and efficient their heavy shells were against tanks. This argument had been used by Geyr von Schweppenburg during the stormy arguments he had had with Rommel about the distribution of armoured divisions. But though this was a real danger, does it follow that they should have abstained from any attack at all on D-Day and that they should not have taken advantage of the fleeting moment when the enemy had not yet consolidated his bridgeheads?

CHAPTER 109
Allied air offensive

Britain's best heavy bomber of
World War II: an Avro
Lancaster B. I of No. 50
Squadron in flight.

1428

By 1943 ruins were piling up from one end of the Third Reich to the other, the effect of night raids by R.A.F. Bomber Command and day raids by the American 8th Air Force, joined by the 15th Air Force from October 9 from their air base at Foggia, hastily brought back into action after its capture by the British 8th Army on September 27. These round-the-clock attacks were the result of a plan adopted at Casablanca late in January 1943 at a meeting of the British and American Combined Chiefs-of-Staff Committee. A list of proposed objectives was drawn up in order of priority:

"(a) German submarine construction yards.
(b) The German aircraft industry.
(c) Transportation.
(d) Oil plants.
(e) Other targets in enemy war industry."

However, this order did not reflect the realities of strategic bombing. In fact the agreed directive specified the general objective of the strategic air offensive as the destruction of the German industrial system and the undermining of the German home morale.

After the complete failure of a series of American bombing raids on German submarine construction yards, followed by a similar British lack of success, it became clear that bombing techniques would need drastic improvement or, at least, that less demanding targets should be selected. Fortunately for the Allies, by the end of 1943 the U-boat menace was no longer pressing. It should be recalled that in order to keep up his U-boat campaign against all opposition Dönitz was at this time claiming that to abandon it would subject Germany's cities to even greater ordeals as enemy bombing raids grew in ferocity. In this he was not mistaken.

Difficulties in co-ordination

It had not been easy for the British and the Americans to come to an agreement over the best use of the U.S. 8th Air Force. The first unit of this force had arrived in Great Britain on July 1, 1942 when the Flying Fortress "Jarring Jenny" had touched down at Prestwick airport in Scotland.

It was the opinion of Air Chief Marshal Sir Charles Portal, Chief of the Air Staff, that the squadrons of Flying Fortresses

◁ Smoke billows up from the Bettenhausen factory in Kassel (outlined in white) as one of the attacking B-17 bombers of the U.S. 8th Air Force passes over the target area.
◁▽ The crew of the Flying Fortress "Blue Dreams" in cheerful mood after completing a mission.
△ General Carl A. Spaatz, head of the 8th Air Force in 1942 and of the U.S. Strategic Air Forces, comprising the 8th and 15th Air Forces, from January 1944.
▽ A damaged Flying Fortress under repair at a Mobile Machine Shop.

The American Boeing B-17G Flying Fortress heavy bomber

Engines: four Wright R-1820 Cyclone radials, 1,200-hp each.
Armament: thirteen .5-inch Browning machine guns and up to 17,600 lbs of bombs.
Speed: 300 mph at 30,000 feet.
Ceiling: 35,000 feet.
Range: 1,850 miles with typical bomb-load.
Weight empty/loaded: 32,720/55,000 lbs.
Span: 103 feet 9½ inches.
Length: 74 feet 4 inches.
Height: 19 feet 1 inch.
Crew: 10.

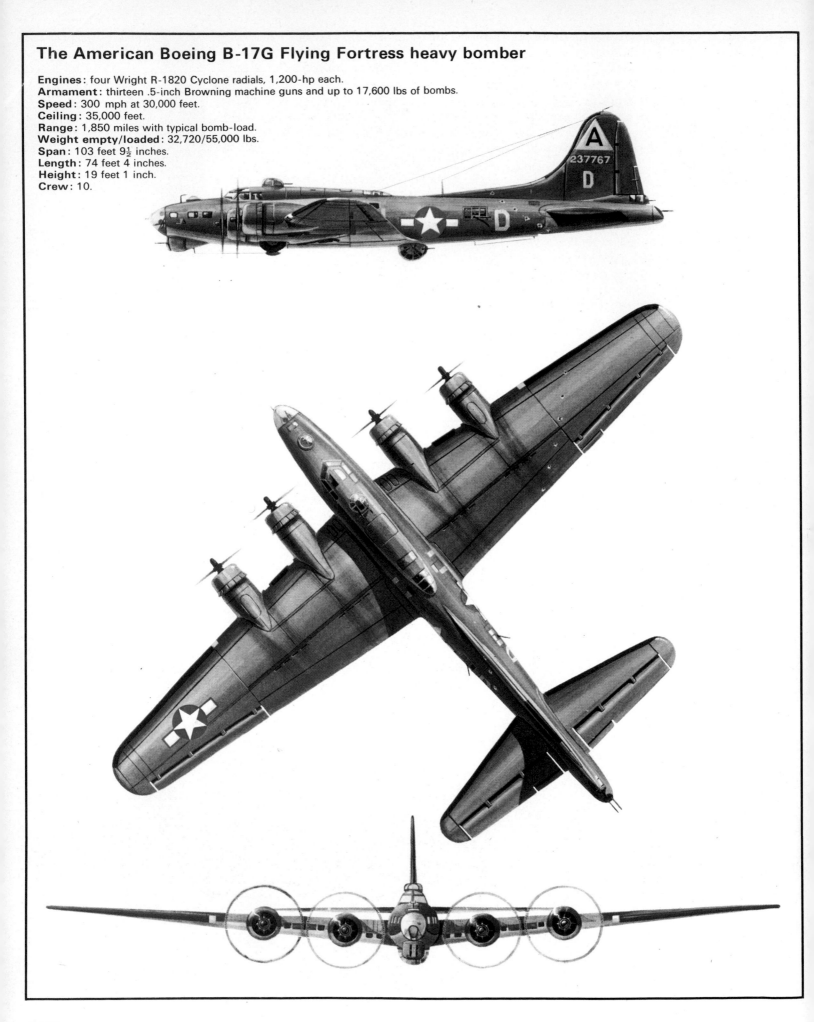

1430

should take part in the night bombing raids of Bomber Command, whose C.-in-C. naturally welcomed the idea of having eventually twice or three times as many planes at his disposal. Both men thought that day bombing against A.A. and Göring's fighters would suffer unbearable losses for a very mediocre profit. But in Washington, General H. H. Arnold, U.S.A.A.F. Chief-of-Staff, and at H.Q. 8th Air Force, Lieutenant-General Ira C. Eaker both disagreed with British optimism about night operations. If the Anglo-American strategic force was to carry out its mission successfully it would, in their opinion, have to attack by day and nothing would make them change their minds. But if, under certain conditions,

△ *Ammunitioning the ball turret, aptly named "The Morgue", of a B-17 with .5-inch armour piercing tracer rounds. Once ensconced in the cramped turret, sitting on a bicycle seat and braced against padded knee-rests, the ball gunner was condemned to spend the whole flight there, with little chance of escape in the event of his aircraft being shot down.*

◁ *G. C. Wilson, of Minneapolis, Minnesota, in the rear turret of his Fortress. The swastikas show that he was credited with shooting down of two German fighters. American rear turrets were usually armed with two .5-inch guns, compared with the British armament of four .303-inch weapons.*
▽ *An 8th Air Force Liberator is christened.*

△ *Flying Fortress of the 533rd Bombardment Squadron, 381st Bombardment Group, 1st Combat Wing, 1st Air Division, 8th Air Force, over England.*

▷ *Armourers bomb up a drab-camouflaged B-17F. Note the provision of mounts for machine guns in the plexiglass nose, much improved upon by the fitting of a two-gun chin turret in late production F and all G models.*

△ *Captain Donald S. Gentile seated on the wing of his North American P-51 Mustang "Shangri-La". He was one of the 8th Air Force's highest scoring aces, with 20 "kills". Until the advent of the Mustang, with long range tanks, American daylight bomber formations were appallingly vulnerable to the German fighter defences.*

which were not all fulfilled late in 1942, the Flying Fortresses and the Liberators were to take on the considerable risks of day bombing, this was not to be so for the R.A.F., whatever the courage or the state of training of its crews.

R.A.F. by night, U.S.A.A.F. by day

And so that task was divided round the clock equally between the British and the Americans, the former taking off at nightfall and the latter by day, each sticking to his task with ruthless obstinacy and without complaining of his losses. This was the system adopted after heated discussions. For Generals Arnold and Eaker there was the additional advantage (though perhaps not admitted) that the Americans would still retain their autonomy though working under a joint command. This division of labour meant that the two air forces came to use totally different methods of action.

By day the 8th Air Force performed what it called precision bombing. Well-defined objectives were thus allotted: a particular factory, construction-yard, assembly-shop in Germany or in an occupied country, in the latter of which only where civilian casualties could be spared as far as was compatible with the successful completion of the mission. The American crews nevertheless greatly exaggerated the degree of precision they could obtain with their Norden bomb-sights.

As it operated by night, Bomber Command could not expect results like these, and so performed area bombing, applying to Germany what nuclear arms specialists today have come to call "anti-city" strategy. In addition to H.E. bombs, they used a great variety of incendiary devices, some packed with jellied products of horrifying efficiency. Air Chief Marshal Sir Arthur Harris, A.O.C. Bomber Command, did not limit his task to the simple destruction of the Third Reich's war potential, but aimed also at destroying the morale of the German people. In

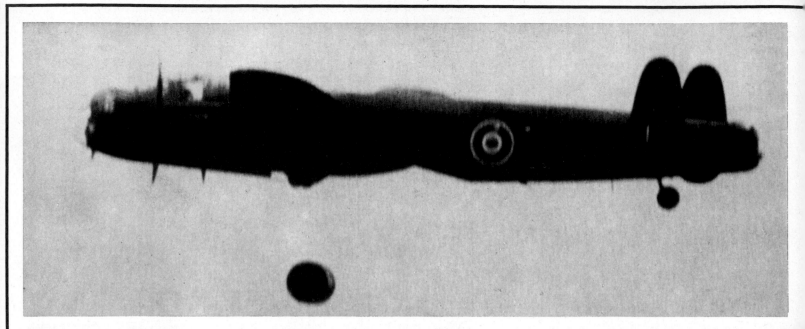

THE DAMBUSTERS

The famous "Dams Raid" of May 16, 1943 was intended to breach the Möhne (right), Eder, Sorpe, Lister, and Schwelme dams. Converted Lancasters of 617 Squadron (top) attacked with special bombs designed by Mr. Barnes Wallis (above) which, when released at a precise speed and height, skipped over the dams' net defences and rolled down the inside wall of the dam to explode at a predetermined depth. The shock wave then caused the dam to break. The Schwelme dam was not attacked, and only the Möhne and Eder dams were breached.

△ △ ◁ Water pours through the gap in the Eder dam, causing severe, but only local, damage to agricultural land.

△ △ ▷ The last of the water held back by the Möhne dam streams through the breach.

△ Below the Möhne dam: the flood waters spread over the river valley. But only if all five targets had been destroyed would German industry have felt any long-term effects.

◁ Wing-Commander Guy Gibson, V.C. (centre), commander of 617 Squadron.

▷ The King, with Gibson looking over his shoulder, inspects photographs of the results.

in spite of the loss during the year of 1,261 four-engined planes and most of their crews, the growing strength of the 8th Air Force is shown in the following table:

| | Groups | |
	B-17 Flying Fortresses	B-24 Liberators
January 1	5	2
April 1	5	2
July 1	11	—
October 1	17	4
December 1	19	7

This shows that the number of four-engined bombers at the disposal of Major-General James H. Doolittle, who succeeded Eaker as 8th Air Force commander at the end of the year, increased over three and a half times in 12 months. The number of sorties made by these planes rose at an even faster, one could say spectacular, rate:

January	279
April	379
July	2,334
October	2,159
December	5,618

Flying Fortresses in action

Compared with the Consolidated B-24 Liberator, the American crews operating over Germany preferred the Boeing B-17 Flying Fortress, of which over 12,000 were finally made by a consortium of the original builders with Douglas and Lockheed-Vega. Weighing 24 tons loaded, this four-engined plane could reach a top speed of 325 mph and had a range of 2,000 miles. The B-17E had eleven .3- and .5-inch machine guns which the Americans believed gave it all-round fire-power. This optimism was proved false by experience. For example, on August 17, 1943 the 8th Air Force lost 60 out of the 376 Flying Fortresses sent on raids on the Schweinfurt ball-bearing factory and the Messerschmitt assembly plant at Regensburg. On October 14 a new attack on the first of these objectives cost another 60 planes out of the 291 which had taken off, and altogether the loss of aircraft on these raids over the month was running at the intolerably high level of 9.1 per cent. Under these conditions it can be imagined that questions were raised as to whether or not the methods advocated by General Arnold were failing for, if it was relatively easy to replace the planes, it was not the

this he was free to act. Returning to the matter after the event, he wrote that the Casablanca Conference released him from his last moral scruples. His hands from that time forward were free as far as the bombing war was concerned.

After this account of the basic methods used by the Anglo-American forces in their air offensive against Germany we must now consider briefly the material means which they used with varying success.

From January 1 to December 31, 1943,

△ △ Bombing up a Handley-Page Hampden, Britain's best bomber, together with the Vickers Wellington, during the first two years of the war. The Hampden could carry a worthwhile load a considerable range, but had a completely inadequate defensive armament. The type was phased out of service with Bomber Command by September 1942, but continued as a minelayer and torpedo bomber with Coastal Command until 1944.

△ In the cockpit of an R.A.F. bomber.

▷ The bomb-aimer's position in the nose of a Short Stirling.

▷ △ Armstrong-Whitworth Whitley, another of Britain's standard bombers early in the war.

▷ ▷ Two Stirling bombers. Britain's first war-time four-engined heavy bomber, the type entered service in 1940. Note the long under-carriage legs, to give the wings the right angle of attack at take-off.

▷ ▽ Avro Manchester (right), the unsuccessful two-engined precursor of the Lancaster. Note the Wellington in the background.

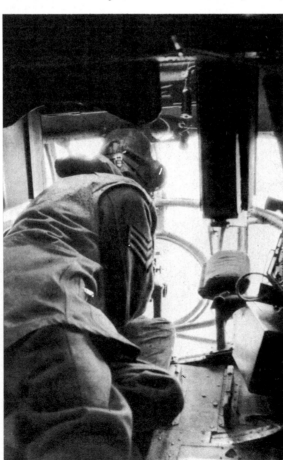

same thing for the crews and, after the second attack on Schweinfurt some loss of morale was noticeable among their ranks. This can be illustrated by one anecdote quoted by Werner Girbig in his *1000 Tage über Deutschland*. There was a manufacturer's advertisement in a magazine which, occupying a complete page, showed an Army Air Force machine gunner, his eye staring fiercely through the back-sight of his .5-inch gun, which he was aiming at a swarm of Focke-Wulf 190's. The caption read: "Who's afraid of the Big Bad Wolf?"

"An 8th Air Force pilot tore the page out, pinned it up on the blackboard in the Orderly Room and stuck on it a long strip of paper on which he wrote in red ink 'WE ARE'. Every officer, including the Station Commander, added his signature. Then the whole lot was sent back, without comment, to the manufacturer."

By the autumn of 1943 the Luftwaffe had won a major victory over the 8th Air Force. On deep penetration raids the German day fighters were shooting the U.S.A.A.F. out of the sky. It was during the period leading up to the bombing run that the Luftwaffe struck hardest. The German fighter commanders had discovered the American practice of formation bombing by order of the bombardier in the lead

plane. Thus the lead groups in large formations suffered mercilessly from fighter attacks, as was the case on the "second" Schweinfurt raid when the lead formation was virtually wiped-out. On one notorious raid against the Ploeşti oil refineries in Rumania, the casualty rate was nearly a third of all planes involved.

Deep penetration raids had to be abandoned, with the clear result that the 8th Air Force's losses fell by more than half: in November they were 3.9 per cent, in December 3.4 per cent.

But in the early months of 1944 increasing numbers of long range Mustang P-51 fighters enabled the U.S. Air Force to renew its deep penetration bombing—and decimate the German fighter force.

The British offensive

Bomber Command continued its area-bombing offensive against Germany's cities during 1943. Improved equipment was now making possible greatly improved standards of navigational and bombing accuracy.

The R.A.F.'s night offensive was based on three types of four-engined plane:
1. the Avro Lancaster: 28 tons, 287 mph, 1,660 mile range, and eight .303-inch machine guns;
2. the Handley-Page Halifax: 27 tons, 282 mph, 1,030 mile range, and nine .303-inch machine guns; and
3. the Short Stirling: 26.5 tons, 260 mph, 1,930 mile range, and eight .303-inch machine guns.

With the help of Canadian industry 16,000 bombers of these three types were built. Nearly half of them were Lancasters. As will be seen, their armament was insufficient to allow them to carry out daylight raids. They took off at dusk and the device for guiding bombers known as "Gee" then, after March 5, 1943, the "Oboe" blind bombing device, gave them their position at all times and then enabled them to locate their targets with considerable accuracy.

The objective was also indicated by pathfinders using coloured flares. As soon as they came into service they were fitted with the new "H₂S" radar which presented an image of the ground below rather like a fluorescent map.

◄ ◄ *Hamburg. The raids between July 24 and August 3, 1943 cost the city some 40,000 dead and informed the Germans of what they could expect in the future.*
◄▽ *Hamburg under the Allied bombardment: in three days 9,000 tons of bombs destroyed 277,000 houses in the city.*
◄ *A low-level photograph taken from a Mosquito during a raid on Hengelo in Holland. Just to the left of the locomotive is a wooden flak tower. Operating at these low altitudes, the speedy Mosquito could drop its bombs with devastating accuracy after passing below the German radar screen on the coast.*
▽ *Reconnaissance photograph of the Focke-Wulf factory at Marienburg in East Prussia, taken on October 9, 1943. The one building not destroyed by direct hits was severely damaged by blast.*

The British Handley-Page Halifax B. II Series Ia heavy bomber

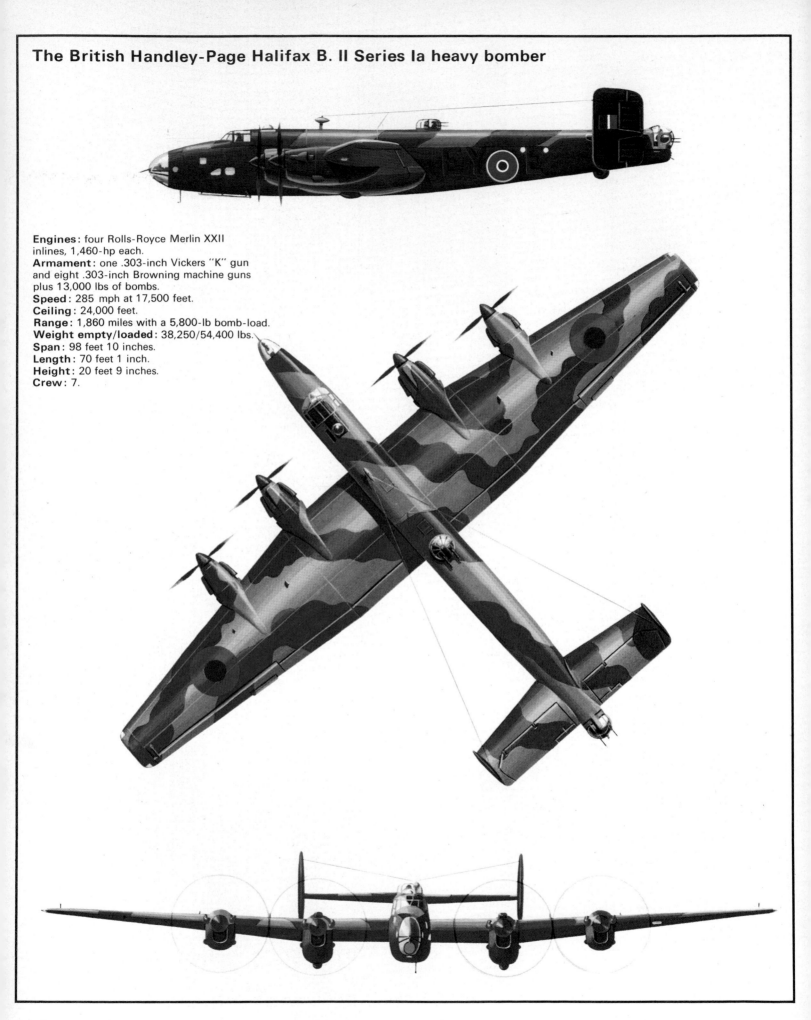

Engines: four Rolls-Royce Merlin XXII inlines, 1,460-hp each.
Armament: one .303-inch Vickers "K" gun and eight .303-inch Browning machine guns plus 13,000 lbs of bombs.
Speed: 285 mph at 17,500 feet.
Ceiling: 24,000 feet.
Range: 1,860 miles with a 5,800-lb bomb-load.
Weight empty/loaded: 38,250/54,400 lbs.
Span: 98 feet 10 inches.
Length: 70 feet 1 inch.
Height: 20 feet 9 inches.
Crew: 7.

◄ *Handley-Page Halifax. This was the second of Britain's trio of four-engined bombers to enter service during the war, and served with great distinction in Europe and the Mediterranean. A total of 6,176 was built, in bomber, maritime reconnaissance, glider towing, paratroop dropping, and transport versions.*

Germany's cities devastated by bombs

Not only was radar used by the Allies for target identification, it was used in jamming the enemy's radar. From July 1943 the British used a device called "Window". This consisted of thousands and thousands of strips of metallic paper which confused the echoes of the Germans' *Würzburg* apparatus for directing A.A. and fighters. Even better, the British succeeded in breaking in on the enemy radio-traffic between ground control and the fighters up in the air, sending his planes off in the wrong direction by mimicking exactly the ground-controller's voice. In the night of October 22-23, during an attack on Kassel, the authentic German controller, infuriated by the interference, let out an oath and the Luftwaffe pilots heard the "phantom voice" exclaim: "That cretin of an Englishman's starting to swear!" Whereupon the German, beside himself with

rage, shouted into the microphone: "It's not the Englishman who's swearing, it's me!"

For evident reasons, on their day raids, the Americans rarely sent in more than 200 planes on the same objective. By night the British attacked the towns of the Reich with three and sometimes five times as many and made the raids as brief as possible so as to saturate the active and the passive defence, particularly the latter which, within two hours after the raids had begun, was faced with hundreds of fires concealing delayed-action bombs. The theory was simple: the leading planes would drop High Explosive with the intention of causing structural damage and keeping the fire-fighting teams underground. Incendiaries would follow, setting light to the buildings, creating fires of sufficient intensity to develop into an all-consuming fire-storm. In practice, however, this ideal was seldom realised; the practical problems being too great.

And so by September 1, according to the figures given by Georg W. Feuchter in his excellent book *Der Luftkrieg,* Bomber

Air-Marshal Sir Arthur 'Bomber' Harris, born in 1892, firmly believed in the decisiveness of air power. From February 1942 he directed R.A.F. Bomber Command in its onslaught on Germany. He deployed all available aircraft in the first 1,000-bomber raid on Cologne on May 30, 1942, devastating one-third of the city. In September 1942, the first 8,000-lb 'blockbuster' bomb was dropped on Karlsruhe. He initiated night bombing to supplement day raids, and introduced area bombing.

The Avro Lancaster was built in greater numbers than any other British four-engined bomber of World War II, a total of 7,374 being produced. Derived from the twin-engined Manchester, whose performance had been good, but whose engines proved totally unreliable, the Merlin-engined Lancaster first appeared in 1941. It proved an excellent aircraft, capable of carrying enormous loads, and very easy to fly. Besides large loads of conventional bombs, the Lancaster could carry such special stores as "Dambuster" bombs, 12,000-lb "Tallboys" and 22,000-lb "Grand Slams". Its one major failing was lack of ventral protection.
◁ In flight.
▽ A Bomber Command station with Lancasters at their dispersal points.
▷ Bombing up.
▷ ▷ Aircrew.
▷ ▽ Maintenance.
▷ ▽ ▽ Debriefing.

of the German Foreign Office, were lost without trace.

9,000 tons on Hamburg

In the last week of July 1943, Hamburg and its port were reduced to ruins by the concerted efforts of Bomber Command and the 8th Air Force, a combined operation unique of its kind. The operation was called "Gomorrah" and started on the evening of July 24 with an enormous release of "Window". To follow the effect of this decoy device, let us go with Cajus Bekker to Stade on the lower Elbe and into the command post where Lieutenant-General Schwabedissen was about to send up the fighters of his 2nd *Fliegerdivision*:

"But on this July 24 the inconceivable took place. It was shortly before midnight when the first reports reached Stade, and the projections on the screen showed the enemy bomber formations flying eastwards over the North Sea, parallel to the coast. The Bf 110's of NJG [*Nachtjagdgeschwader*] 3 were duly ordered off from their bases at Stade, Vechta, Wittmundhaven, Wunstorf, Lüneburg and Kastrup, and took up their positions over the sea under *"Himmelbett"* control. Meanwhile it was confirmed that the initial Pathfinders were being followed by a bomber stream of several hundred aircraft, all keeping to the north of the Elbe estuary. What was their objective? Would they turn south to Kiel or Lübeck, or proceed over the Baltic for some target as yet

Command had attacked the following German cities with the amounts of bombs shown over the previous eight months:

	tons		tons
Hamburg	11,000	Berlin	6,000
Essen	8,000	Dusseldorf	5,000
Duisburg	6,000	Nuremberg	5,000

The massive attacks on the capital of the Third Reich began again on November 18 and between that date and January 1, 1944 no less than 14,000 tons of bombs transformed it into an immense heap of rubble. It was during this period that the archives of the French G.H.Q., discovered in the station at La Charité-sur-Loire on June 19, 1940 by the 9th Panzer Division and then preserved in an annexe

The British Avro Lancaster B. I heavy bomber

Engines: four Rolls-Royce Merlin XXII inlines, 1,460-hp each.
Armament: eight .303-inch Browning machine guns and up to 18,000 lbs of bombs.
Speed: 287 mph at 11,500 feet.
Ceiling: 24,500 feet.
Range: 2,530 miles with 7,000-lb bomb-load, 1,730 miles with 12,000-lb.
Weight empty/loaded: 36,900/68,000 lbs.
Span: 102 feet.
Length: 69 feet 6 inches.
Height: 20 feet 6 inches.
Crew: 7.

The de Havilland Mosquito, of laminated wood construction, was one of the most versatile aircraft to see service in the war. It served as a bomber, fighter-bomber, reconnaissance aircraft, night fighter, strike fighter, and in several other rôles. Illustrated are aircraft of 139 Squadron.

unknown? All now depended on closely following their course without being deceived by any feint attack.

"Suddenly the Stade operations room throbbed with disquietude. For minutes the illuminations on the screen representing the enemy had stuck in the same positions. The signals officer switched in to the direct lines to the radar stations and asked what was the matter. He received the same answer from all of them: 'Apparatus put out of action by jamming.'

"The whole thing was a mystery. Then came reports from the 'Freya' stations, operating on the long 240-cm wave, that they too were jammed. They at least could just distinguish the bomber formation's echo from the artificial ones. But the screens of the 'Würzburgs', operating on 53-cm, became an indecipherable jumble of echo points resembling giant insects, from which nothing could be recognised at all.

"It was a portentous situation, for the control of the night fighters entirely depended on exact information as to position and altitude being given by the 'Würzburgs'. Without it the controllers were powerless and the fighters could only fumble in the dark.

"2nd *Fliegerdivision* had to turn for help to the general air-raid warning system–to the corps of observers watching and listening throughout the land. These could only report what they saw. At Dithmarschen, not far from Meldorf, they saw yellow lights cascading from the sky; more and more of them all in the same area. Presumably they marked a turning point. The bomber stream had veered to the south-east, as fresh reports confirmed. In close order the enemy was heading parallel with the Elbe–direct to Hamburg."

Similarly handicapped, the 54 batteries of heavy (8.8-cm) A.A. and the 26 batteries of light A.A. defending the great city of Hamburg could only fire in barrage. They thus claimed only 12 victims out of the 374 Lancasters, 246 Halifaxes, 125 Stirlings, and 73 Wellingtons which had taken off that evening, 721 of which reached their objective. On the following morning 235 Flying Fortresses took over from their R.A.F. comrades and on the 26th started their attacks again, concentrating their efforts on the shipyards and port installations. During the night of the 27th-28th Air Chief Marshal Harris sent up 722 four-engined bombers against Hamburg

and 48 hours later another 699. As weather conditions had deteriorated, only 340 reached their objective during the night of August 2-3. During these six attacks nearly 3,000 British and American planes dropped 9,000 tons of bombs. In the resulting holocaust half the city was devoured by flames which ravaged 277,330 dwellings. Civilian victims totalled some 43,000 men, women, and children. All this was achieved at the cost of 89 British bombers shot down by fighters and A.A. These losses were light, of course, but this was not always to be the case for Bomber Command. In fact, between March 1 and July 1, 1943 the night attacks on the industrial complex of the Ruhr, when 18,506 sorties were made, cost 872 four-engined bombers and 5,600 crew. Replacements at the right time were not always easy, in spite of the efforts of the Dominions and the Allied powers.

A British success: the Mosquito

For its day operations over the Reich, which consisted of harassment or diversionary raids, the R.A.F. used principally the de Havilland Mosquito. Constructed almost entirely of wood, in which the firm had considerable experience, it was nevertheless one of the most successful of all the weapons which left British workshops. It weighed nine tons on take-off and its two motors delivered 2,500 hp, giving it a top speed of 400 mph, thus putting it virtually out of reach of enemy fighters. The Mosquitoes took part in 1,000 raids in 1943, attacking 40 German towns, including Berlin 27 times.

Hitler paralyses German reaction

When Hitler heard from Colonel Christian, his Luftwaffe A.D.C., about the first attack on Hamburg, he poured recrimination on the Luftwaffe for its shortcomings. From the shorthand transcript of this interminable indictment we quote only one passage, significant however in the way it reveals the way of thinking and reasoning of the master of

Air Chief-Marshal Sir C. Portal was born in 1893 and was head of Bomber Command in 1939 before becoming Chief of Air Staff in 1940. As such he realised that Bomber Command would have to play an important part in the war before the Allies could invade the continent, and laid the foundations of its expansion well. He was greatly respected by the Americans and had great influence at all conferences.

Lieutenant-General James R. Doolittle was born in 1896, and first came to prominence with the "Doolittle Raid" on Japan in April 1942. Later that year he commanded the 12th Air Force in the "Torch" operations, and in 1943 the Strategic Air Forces operating against Italy. During August he led a major raid on Rome. In 1944 he assumed command of the 8th Air Force in Britain, and later commanded U.S. air forces in the Pacific. Between the wars Doolittle had been a record breaker, and was the only non-regular officer to command a major air force in combat.

△ *A German town begins to burn. By now the boot was firmly on the other foot, and with the arrival of the 8th Air Force in Europe the Allied bombing offensive would go from strength to strength.*

▷ *Ruins in Nuremberg, one of the Nazi party's spiritual homes, devastated by an Allied raid.*

enough planes!' well, we have enough to do other things than what we are doing. On another occasion someone said: 'It wouldn't have the effect we want anyway,' and then he added: 'We must sow mines,' and another time: 'The A.A. was very heavy' and the next day: 'The A.A. fire was no good!' Most of what I hear all the time means: 'We can't find our objective'. Not to find London, that's shameful! And then I have to hear some idiot tell me: 'Yes, *mein Führer,* when the British planes come over Dortmund with their ray-guided bomb-aimers they can drop their bombs precisely on blocks of buildings 500 yards wide and 250 yards long.' Fool! But we can't even find London which is 35 miles across and less than 100 miles from the coast! That's what I told those gentlemen. I'm not saying this for your benefit Christian. You can't do anything about it. You're an A.D.C. I'm saying it also for other interested persons."

As we can see, Hitler accused the Luftwaffe of "beating about the bush" when he had asked for reprisals against English cities. Shortly before this he had said to Christian: "You can only break terror with terror. We must get to counter-attack; everything else is folly."

But how could the *Reichsmarschall* counter-attack with the means then at his disposal? The fear of a raid on London by 50 two-engined bombers was not

△ *A German air raid poster exhorts the civilian population to watch out for shell splinters from A.A. fire.*

▽ *Focke-Wulf 190s line-up. With later models of the Bf 109, this superb fighter formed the backbone of the Luftwaffe's day fighter force.*

the Third Reich: "That they should attack our aerodromes, I care little; but when they demolish the cities of the Ruhr! And they [the British] are very easily upset: a few bombs filled with the new explosives soon put the wind up them. 'The Germans have got a new weapon!' I don't know why we're beating about the bush here in Germany. The only way to stop this is to impress those on the other side; otherwise people will go mad here. In time things will come to such a pass that they will lose all confidence in the Luftwaffe. Anyway that confidence is partly gone already. Then you can't come and say 'We've laid mines in the enemy's waters!' For whether he comes over Hamburg with 400 to 500 planes, or only 200 to 300 it's all the same. But look at us dithering about! The only way we can make any impression is ourselves to bomb the towns on the other side methodically. But when I hear people say: 'We didn't find our objective,' and then the next time: 'We haven't got

likely to put Harris off sending 700 or 800 four-engined bombers over Berlin the next day. Hitler's grievance was thus imaginary. But for all that, the high-ranking officers of the Luftwaffe were not without blame, though Hitler in his diatribe did not touch on the real reason: the failure to take advantage of the brilliant team of scientists and technologists then working in Germany on jet and rocket propulsion.

The aircraft manufacturer Ernst Heinkel had prospected in both these directions as early as 1935 with the collaboration of the young Wernher von Braun in the field of the rocket and of the engineer

△ △ *A stick of bombs starts its long fall into Germany.*
△ *A B-24 Liberator heads for home over the Luftwaffe airfield at Saint-Didier. The airfield itself (centre right) seems relatively undamaged, but the administrative buildings (top right) and dispersal areas (bottom centre) appear to have been hit severely.*

Pabst von Ohain in that of the turbojet. The rocket-powered Heinkel 176, using a liquid propellant, was the first to be ready and it was demonstrated to Hitler, who was accompanied by Generals Göring, Milch, Jeschonnek, and Udet of the Luftwaffe, on July 3, 1939 by test pilot Erich Warsitz. On the following August 27, three years ahead of the British Frank Whittle's plane of the same type, the Heinkel 178, the first jet aeroplane in the world, took off from a landing strip near Berlin. On October 27, 1939, in the absence of Göring, who could not be bothered to attend, it was seen by Secretary of State Milch and General Udet, who were not impressed.

The idea was taken up again by Messerschmitt and on July 26, 1943 Major-General Adolf Galland, who in the previous year at the age of 30 had been appointed head of the German Fighter Command, was invited by the makers to fly the twin-

engined jet propelled Me 262. "It's like being driven by an angel," he said when questioned on his impressions after the test flight, but in his memoirs he added: "On landing I was more enthusiastic than I had ever been before. Feelings and impressions were, however, no criterion; it was the performance and characteristics that mattered. This was not a step forward, this was a leap!"

In fact the Messerschmitt Me 262 could do 540 mph in level flight, twice the speed, that is, of the British and American four-engined bombers. It could climb at record speed, had a range of 50-70 minutes' flying time, and used low-grade fuel.

Was Germany going to have another chance, then, after the inconceivable indifference shown by Göring, Milch, Jeschonnek, and Udet towards Heinkel's revolutionary plane? Evidently not, for at the first demonstration of Messerschmitt's pure-bred interceptor Hitler demanded that it be changed into a fighter-bomber. And in what terms! "For years," he said in front of Göring, Galland, and Messerschmitt, "I have demanded from the Luftwaffe a Speed Bomber which can reach its target in spite of enemy defence. In this aircraft you present me as a fighter plane I see the *Blitz* Bomber, with which I will repel the Invasion in its first and weakest phase. Regardless of the enemy's air umbrella, it will strike the recently landed mass of material and troops, creating panic, death and destruction. *At last this is the Blitz Bomber!* Of course none of you thought of that.'"

This meant a whole series of modifications to the prototype, listed by Bekker thus:

"Bombs would make the take-off weight too heavy for the slender legs. Undercarriage and tyres had to be reinforced. For bombing missions the range was inadequate, so auxiliary tanks had to be built in. That displaced the centre of gravity, upsetting the plane's stability. No approved method of bomb-suspension, nor even a bomb-sight, existed for such a plane, and the normal fighter reflector-sight bombs could only be aimed in a shallow angle of dive. For regular dive-bombing the machine was too fast safely to hold on target. An order from Führer H.Q. expressly forbade such dives—or indeed any speed exceeding 470 m.p.h."

And so, instead of taking part in the defence of the skies over Germany from 1943-1944, the redoubtable Messerschmitt

The American Consolidated B-24J Liberator heavy bomber

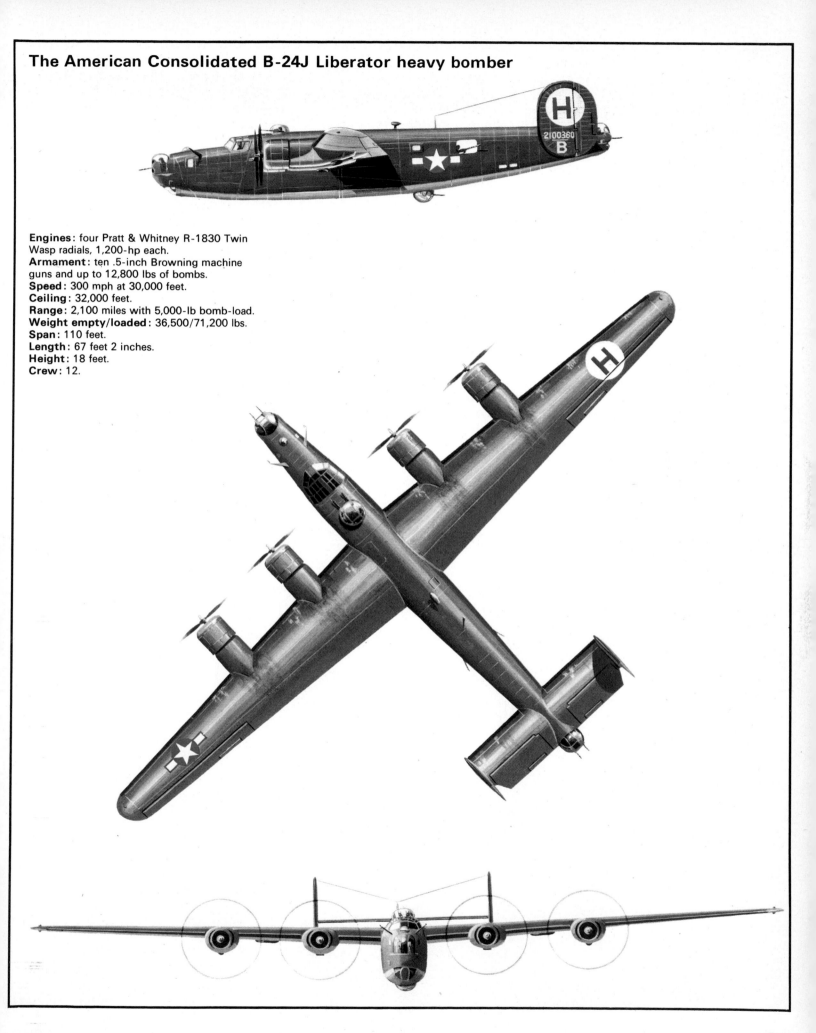

Engines: four Pratt & Whitney R-1830 Twin Wasp radials, 1,200-hp each.
Armament: ten .5-inch Browning machine guns and up to 12,800 lbs of bombs.
Speed: 300 mph at 30,000 feet.
Ceiling: 32,000 feet.
Range: 2,100 miles with 5,000-lb bomb-load.
Weight empty/loaded: 36,500/71,200 lbs.
Span: 110 feet.
Length: 67 feet 2 inches.
Height: 18 feet.
Crew: 12.

Me 262 failed to turn up over the beaches assigned to it by Hitler. It was first seen over the Albert Canal when it was reported in Allied communiqués at the beginning of September 1944. Yet in spite of this disastrous delay it came into use eight months before its R.A.F. counterpart, the Gloster Meteor.

The British attack Peenemünde

Wernher von Braun was born in 1912, and was one of Germany's ablest rocket engineers. Braun became the Technical Director of the German Army's rocket research centre at Peenemünde in 1937. Though great progress on missiles had been made by 1940, Hitler's interference seriously hampered further advances. He was arrested by the Gestapo but released on Hitler's express orders. Operations with V-2s started in September 1944.

"Break terror by terror." When Hitler had said this on July 25, 1943 he was thinking not merely of the counter-attacks which he was demanding from the Luftwaffe, but especially of the retaliatory weapons which were then being perfected at the Peenemünde testing station on the shores of the Baltic under the command of General Walter Dornberger. Since January 1943 the Allies' secret services had been on the alert for a new enemy weapon which French resistance agents were calling the "self-propelled shell". In his memoirs Churchill reports certain boasts which Hitler made about this weapon to reassure his entourage:

"By the end of 1943 London would be levelled to the ground and Britain forced to capitulate. October 20 was fixed as zero day for rocket attacks to begin. It is said that Hitler personally ordered the construction of 30,000 rockets for that day. This, if true, shows the absurd ideas on which he lived. The German Minister of Munitions, Dr. Speer, said that each V2 required about as many man-hours to make as six fighters. Hitler's demand was therefore for the equivalent of 180,000 fighters to be made in four months. This was ridiculous; but the production of both weapons was given first priority and 1,500 skilled workers were transferred from anti-aircraft and artillery production to the task."

As the threat grew more real, the Prime Minister charged his son-in-law Duncan Sandys with the task of centralising all work connected with rockets, their characteristics, their manufacture, and their installation, as well as the best methods of fighting them. On June 11 Duncan Sandys wrote to Churchill:

"The latest air reconnaissance photographs provide evidence that the Germans

are pressing on as quickly as possible with the development of the long-range rocket at the experimental establishment at Peenemünde, and that frequent firings are taking place. There are also signs that the light anti-aircraft defences at Peenemünde are being further strengthened.

"In these circumstances it is desirable that the projected bombing attack upon this establishment should be proceeded with as soon as possible."

The raid recommended in these terms was carried out during the night of August 16-17 by 597 four-engined bombers of Bomber Command which were ordered to drop 1,500 tons of high explosive and incendiaries from the then unusual height of just over 8,000 feet. On take-off the pilots were warned that in case of failure they would begin again without regard to the losses sustained or about to be sustained. The operation was carried out with magnificent dash and spirit and without excessive losses, a diversionary raid on Berlin having drawn off most of the German fighters. At the time the Anglo-American propaganda no doubt exaggerated the results of the raids, yet the operation did appreciably slow down the German V-1 and V-2 programme which, according to Hitler, was going to bring Britain to face the alternative of annihilation or capitulation before the end of the year. It was in fact on the eighth day of Operation "Overlord", that is only on June 13, 1944, that the first V-1 flying bomb took off for London.

The results

Altogether, 135,000 tons of bombs were dropped on Germany between January 1 and December 31, 1943. With what result? As we have seen, following the proclamation of full mobilisation as a consequence of Stalingrad, German war production shattered all records in every variety of weapon. And, in spite of fearful suffering, the morale of the German people was not badly affected by this pitiless offensive.

This is not to say that, accurate though these statements are, the Anglo-American offensive was a failure. On this point Georg Feuchter, in his *Der Luftkrieg*, makes two valuable observations.

The first concerns the ever-increasing ratio of A.A. weapons being made within the German armament industry. This eventually reached first 20 per cent and then 30 per cent of all artillery and brought with it a corresponding inflation in guncrews. In 1942 these amounted to 439,000 men, in 1943 there were 600,000, and there were nearly 900,000 in 1944. The increase was achieved at the expense of the Eastern Front where there were virtually none left. The second observation is equally, if not more, important. The German war industry owed its survival to a system of extreme decentralisation. The maintenance of its production depended in the last resort on keeping open the railways, the rivers, and the roads. On the day when the Anglo-Americans shifted the centre of gravity of their operations to the communications within the Third Reich, Dr. Speer's already overstretched network began rapidly to disintegrate and, once started, this became irreversible. The two Western Allies no longer lacked the means. At the end of the year Lieutenant-General Ira C. Eaker, from whom his colleague James H. Doolittle had taken over in Great Britain, assumed command of the 15th Air Force, a large new American strategic bombing formation.

◁▽ *Peenemünde before and after the Allied visitation on August 16-17. Damage to German installations was heavy, but of the 597 British bombers despatched, 40 failed to return and 32 others were damaged.*
▽ *Germany learns the horrors of the area bombing so beloved by "Bomber" Harris.*

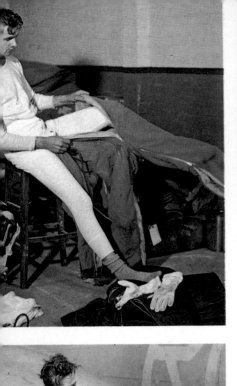

CHAPTER 110
Eisenhower's build-up

Let us cross the Channel and watch the preparations for "Overlord" from London. S.H.A.E.F. (Supreme Headquarters Allied Expeditionary Forces) had been set up under the initiative and the control of the Combined Chiefs-of-Staff Committee. In fact, it did not function with absolute smoothness but it should be noted that, with a few exceptions, the disagreements were not manifest during the preparation period. And up to mid-July 1944, Generals Eisenhower and Montgomery did really work shoulder to shoulder, though the functions that Montgomery took on himself did lead to some misunderstanding and were not understood in the same way by both men.

Writing to General Marshall on this matter on December 23, 1943, Eisenhower expressed his views as follows:

"In the early stages of OVERLORD I see no necessity for British and American Army Group Commanders. In fact, any such setup would be destructive of the

essential co-ordination between Ground and Air Forces."

Consequently, he entrusted Montgomery with the command of British and American land forces taking part in the landing itself and in later operations designed to consolidate and then extend the bridgeheads. Therefore Montgomery would have the responsibility of preparing and leading to its conclusion the offensive which would seal the fate of the German armies engaged in Normandy.

But later, when the Allies were out of Normandy, the victory would be exploited and this would take the Grand Alliance right to the very heart of Germany. This would be preceded by the establishment of two army groups, one Anglo-Canadian and the other American.

Montgomery would assume command of the first and Bradley was called upon to lead the second. Eisenhower would once more take over the command of land operations and remain C.-in-C.

△ *"Somewhere in England"–
the men of an American
artillery unit rest by the roadside
during the great build-up of the
"Overlord" forces in southern
England.*
◁ *Getting ready for the fray.
Staff Sergeant Lusic of the 8th Air
Force shows the preparations
needed by an air gunner before he
even boards his aircraft.*

Montgomery's rôle

Nothing, in the documents we have, indicates that Eisenhower left Montgomery under any misconception about his intention of taking over the reins from him again, but everything goes to suggest that, in his heart of hearts, Montgomery had flattered himself that his superior would change his mind in view of the successes that he (Montgomery) would win for him, and that, until the final victory, Eisenhower would leave him as commander of land forces which he had entrusted to him for the first stages of "Overlord". But even if Eisenhower had resigned himself to playing the rôle of a figurehead, his powerful American subordinates would not have put up with it, nor would his superior General George C. Marshall, and much less still American public opinion, which was influenced by a swarm of war correspondents accredited to S.H.A.E.F. The least that can be said about them is that

they were not very responsive to their British ally's point of view or methods.

British opinions of Eisenhower

But furthermore, and perhaps this is the most important point, it must be noted that, rightly or wrongly, General Eisenhower's talents did not greatly impress Montgomery. The latter had a real superiority complex in matters of strategy towards his chief. But Montgomery was not the only general in the British hierarchy who felt like this in regard to the American supreme commander. On May 15, 1944, leaving a conference during which Eisenhower, together with his subordinates, had explained his operational plans in the presence of George VI, the Prime Minister, and Field-Marshal Smuts, Brooke noted in his diary:

"The main impression I gathered was that Eisenhower was no real director of thought, plans, energy or direction. Just a co-ordinator, a good mixer, a champion of inter-Allied co-operation, and in those respects few can hold the candle to him. But is that enough? Or can we not find all qualities of a commander in one man? May be I am getting too hard to please, but I doubt it."

Re-reading his notes two years later, Lord Alanbrooke changes this portrait only in tone. This is how he depicts him:

"A past-master in the handling of allies, entirely impartial and consequently trusted by all. A charming personality and good co-ordinator. But no real commander . . . Ike might have been a showman calling on various actors to perform their various turns, but he was not the commander of the show who controlled and directed all the actors."

Eisenhower's personality

Unlike Brooke, Montgomery, MacArthur, and Patton, Eisenhower had not taken part in World War I and the highest command he had ever had in the inter-war years had been that of an infantry battalion. So, though he was completely at home with all aspects of staff work, he did not possess the tactical imagination which characterised to a rare degree

men such as Bradley and Montgomery. Certainly, though, he had a remarkable aptitude for assimilating the ideas of others and fitting them into the more general picture of his own sphere of responsibility.

In addition, there is much to admire in the calm authority, the tact, and the psychological deftness of a man who could get on with a subordinate as difficult as Montgomery, who, when asked, "But don't you ever obey orders?" could reply: "If I don't like them I'll go as far as I can in disobedience and try to bluff my way through. But, of course, if I can't get what I want, then I must submit in the end."

Likewise, Eisenhower managed to soften the verbal brutality of the brilliant but at times unbearable George S. Patton, at the same time as he promoted above his head the "serious, zealous and very cultivated" Omar N. Bradley, who had been Patton's subordinate in Sicily, without the least tension between these two soldiers of such great difference in temperament and method. The respect he had for them did not, nevertheless, prevent him from turning a deaf ear when some depreciatory remark about their British allies passed their lips.

It has been said that Eisenhower did not impose his will. It would be more accurate to say that he did not impose

◁△ *British tank crews load their Shermans aboard landing-craft.*
◁▽ *Eisenhower (standing, with binoculars) and Tedder watch American tank men training.*
△ *A stockpile of gun wheels and artillery wheels in southern England.*

▽ *A mobile, swastika-bedecked target for anti-tank gunners on practice shoots.*

The British Churchill VII Crocodile flame-thrower tank

Weight: 41.2 tons.
Other specifications and performance figures: as for Churchill VII.
Flame-throwing equipment: the hull machine gun was replaced by the flame projector, which was fed from the two-wheel trailer via the linkage between the trailer and tank and an armoured pipe under the belly of the tank. The armoured trailer weighed 6.5 tons, and carried 400 gallons of flame fuel, enough for 80 one-second bursts. The trailer could be jettisoned if hit, and the Churchill could then perform as an ordinary tank. The range of the flame projector was between 80 and 120 yards.

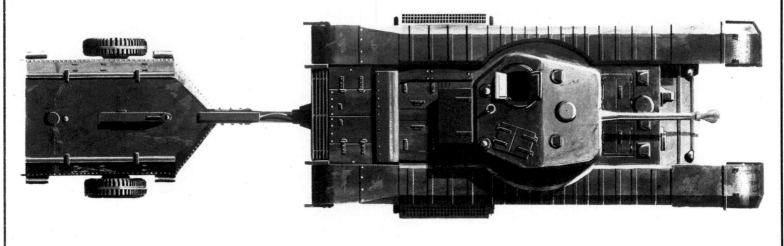

The British Infantry Tank Mark IV Churchill VII

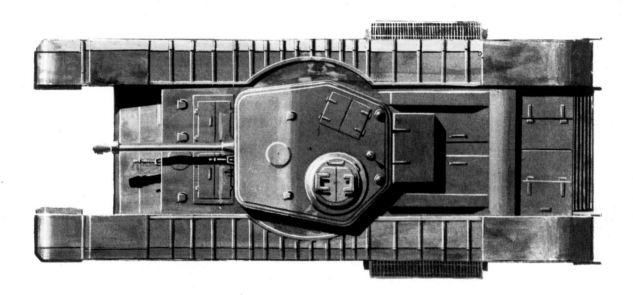

Weight: 40 tons.
Crew: 5.
Armament: one 75-mm Mark 5 gun with 84 rounds plus one .303-inch Bren and two 7.92-mm Besa machine guns with 600 and 6,525 rounds respectively.
Armour: hull front 152-mm, sides 95-mm, rear 50-mm, and decking 19-mm; turret front 152-mm, sides 94-mm, and roof 20-mm.
Engine: one Bedford "Twin-Six" 12-cylinder inline, 340-hp.
Speed: 13.5 mph.
Range: 90 miles.
Length: 24 feet 2 inches.
Width: 10 feet 10½ inches.
Height: 8 feet 10¼ inches.

△ The man who drew the first blueprints for "Overlord": C.O.S.S.A.C., short for "Chief-of-Staff to the Supreme Allied Commander". Lieutenant-General F. E. Morgan was given the post at the time of the Casablanca Conference.
▽ The final team, S.H.A.E.F.–"Supreme Headquarters of the Allied Expeditionary Forces". Left to right: Bradley, Ramsay, Tedder, Eisenhower, Montgomery, Leigh-Mallory, Bedell Smith.

himself often, but that he did so whenever the situation demanded his personal intervention, and then always very decisively. Two examples will suffice to justify this point of view.

One week before the launching of "Overlord", Air Chief Marshal Leigh-Mallory, commanding the tactical air forces, came for the last time to protest that a useless massacre awaited the American 82nd and 101st Airborne Divisions if the command insisted on landing them in the Cotentin peninsula. According to him, losses of glider-borne troops would amount to 70 per cent and half the paratroops would be killed or wounded in the drop. As Eisenhower himself later recorded: "I instructed the air commander to put his recommendations in a letter and informed him he would have my answer within a few hours."

After the few hours had passed, Eisenhower telephoned Leigh-Mallory. As the "Utah" Beach landing could not be abandoned, he was sticking to his deci-sion, but he did not omit to tell Leigh-Mallory that his orders would be confirmed in writing. As events were to prove, Leigh-Mallory's fears were largely unjustified. On December 19, 1944, with the Panzers advancing on Bastogne in the Ardennes, Eisenhower demonstrated the same characteristic *sang-froid* of a great leader. He had gone to Verdun, where he was awaited by Generals Bradley, Devers, and Patton. He said boldly as he opened the sitting: "The present situation is to be regarded as one of opportunity for us and not of disaster. There will be only cheerful faces at this conference table."

What is more, as his deputy he kept Air Chief Marshal Sir Arthur Tedder, who had been attached in this capacity since the end of January 1943. Here he could count on a first class ally, particularly qualified to get him the unreserved support of the British strategic air forces. Another invaluable aid was Eisenhower's Chief-of-Staff, Bedell Smith.

◁ *Key weapon for the assault: the D.D. (Duplex Drive) swimming tank. The D.D. was a waterproofed Sherman with twin propellers driven by the tank's engine. It was supported in the water by a deep, collapsible skirt which was lowered on reaching the beach, enabling the gun to come into action at once while the drive was shifted from the propellers to the tank tracks. The D.D. was a classic example of the British adapting a proved American weapon to a specialist rôle. At Bradley's headquarters these novel weapons were viewed with scepticism – which was to have bloody results on "Omaha" Beach.*
▽ *American Shermans on field manoeuvres.*

The C.O.S.S.A.C. plan criticised

On January 2, 1944 Eisenhower returned to the U.S. capital, where he had been summoned by General Marshall, and then went to the bedside of President Roosevelt, who was incapacitated for a few days. He would willingly have foregone having to go so far out of his way on his journey from Tunis to London, for time was pressing and what he knew of the plan drawn up by Lieutenant-General Sir F. E. Morgan and the C.O.S.S.A.C. group (Chief-of-Staff Allied Supreme Commander) was only partly to his liking.

"I was doubtful about the adequacy of the tactical plan because it contemplated an amphibious attack on a relatively narrow, three-division front with a total of only five divisions afloat at the instant of assault . . . In addition to being disturbed by the constricted nature of the proposed manoeuvre, I was also concerned because the outline I had seen failed to provide effectively for the quick capture of Cherbourg. I was convinced that the plan, unless it had been changed since I had seen it, did not emphasize sufficiently the early need for major ports and for rapid build-up."

Therefore, even before he flew off to the

United States, he instructed Montgomery to get together with Bedell Smith and begin an analysis and, if necessary, a revision of the C.O.S.S.A.C. plan and to report to him on the results of this on his return to London in mid-January.

As soon as his eye fell on the documents submitted to him, Montgomery made up his mind. The plan was "impracticable". This abrupt opinion was based on the following considerations:

"The initial landing is on too narrow a front and is confined to too small an area.

"By D+12 a total of 16 divisions have been landed on the same beaches as were used for the initial landings. This would lead to the most appalling confusion on the beaches, and the smooth development

△ and ▷ *Paratroops, who would form the airborne spearhead of the assault, in training. Heavy paratroop attacks were scheduled for both flanks of the invasion front.*

▽ *British airborne troops are given glider instruction.*

of the land battle would be made extremely difficult–if not impossible.

"Further divisions come pouring in, all over the same beaches. By D+24 a total of 24 divisions have been landed, all over the same beaches; control of the beaches would be very difficult; the confusion, instead of getting better, would get worse."

It will be noted that the objections which Montgomery raised about the C.O.S.S.A.C. plan, which he submitted confidentially to Churchill, convalescing in Marrakesh at the time, were based on considerations different from Eisenhower's. Nevertheless, they reinforced his determination to throw the whole project back into the melting-pot when he returned to London on January 14.

Montgomery's views prevail

Here, as Montgomery was responsible for the landings and their initial advance, he was not content with the severe analysis just quoted from, but proposed

another plan. Considering only the land forces, Montgomery's memorandum concluded that the following points were vital:

"*(a)* The initial landings must be made on the widest possible front.

(b) Corps must be able to develop operations from their own beaches, and other corps must NOT land *through* those beaches.

(c) British and American areas of landing must be kept separate. The provisions of *(a)* above must apply in each case.

(d) After the initial landings, the operation must be developed in such a way that a good port is secured quickly for the British and for American forces. Each should have its own port or group of ports."

Having laid down these principles, which were eminently sensible, Montgomery proceeded to deduce from them a plan of operations, one of whose many merits was the inclusion of a properly co-ordinated plan for co-operation by the tactical and strategic air forces available:

"The type of plan required is on the following lines:

(a) One British army to land on a front of two, or possibly three, corps. One American army similarly.

(b) Follow-up divisions to come in to the corps already on shore.

(c) The available assault craft to be used for the landing troops. Successive flights to follow rapidly in any type of unarmoured craft, and to be poured in.

(d) The air battle must be won before the operation is launched. We must then aim at success in the land battle by the speed and violence of our operations."

Eisenhower agrees with his subordinate

General Eisenhower is to be praised for siding with his subordinate. And so the plan which was put into effect on June 6, 1944, was a very much amended form of the C.O.S.S.A.C. project:

1. The narrow front which had aroused criticism was widened to take in Saint Martin-de-Varreville ("Utah" Beach) on the right, and Lion-sur-Mer ("Sword" Beach), on the left.
2. The taking of a bridgehead on the eastern side of the Cotentin peninsula

△ *How to lift an airborne division: Horsa gliders and Halifax and Stirling tugs.*

continued on page 1468

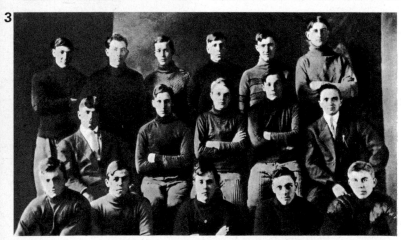

EISENHOWER ALLIED SUPREMO

Dwight D. Eisenhower: Allied supreme commander, soldier, diplomat; figurehead of the Anglo-American victory in Europe—all summed up in the three letters which spell "Ike".

Eisenhower was born on October 14, 1890, at Denison, Texas, the third son of a poor and hard-working family. In 1911 he entered the West Point Military Academy and passed out in the top third of his class. He commanded a tank training centre during World War I and was promoted major after the war.

From 1922 to 1924 Eisenhower served in the Panama Canal Zone; and then, in 1926, he took the first important step up the ladder to high command, graduating from the U.S. Army's command and general staff school first out of a class of 275. In 1928 he added to his laurels by graduating from the Army War College. This was followed by a year in France, up-dating a guide-book to American battlefields. Subsequent posts in Washington, D.C., culminated in his appointment in 1933 to the office of General MacArthur, Army Chief-of-Staff. When Mac-Arthur went to the Philippines in 1935 as military adviser, Eisen-

1. *Ike in the cockpit of a Marauder bomber.*
2. *At the age of two* (lower right) *with three of his brothers.*
3. *Member of the Abilene football team* (back row, third from left).
4. *Family reunion, 1926. Lieutenant-Colonel Eisenhower at left, standing.*
5. *Ike samples Army "C" rations in Tunisia.*
6. *Supreme commander. Watching manoeuvres with Montgomery.*

hower went with him.

When war broke out in September 1939 Eisenhower returned to the United States. In the summer manoeuvres in 1941 he made his mark as chief-of-staff of the 3rd Army and was soon promoted to brigadier-general. After Pearl Harbor he was recalled to Washington to serve as assistant chief of the war plans division of the general staff. This work naturally involved planning for the eventual invasion of Europe, which in turn required close discussion with the British, carried out by Eisenhower in April-May 1942. The following month Eisenhower returned to London as commander of the European Theatre of Operations (E.T.O.).

Eisenhower's baptism of fire in the "Torch" landings was severe. In Algeria and Tunisia he had to co-ordinate the movements of the 1st and 8th Armies – and cope with Rommel's push at Kasserine. The Tunisian campaign, however, proved conclusively that he really did have the magic blend of talents which got the best out of his wildly differing subordinates while coping with the all-time incalculable factor in war: unexpected and dangerous moves by the enemy at the worst moment.

Eisenhower's next task was the conquest of Sicily. Here he had to co-ordinate the 7th and 8th Armies and the differing talents of Patton and Montgomery. He showed his firmness as the "man in charge" by his disciplining of Patton over the "slapping incident" – when Patton slapped soldiers whom he believed to be cowards. But Sicily was only the

prelude to the negotiations for the surrender of Fascist Italy and the invasion of the Italian mainland.

Italian vacillation made these negotiations extremely tense, but Eisenhower finally tipped the scales by losing his temper. In the words of a British staff officer, he "demanded to be led to a telephone to speak to his Chief-of-Staff in Algiers. I took him to mine and waited while he bellowed down it, dictating on the spot a remarkably incisive telegram to be sent forthwith to Marshal Badoglio." This well-timed crack of the whip by Eisenhower had the desired effect and the surrender and landings both went ahead as planned.

The successful campaigns in Tunisia, Sicily, and Italy made Eisenhower an obvious contender for the supreme command of "Overlord"; but it took Roosevelt much soul-searching before he decided that the U.S. Army Chief-of-Staff, General Marshall, could not be spared from his current duties. The President made his decision on December 5, 1943. "Ike" would command the "Overlord" forces.

Eisenhower had formidable advantages when he took up his task. He had the fruits of all the preliminary work which had been put in on the subject. He had all the expert advice he needed, plus the knowledge that his forces would have technical and material superiority. And he had a sound team of subordinates. Yet all his tact and patience was still required to get those subordinates to give of their best – and at this "Ike" was a past master.

7. *With Mark Clark in London, returning a ranker's salute.*
8. *Chatting with paratroops.*
9. *The soldier-diplomat; Ike with the formidable combination of Churchill and de Gaulle.*
10. *Head of the S.H.A.E.F. team – with his hand on Berlin.*
11. *At a rubber dinghy demonstration.*
12. *Presenting a U.S. Army carbine to Montgomery.*
13. *A talk with the bomber chiefs – Brereton (left) and Spaatz.*
14. *Making a point on field manoeuvres.*
15. *Loneliness of command.*

continued from page 1463

allowed the Allies to deal with the problem of Cherbourg at their ease and not to have to worry later about the serious obstacle presented by the River Vire.

3. Plan C.O.S.S.A.C. allowed for the initial landing of three divisions supported by a "floating reserve" against the 716th and 352nd Infantry Divisions of the German LXXXIV Corps. On the day that "Overlord" began, there were eight Allied divisions facing four German divisions. Moreover, in the "Utah" sector, the 91st and 709th Divisions would only be engaged in part. In addition, the second stage of the landing had been increased to include seven divisions.

From all this, should it be concluded

that Sir Frederick Morgan and the staff of C.O.S.S.A.C. had not looked far enough ahead and had come up with a plan which was too narrow and unambitious? If this is the conclusion, it can only be reached if one does not know that they were caught in an impossible situation.

Operation "Anvil", which, according to the decision of the Combined British and American Chiefs-of-Staff, confirmed by the Teheran Conference, was to precede "Overlord" and retain considerable quantities of landing equipment in the Western Mediterranean.

That is why on February 21, Montgomery wrote to Eisenhower: "I recommend very strongly that we now throw the whole weight of our opinion into the scales against ANVIL."

"Anvil" postponed

For strictly strategic reasons, Eisenhower refused to accept this point of view, for the mission which had been entrusted to him had read:

"You will enter the Continent of Europe and, in conjunction with the other Allied Nations, undertake operations aimed at the heart of Germany and the destruction of her Armed Forces."

This instruction seemed to Eisenhower to demand an advance up the valleys of the Rhône and the Saône, linking up somewhere in France with the right wing of the armies which had crossed the Channel. Nevertheless, he gave in to the argument that the success of "Overlord" could only be assured by the postponement of "Anvil" until after July 15.

◁ △ and ◁ British engineers train in the building of pontoon bridges.
△ △ "Wasps" (top), which were flame-throwing Bren-gun carriers, and a standard infantry flame-thrower.
△ More flame-thrower support for the "poor bloody infantry".

"Overlord" put back to June

However, the alterations which came with the re-shaping of the C.O.S.S.A.C. plan forced the initial landing date to be put back from early May to early June. The actual date was subject to these considerations:

1. The parachute drop at night on both flanks of the attacking front required a date as close as possible to the full moon.
2. As three airborne divisions would be in action from midnight onwards, they

1469

▽ *American engineers lay a corduroy track, intended to carry vehicles in the assault wave over sticky going.*
▽▽ *Counterpart of the German Panzerschreck – the American "Bazooka" rocket gun.*
▷ *American gunners train in Scotland.*

had to be supported as soon as possible. Between dawn and the landing, a small interval of time would, nevertheless, be left free for the air forces and warships to neutralise and saturate the enemy's coastal defences.

3. Rommel's energetic multiplication of the quantity of mined obstructions on the beaches made it essential that Allied troops should reach them while the tide was still low enough not to have covered them, in order that the sappers in the first wave might have the utmost opportunity of dealing with the danger.

All these elements taken together timed the mighty enterprise within the dates of June 5 and June 7. It is worth noting in this connection that the Germans were taken unawares, for at every level of the Wehrmacht's hierarchy (Army Group "B", O.B.W., and O.K.W.), all were agreed that the invasion would be launched on the morning tide.

Eisenhower could not conceive of any later date for the landing which would not bring the whole Allied cause into serious danger. From the reports of his Intelligence network and from photographic reconnaissance, it appeared that there was a great increase in the number of V-1 launching ramps under construction in the Pas-de-Calais and the Cotentin peninsula, and that, within a few weeks, England would come under a new type of Blitz. Moreover the information he

received from the U.S.A. concerning the advanced stage of development reached by bacteriological and atomic weapons encouraged him to make haste, because there was, of course, no guarantee that German science was not working in the same direction.

Montgomery's plan

In his memoirs, which appeared in 1958, Lord Montgomery explains his plan of attack:

"It is important to understand that, once we had secured a good footing in Normandy, my plan was to *threaten* to break out on the eastern flank, that is in the Caen sector. By pursuing this threat relentlessly I intended to draw the main enemy reserves, particularly his armoured divisions, into that sector and to keep them there – using the British and Canadian forces under Dempsey for this purpose. Having got the main enemy strength committed on the *eastern* flank, my plan was to make the break-out on the *western* flank – using for this task the

△ *This is the enemy – American troops are briefed on German uniform recognition. The photograph is a typical example of pre-D-Day security measures; the background of this picture has been erased.*
▷ *Fighters roll through an English town. Security again: not only the street name but the tram number and the name of the city transport corporation have been removed.*
▷ ▷ △ *Armour aboard ship. The tank in the centre is an "Ark", carrying a box-girder bridge for dropping over anti-tank ditches.*
▷ ▷ *Heavily camouflaged against prying German air reconnaissance: Allied trucks in an open field.*

American forces under General Bradley. This break-out attack was to be launched southwards, and then to proceed eastwards in a wide sweep up to the Seine about Paris. I hoped that this gigantic wheel would pivot on Falaise. It aimed to cut off all the enemy forces south of the Seine, the bridges over the river having been destroyed by our air forces."

Some critics have said that as Montgomery was writing after the war, he was constructing long-term aims of which he was not thinking at the time, so that he could say that Rommel had been forced to dance to his tune in France as well as in North Africa.

Martin Blumenson, one of the contributors to the monumental *U.S. Army in World War II,* put the question in this way in 1963:

"Did Montgomery, from the beginning of the invasion, plan to attract and contain the bulk of the German power to facilitate an American advance on the right? Or did he develop the plan later as a rationalisation for his failure to advance through Caen? Was he more concerned with conserving the limited British manpower and was his containment of the enemy therefore a brilliant expedient that emerged from the tactical situation in June? The questions were interesting but irrelevant, for the Germans had massed their power opposite the British without regard for General Montgomery's original intentions."

Questions like these are not idle, for other great captains, notably Napoleon and the older Moltke, have posed for posterity by remodelling their victories in order to attribute their successes to long and brilliant preparation, when really they were due to their facility for improvisation, and, in a situation which upset their careful calculations, to their aptitude for taking maximum advantage of the smallest favourable circumstances. In this argument, we do not hesitate to come down on the side of Lord Montgomery, and this can be proved with the aid of three texts contemporary with the events. They come from Sir Arthur Bryant's *Triumph in the West* which clothes, as it were, Brooke's daily notes:

1. On June 15, 1944 Montgomery wrote to Brooke: "When 2nd Panzer Division suddenly appeared in the Villers-Bocage–Caumont area, it plugged the hole through which I had broken. I think it had been meant for offensive action against I Corps in the Caen area. So long as

Rommel uses his strategic reserves to plug holes, that is good."

2. On June 18, Brooke noted, from a message sent by Montgomery to his army commanders: "Once we can capture Caen and Cherbourg and all face in the same direction we have a mighty chance–to make the German Army come to our threat and defeat it between the Seine and the Loire."

3. On June 27 Montgomery wrote to Brooke: "My general broad plan is maturing . . . All the decent enemy stuff, and his Pz. and Pz. S.S. divisions are coming in on the Second Army front–according to plan. That had made it much easier for the First U.S. Army to do its task."

The case seems proved.

Air power's rôle

The British and American strategic and tactical air forces were a vital element in the success of Operation "Overlord", after five months of intensive training.

For this purpose, General Eisenhower

△ *A group pose for G.I.s on the quayside.*
▷ *Embarkation drill in full kit. Barrage balloons for the invasion fleet in the background.*
▽ *Formation manoeuvres in landing-craft.*

had managed to have all strategic bomber formations, based in Great Britain and southern Italy, placed at his disposal. Under the immediate command of Lieutenant-General Carl A. Spaatz, they comprised:

1. R.A.F. Bomber Command (Air Chief Marshal A. T. Harris);
2. The American 8th Air Force (Lieutenant-General James H. Doolittle) in Britain; and
3. The American 15th Air Force (Lieutenant-General Nathan F. Twining) in Italy.

In addition, through Air Chief Marshal Leigh-Mallory, he was able to use the American 9th Air Force (Major-General Hoyt S. Vandenberg), and the British 2nd Tactical Air Force (Air Marshal Sir Arthur Coningham).

For this air assault, American industry smashed all previous records. Between 1942 and 1943, its annual production had gone up from 48,000 to 86,000 machines of all types, until it reached a daily average of 350 in February 1944, i.e. close to one aeroplane every four minutes.

For its part, the R.A.F. had received 28,000 aircraft in 1943, of which 4,614 were four-engined bombers, 3,113 two-engined bombers, and 10,727 fighters and fighter-bombers. But by then British industry was working to its limit.

As regards the bombing of Germany, the division of labour between the British and the Americans worked according to a system established in 1943. Nevertheless, though Air Chief Marshal Harris stuck obstinately to his theory that the Third Reich could be forced into defeat merely by the effects of mass area bombing, General H. H. Arnold, commanding the U.S. Army Air Force, saw another objective for the daytime raids of his Flying Fortresses and Liberators, escorted further and further into the heart of Germany by ever-increasing numbers of long-range fighters.

The idea was to force Göring's fighters to stretch themselves to the limit to defend the Reich's centres of industrial production and to destroy them there. Thus total mastery of the air would be gained, and this would guarantee success for the troops who were preparing to cross the Channel and invade the continent.

▽ *Battle training. This particular assault course consists of a 200-yard obstacle race with rifle and pack, to be covered in four minutes.*

1475

CHAPTER III
On the brink

In the space available it is not possible to present a complete picture of the operations carried out by the British and American strategic air forces against the German industrial machine. The following is a summing-up of these operations and an analysis of the results achieved by June 1944.

On January 11, some 720 four-engined bombers of the 8th Air Force, forming a column of more than 200 miles long, shared between them the targets of Halberstadt, Brunswick, Magdeburg, and Aschersleben. During the battles in the Westphalian sky, no less than 59 American bombers were shot down. It would still have been a great success if 152 German aircraft had shared the same fate, as was announced by General Doolittle's headquarters. However, it was learnt after the war that the Luftwaffe's losses that day were no more than 40 aircraft.

United States airmen refer to the week of February 20 to February 26 as the "Big Week". For seven days the 8th and 15th Air Forces, relieved at night by R.A.F. Bomber Command, concentrated on the German aircraft industry. In a report to Stimson on February 27, 1945, General Arnold declared:

"The week of February 20-26, 1944 may well be classed by future historians as marking a decisive battle of history, one as decisive and of greater world importance than Gettysburg."

After calm appraisal, though, the historian cannot ratify this opinion, which puts the "Big Week" on the same level as July 3 and 4, 1863, days that saw Robert E. Lee and the cause of the Confederacy falling back finally before the superiority of the Union. Flying 3,000 sorties, the Americans suffered the loss of 244 bombers and 33 fighters while the R.A.F. lost 157 four-engined aircraft. The communiqué from London which announced, when the operations had finished, that 692 enemy aircraft had been shot down or destroyed on the ground, was very much mistaken in its figures. Nevertheless, thanks to the new Mustang long-range fighter escorts, American bomber losses were only 3·5% of aircraft despatched, while the rate of German fighter losses began to rise steeply. The heart of the Luftwaffe was

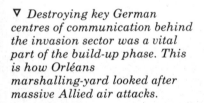

▽ *Destroying key German centres of communication behind the invasion sector was a vital part of the build-up phase. This is how Orléans marshalling-yard looked after massive Allied air attacks.*

being gradually torn out—inside the Reich itself.

However, in spite of the carpet of bombs which fell on the factories of Brunswick, Aschersleben, Bernburg, Leipzig, Augsburg, Regensburg, Stuttgart, Fürth, Gotha, Schweinfurt, Tutow, and Posen, German industry continued to build aircraft, by an elaborate process of decentralising production away from major cities. By August 1, 1944, the average monthly figure for the first seven months of the year had reached 3,650, of which 2,500 were day fighters, 250 night fighters, and 250 bombers. All the same, Göring had to defend the vital targets, and to do this he was forced to make painful decisions and to take aircraft away from the fighter squadrons behind the Atlantic Wall. Here it is true to say that the American attack on the German aircraft industry helped the Allied landings in France.

For 36 days and 55 nights, from January 1 to June 5, 1944, the great cities of the Reich suffered 102 serious attacks which devastated Berlin (17 raids), Brunswick (13 raids), Frankfurt (eight raids), Hanover (five raids), Magdeburg, Leipzig, Duisburg, and many others. In January, the 15th Air Force bombed Klagenfurt; on March 17, Vienna was raided for the first time. May 18 saw the port of Gdynia and the East Prussian city of Marienburg under attack. As can be seen, the whole of Germany was now vulnerable.

The right targets

Though General Spaatz's success in the battle against Germany's aircraft industry had only been partial, he unquestionably won a great victory in the attack he launched at the beginning of April 1944 against the Reich's sources of liquid, natural, and synthetic fuel.

On August 1, 1943, 179 B-24 Liberators of the American 9th Air Force had taken off from Benghazi and bombed the oil-wells and installations at Ploiești. But the success of the raid had not been equal to its boldness, for the Americans had lost 53 aircraft, eight of which were interned in Turkey. On April 4, 1944, the 15th Air Force, based around Foggia, made a fresh start with 230 four-engined bombers and produced far better results. The bombers extended their raids to refineries in Bucharest, Giurgiu, Budapest, and

Vienna, to the Danube ports and the convoys of barges going up the river, and this managed to reduce the amount of oil that Germany was drawing from Rumania by 80 per cent. From 200,000 tons in February 1944, the amount had fallen to 40,000 in June.

But the most important aspect was the plan approved on April 19 by General Eisenhower, by which the 8th Air Force and Bomber Command began a systematic attack on the German synthetic fuel industry. On May 12, 935 American bombers dropped a hail of high-explosive and incendiary bombs on plant at Leuna,

△ *A smashed German supply-train in France. Obviously the Germans would try to prevent the Allies from building up a local superiority in the beach-head; the Allies must therefore keep the flow of German reinforcements to the utter minimum or shut it off altogether.*

△ *B-24 Liberators unload.*
▷ *A direct hit on the viaduct at Poix. A train can be seen steaming on to the viaduct at the bottom of the picture, but subsequent air reconnaissance did not establish whether its brakes were good enough.*
▽ *Another smashed station.*

Böhlen, Zeitz, Lützkendorf, and Brüx. On May 28 and May 29, the well-defended American four-engined bombers returned to the targets and completely laid waste the great coal hydrogenation plants of Politz in Pomerania. In their struggle against the German war sinews, the 8th Army Air Force had found the right target. This was seen clearly by General Spaatz, though perhaps not by others, when on June 8 he sent a directive to the 8th and 15th Air Forces ordering them to concentrate on Germany's fuel production centres. Bomber Command also joined this offensive.

In a memorandum to the Führer on June 30, Speer, the German Minister of War Production, wrote:

"If we cannot manage to protect our hydrogenation factories and our refineries by all possible means, it will be impossible to get them back into working order from the state they are in now. If that happens, then by September we shall no longer be capable of covering the Wehrmacht's most urgent needs. In other words, from then on there will be a gap which will be impossible to fill and which will bring in its train inevitable tragic consequences."

Albert Speer, whose organisational gifts are recognised by all, did not exaggerate matters in Hitler's style. This is clearly evident from the following table, the figures for which are taken from the book which Wolfgang Birkenfeld wrote in 1964 on the history of the manufacture of synthetic fuel during the Third Reich.

Aviation fuel (in thousands of tons)

	Pro-grammed	Produced	Con-sumed
January	165	159	122
February	165	164	135
March	169	181	156
April	172	175	164
May	184	156	195
June	198	52	182
July	207	35	136
August	213	17	115
September	221	10	60
October	228	20	53
November	230	49	53
December	223	26	44

Similar conclusions could be reached from the figures for ordinary petrol and diesel fuel. It is calculated that a Panzer division, according to its 1944 establishment, consumed in battle some 55,000 gallons of fuel a day. Towards the end of summer 1944, the aircraft and tanks of the Third Reich were running on almost empty fuel tanks.

Occupied areas to be bombed?

Sir Trafford Leigh-Mallory's air forces had the mission of preparing for the landings and creating conditions which would permit the British and American armies fighting in Normandy to win the great air and ground battle over the Reich which, it was expected, would lead to final victory.

Even so, all General Eisenhower's energy and power of argument was required to get the green light from Churchill for the bombing planned, for the Prime Minister hated the idea of bombing the peoples whom Operation "Overlord" was to free from the German yoke.

German communications

While attacks on the V-1 launching sites and on German industry continued, the bulk of the Allied effort, including Bomber Command whose aircraft could now bomb more accurately, and with heavier loads than American bombers, was to be devoted to destroying enemy communications in France, to inhibit the free movement of German troops after the landings.

Bombing objectives in Western Europe

1. To halt the movement of reserves

The systematic attack on communications was aimed at preventing O.K.W. and Army Group "B" reserves from reaching the battlefields. But at the same time it was at all costs essential to avoid revealing, by the choice of targets, the primary objectives of Operation "Overlord".

Bearing in mind these two contradictory requirements, which had to be satisfied at the same time, the Allied squadrons began by dropping two curtains of bombs, one along the Seine between Rouen and Paris and the other following the line of the Albert Canal from Antwerp to Liège, finishing at Namur. Within these lines, about 20 principal railway junctions were completely wiped out. As the Allies did not wish to inflict this treatment on Paris, they restricted themselves to destroying the marshalling yards of its outer suburban area: Trappes, Juvisy, and Villeneuve Saint Georges. In this way the Allies counted on preventing the German 15th Army from intervening on the left bank of the Seine and at the same time convincing German high command that the probable landing-zone was the Pas-de-Calais far from the planned attack on Normandy.

2. To cut lines of communication

Even so, Rundstedt had to be prevented from reinforcing the Normandy battlefields with the eight divisions he had in Brittany, or from Army Group "G" (Colonel-General Blaskowitz), which had 15, including three Panzer, divisions between Nantes and Hendaye and between Perpignan and Menton. This was the reason for the hail of bombs which fell at intervals on Rennes, Nantes, Le Mans, Angers, and the most important towns of the Loire valley, while the bombing of Lyons, Saint Etienne, Avignon, Marseilles, and Toulon made Hitler think an attack on the Côte d'Azur was being prepared. Finally, in Lorraine, Alsace, and Champagne, the lines along which O.K.W. might route its reserves to reinforce the Western Front were also cut.

On May 4, the bridge at Gaillon collapsed under the very eyes of Rommel, who had just completed an inspection at Riva Bella. Mantes bridge had also been

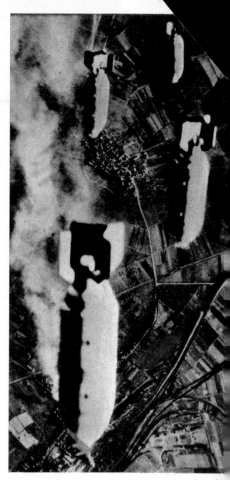

△ *A stick of "heavies" makes for its target.*

▽ *A German housewife, clutching hastily-snatched belongings, runs from her burning home.*

△ *The spectre that hung over "Fortress Europe" – Boeing B-17's in mass formation.*
▷ *Bitter German propaganda stressing the inevitable by-product of strategic bombing: civilian deaths and maimings.*

EN 6 MOIS
L'AVIATION ANGLO-AMÉRICAINE
A TUÉ
3.112 FRANÇAIS, HOMMES, FEMMES
ENFANTS
5.228 PERSONNES
25 HOPITAUX 44 EGLISES 118 ECOLES
31.177 MAISONS

destroyed on the same day, leaving no other passable bridges over the Seine below Paris. On the same day the Loire bridges downstream from Blois had met the same fate.

This campaign against the railway communications of Western Europe met with absolute success, particularly because from May 1 onward the British and American tactical air forces harried locomotives, both on the track and in the repair sheds. So intense and accurate was this offensive that by June 6, railway traffic had fallen to half its January 1943 level in the rest of France and to only 13 per cent in the area north of the Loire. Catastrophic consequences for German strategy followed. Here the example often given is that of the *Waffen*-S.S. II Panzer Corps, which had been lent to Model to re-establish the line in Eastern Galicia. When the invasion was reported, the corps was entrained at L'vov and took five days to reach Nancy. After here, the railways were in such a state that the corps had to be detrained and sent to the Normandy front by road. At a time when every hour was vital, this brought it into battle four days later than calculated.

Another result of the bombing had not been foreseen by S.H.A.E.F. Because of the destruction and the absolute priority given to military transport, iron ore ceased to flow into the Saar factories, while the coal stocks at the pit-heads mounted up.

3. To destroy coastal radar and guns
Another success for British and American air forces was the action they took against the radar network set up by the Germans between Cape Gris-Nez and Cape Barfleur. Also the attack on the coastal batteries placed or in course of emplacement between Le Havre and Cherbourg brought about the destruction of a certain number of large-calibre guns or caused the Germans to move them back inland, with the result that they took no part in repelling the landings. In any case, there had been so much delay in building the concrete shelters intended to house them that they were not usable.

Sperrle's air force in France had been defeated in the air or wiped out on the ground and was almost destroyed. And so, as they instructed raw recruits moving up to the front, the old soldiers of the Wehrmacht would say: "If you see a white plane, it's an American; if it's black, it's the R.A.F. If you don't see any planes, it's the Luftwaffe."

Assault and lodgement

Cornelius Ryan, in his book *The Longest Day,* emphasises the importance of the H-hour decision when he described the historic scene:

"Eisenhower now polled his commanders one by one. General Smith thought that the attack should go in on the sixth – it was a gamble, but one that should be taken. Tedder and Leigh-Mallory were both fearful that even the predicted cloud cover would prove too much for the air forces to operate effectively . . . Montgomery stuck to the decision that he had made the night before when the June 5 D-Day had been postponed. 'I would say Go,' he said.

"It was now up to Ike. The moment had come when only he could make the decision. There was a long silence as Eisenhower weighed all the possibilities. General Smith, watching, was struck by the 'isolation and loneliness' of the Supreme Commander as he sat, hands clasped before him, looking down at the table. The minutes ticked by; some say two minutes passed, others as many as five. Then Eisenhower, his face strained, looked up and announced his decision. Slowly he said, 'I am quite positive we must give the order . . . I don't like it, but there it is . . . I don't see how we can do anything else,' Eisenhower stood up. He looked tired, but some of the tension had left his face."

When one reviews the first 24 hours of Operation "Overlord", the rôle of the Resistance must first be mentioned. It was in fact vital. This opinion is based on the evidence of the Allied and German combatants, and the works on the Resistance by Colonel Rémy, Pierre Nord, and George Martelli should also be carefully considered. No military operation was ever based on such comprehensive Intelligence as "Overlord". Evidence for this is offered by the remarks of the operations officer of the 12th *"Hitlerjugend"* S.S. Panzer Division when he examined a map which had been found on June 8 in the wreck of a Canadian tank. "We were astounded at the accuracy with which all the German fortifications were marked in; even the weapons, right down to the light machine guns and mortars, were listed. And we were disgusted that our own Intelligence had not been able to stop this sort of spying. We found out, later on, that a Frenchman had been arrested who admitted that he had spied for years in the Orne sector, appearing every day in his greengrocer's van on the coastal road. We could clearly see on this map the result of his activities, and that of other spies also."

These were the results obtained by the networks organised by Colonel Rémy from 1942 onwards. Admittedly there were some slight errors and omissions in their summaries: these were inevitable. The English would probably not have embarked on the dangerous airborne attack on the Merville battery if they had known that instead of the 4-inch guns it was thought to have had, it had four 3-inch guns which were not powerful enough to affect the landing of the British 3rd Division at Riva-Bella. Similarly, the Rangers would not have scaled Pointe de Hoe had they known that its casemates were without the six long range guns they were reported to have.

General Bradley moreover did not know that Rommel had advanced five battalions from the 352nd Division to support the regiment on the left wing of the 716th Division. The two carrier-pigeons bringing news of this considerable reinforcement of the enemy's defences had been shot down in flight. However, the Allies' otherwise excellent information concerning the German army's plans was gained at the expense of considerable personal sacrifice and much loss of life.

Weather conditions against the Allies

It is well known that weather conditions played an important part in the way that the Germans were taken by surprise at dawn on June 6. They had a paralysing effect. Rommel's opinion, that the landing would only take place when dawn and high tide coincided, was also mistaken. His naval commander, Vice-Admiral Ruge, noted in his diary on June 4: "Rain and a very strong west wind". Moreover, before leaving la Roche-Guyon via Herrlingen for Berchtesgaden, Rommel noted in the Army Group "B" diary at 0600 hours on the same day that "he had no doubts about leaving as the tides would be very unfavourable for a landing in his absence,

and air reconnaissance gave no reason to think that a landing could possibly be imminent." At the same time, on the other side of the Channel, Eisenhower had just postponed "Overlord". On the next day, owing to the temporary spell of good weather forecast by Group-Captain Stagg, Eisenhower decided to cross on June 6, while the German weathermen at O.B.W. still maintained that a landing was out of the question.

Up to now the weather conditions had favoured the Allies. After midnight on June 5, the weather turned against them;

▽ *The Allies present the world's account at Germany's Atlantic Wall.*

The American/British Sherman Duplex Drive tank

Performance and specifications: basically similar to that of the unconverted model.

Duplex Drive: Lacking sufficient buoyancy in itself, the Sherman was fitted with the flotation device invented by Nicholas Straussler earlier in the war. This flotation device consisted of a boat-shaped platform attached to the hull of the tank, which had to be waterproofed, and a collapsible canvas screen. When it was desired to enter the water, 36 rubber tubes inside the screen were inflated from two air bottles on the tank's rear decking. These tubes lifted the screen, which was then held fully up by metal struts. The process took about quarter of an hour. In the water the tank turret was level with the water, the screen providing about three feet of freeboard. The propellers at the rear of the vehicle were driven off the tracks and gave the tank a speed of 4 knots in the water. Steering was by swivelling the propellers.

although the wind had fallen a little, as Group-Captain Stagg had predicted, it was blowing strongly enough to scatter widely the paratroopers of the 82nd and 101st American Airborne Divisions, who had dropped over the Cotentin peninsula, and the British 6th Airborne Division which had dropped between the Orne and the Dives.

A few hours later, the bomber attack failed for the same reason to neutralise the "Omaha" Beach defences. In the same sector, disaster met the amphibious tank formation which was to support the left wing of the American 1st Division: of the 32 tanks which were launched into the water 6,000 yards from the shore, 27 sank like stones with most of their crews; the canvas flotation skirt supported by a tubular framework gave the tanks only about 3 feet free-board–but the sea was running with a swell of more than 3 feet. The Americans who landed between Vierville and Saint Laurent were therefore put to a gruelling test.

One other apparently accidental factor this time favoured the attackers. On the evening of June 5 Lieutenant-Colonel Hellmuth Meyer, chief Intelligence officer of the German 15th Army, interrupted Colonel-General von Salmuth's game of bridge and told him that the B.B.C. had just broadcast a special message for the French resistance networks:

"Blessent mon coeur
D'une langueur
Monotone"
(a quotation from Verlaine's poem Chanson d'automne).

The Abwehr had found out, though it is not yet known how, that the code message meant that the landing would take place within 48 hours after midnight of the day of the message.

When he received this news, the commander of the 15th Army not only alerted his staff without delay, but also transmitted this vital information to his superiors at Army Group "B", O.B.W., and O.K.W. At la Roche-Guyon Lieutenant-General Speidel, who was deputising in Rommel's absence, did not think of urging the 7th Army at Le Mans to prepare for action, and at St. Germain-en-Laye no one checked that he had done so.

In his book, Invasion–They're Coming, Paul Carell comments:
"Here is the well-nigh incredible story of why, nevertheless, they were caught unawares." Can we do better than the author of Invasion–They're Coming? Field-Marshal von Rundstedt can be exonerated, since he had just signed an Intelligence report for the German High Command. The following excerpts are taken from Cornelius Ryan's book:
"The systematic and distinct increase

△ Men and vehicles of the U.S. 1st Army land on the coast of Normandy. The Americans, putting their amphibious tanks into the water further out than the British, suffered fairly heavy losses when the swell proved too much for the D.D. tanks and sank all but five at Omaha.

The British Churchill Carpet-Layer Type D Mark III armoured vehicle

This was a converted Churchill designed to unroll a length of 9 feet 11 inches-wide matting over soft ground and barbed wire to facilitate the advance of other armoured vehicles, soft-skinned vehicles, and troops. The matting was carried on the "bobbin" and unrolled under the tank. When the full length of matting had been used, the "bobbin" could be jettisoned with a small explosive charge. Laying speed was 2 mph. The vehicle illustrated is fitted with deep wading gear.

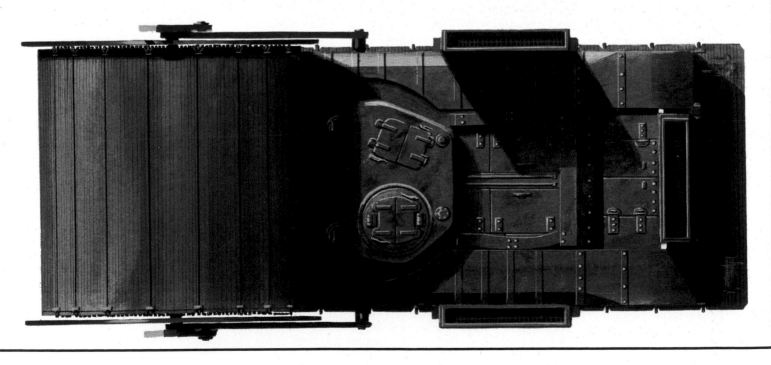

The American/British Sherman Crab mine-clearing flail tank

This was an adaptation of the basic Sherman fitted with a whirling flail to set off mines in the tank's path. Based on the ideas of a South African officer, Major A. S. du Toit, the Crab was fitted with twin booms projecting in front of the vehicle to carry the rotor drum and heavy flailing chains. The drive was taken from the main engine via a chain drive and thence to a drive shaft in the right-hand boom. The whole flailing device could be lifted hydraulically to allow the vehicle to operate as a conventional gun tank. The "antennae" on the tank's rear are dim lights to guide other tanks following behind, and the containers (angled at 45 degrees) held powdered chalk to mark the cleared path.

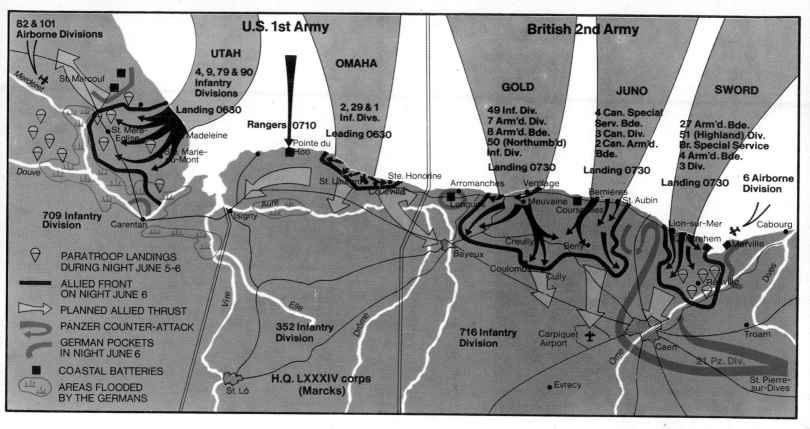

U.S. 1st Army — British 2nd Army

82 & 101 Airborne Divisions

UTAH
4, 9, 79 & 90 Infantry Divisions
Landing 0630

Rangers 0710

OMAHA
2, 29 & 1 Inf. Divs.
Leading 0630

GOLD
49 Inf. Div.
7 Arm'd. Div.
8 Arm'd. Bde.
50 (Northumb'd) Inf. Div.
Landing 0730

JUNO
4 Can. Special Serv. Bde.
3 Can. Div.
2 Can. Arm'd. Bde.
Landing 0730

SWORD
27 Arm'd. Bde.
51 (Highland) Div.
Br. Special Service
4 Arm'd. Bde.
3 Div.
Landing 0730

6 Airborne Division

709 Infantry Division

352 Infantry Division

716 Infantry Division

Carpiquet Airport

H.Q. LXXXIV corps (Marcks)

21 Pz. Div.

PARATROOP LANDINGS DURING NIGHT JUNE 5-6

ALLIED FRONT ON NIGHT JUNE 6

PLANNED ALLIED THRUST

PANZER COUNTER-ATTACK

GERMAN POCKETS IN NIGHT JUNE 6

COASTAL BATTERIES

AREAS FLOODED BY THE GERMANS

of air attacks indicates that the enemy has reached a high degree of readiness. The probable invasion front remains the sector from the Scheldt (in Holland) to Normandy ... and it is not impossible that the north front of Brittany might be included ... it is still not clear where the enemy will invade within this total area. Concentrated air attacks on the coast defences between Dunkirk and Dieppe may mean that the main Allied invasion effort will be made there . . . (but) imminence of invasion is not recognisable."

After accepting the report's rather vague conclusions (it was called *The Allies' Probable Intentions*), Rundstedt, it can be assumed, considered that the 15th Army's alert position, with its right on the Escaut and its left at Cabourg, was ready for any emergency.

One may also assume that Speidel, the chief-of-staff of Army Group "B", was still influenced by Rommel, who had said definitely the day before that the Allies could not possibly make the big attempt in his absence. Moreover, there is no doubt that too frequent alerts would have harmed the troops' morale and prejudiced their training, as well as interrupting the fortification work in which they were engaged.

Admittedly, if the 7th Army and LXXXIV Corps had been alerted at about 2300 hours on July 5, the *coup* attempted by a glider detachment of the British 6th

Airborne Division and the U.S. 82nd Airborne Division's attack on Sainte Mère-Eglise would almost certainly have failed.

Allied air supremacy all important

Admiral Sir Bertram Ramsay, the commander of the naval Operation "Fortune" supporting "Overlord", is said to have likened the invasion army to a shell fired by the navy, but Montgomery asserted that only air supremacy would ensure naval supremacy.

On June 6, 1944, the Anglo-American forces conformed to the two conditions laid down by the two British war leaders. In the air General Eisenhower, faced with 419 Luftwaffe planes, had more than 10,500 fighting planes at his disposal:

    3,467 four-engined bombers
    1,645 twin-engined bombers
    5,409 fighter bombers and interceptor fighters

Therefore he was in a position to use 2,355 transport planes and 867 gliders carrying about 27,000 troops and their *matériel* including light tanks, with no risk of attack by German fighters, though there was still the threat of anti-aircraft defences.

◁ *American infantry come ashore.*
△ *Hitler's fond dream that the Allies' "European adventure" would be "fatal". It could have been, but for Hitler's foolish insistence that the landings in Normandy were only a feint.*

△ *Part of the vast Allied invasion force wallows in the Channel off Normandy, unhindered by the weather and virtually undisturbed by the Luftwaffe.*

▽ *Men of the 3rd Canadian Division disembark at Courselles, on "Juno" Beach.*

The Allied invasion fleet

At sea, the embarkation fleet from British ports consisted of 4,126 transport vessels, including converted liners acting as floating headquarters to the major units being landed, and the LCT(R) support craft firing salvoes of 792 5-inch rockets which saturated an area of 750 by 160 yards. This fleet included 1,173 large and small ships transporting armoured vehicles, which shows how important it was for the infantry attacking the Atlantic Wall to have support from tanks and their guns. The fleet for the initial assault consisted (it is reliably reported) of 1,213 ships of all sizes flying seven different flags; three-quarters of them flew the Royal Navy's White Ensign. They included:

- 7 battleships (3 American)
- 2 monitors
- 23 cruisers (3 American, 2 French, 1 Polish)
- 80 destroyers (34 American, 2 Polish, 2 Norwegian)
- 25 torpedo-boats (1 French, 2 Polish, 1 Norwegian)
- 63 corvettes (3 French, 2 Norwegian, 2 Greek)
- 2 Dutch gunboats
- 98 minesweepers (9 American)

Of this fleet, all the warships, monitors and gunboats, 18 cruisers and about 50 destroyers had been assigned fire targets of the German batteries between Villerville (opposite Le Havre) and the Barfleur cape: these batteries were therefore engaged by 52 12-inch, 14-inch, and 15-

inch guns and more than 500 medium calibre guns whose fire was all the more effective as it was controlled from the air by Spitfire fighters especially detailed for this purpose.

This huge fleet of 5,339 ships was in the Channel on Sunday June 4 when it received the signal that the assault was deferred from the following day to June 6; a part of the fleet spent the day cruising in the area. But the bad weather which caused the postponement also kept the Luftwaffe patrols grounded; otherwise they would have spotted and reported this unusual concentration of ships. On the evening of June 5 the fleet assembled south of the Isle of Wight and made for its objectives in ten columns.

Admiral Lemonnier, who was on the bridge of the *Montcalm,* described the night crossing: "Spotted the buoy at the entrance to the channel which we must follow for four hours behind a flotilla of minesweepers.

"Now we are only doing 6 knots. The sweepers aren't moving. Possibly they've found some mines and the rough sea is hampering them in their work.

"We have to stop continually. We can only move forward in fits, as we have to take care to stay in our narrow channel. This isn't the time to be put stupidly out of action by a mine.

"We feel as though we are in one of those endless rows of cars blocked outside a big city on a Sunday evening, moving forward by pressing the accelerator slightly, then putting the brake on, touching the rear light of the car ahead – with one difference, that here there is not the slightest light to mark the stern of the ship ahead. Luckily there is just enough light to make out the outlines of the *Georges Leygues* and to keep a look-out."

△ *British Infantrymen start on their dangerous trek to the dubious shelter of the shore through heavy German machine gun and mortar fire.*

Ramsay's objectives

Admiral Ramsay had divided his forces into two:
1. Under the American Rear-Admiral A. G. Kirk, the Western Naval Task Force was to land and support the American V and VII Corps on the "Utah" and "Omaha" Beaches on both sides of the Vire estuary. All ships flying the Stars and Stripes, including the *Nevada,* a survivor from Pearl Harbor, had appropriately been assigned to him.
2. Under Rear-Admiral Sir Philip Vian,

the Eastern Naval Task Force was to perform identical services for the British I and XXX Corps which were to come ashore between Ver-Plage and Ouistreham on the beaches called (from west to east), "Gold", "Juno", and "Sword".

When reviewing the Allied air and naval forces, the power and quality of the support they gave the land forces in the hard fighting against the defenders of the Atlantic Wall must be emphasised. For example, two of the three Czechoslovak 8-inch guns comprising the Saint Marcouf battery had been destroyed; similarly the four 6-inch guns of the Longues battery, near Port-en-Bessin, were silenced by the fire of the cruisers *Ajax, Montcalm,* and *Georges Leygues.* In addition, Allied air forces over the battle sector had been increased and they responded rapidly, accurately and efficiently to all requests from the ground forces. From dawn to dusk they had made over 4,600 sorties, while only about 50 planes reminded both sides of the Luftwaffe's existence.

The Germans guarding the coast on the night of June 5-6 were frequently caught off their guard, and several comic incidents were reported. Paul Carell gives an example:

"Hoffman stepped outside the bunker. He gave a start. Six giant birds were making straight for his battle head-quarters. They were clearly visible, for

the moon had just broken through the clouds. 'They're bailing out.' For an instant Hoffman thought the aircraft had been damaged and its crew was going to jump. But then he understood. This was an airborne landing by para-troops. The white mushrooms were floating down–straight at his bunker.

"'Alarm! Enemy parachutists!' The men at 3rd Battalion head-quarters had never pulled on their trousers so fast before.

"Besides reports of parachute landings, radar stations began to signal huge concentrations of aircraft.

"But both in Paris and in Rastenburg the news was received sceptically. 'What,

△ *Safe landing for a British Horsa glider beside a tree-lined road.*
Overleaf: *The American landings.*

in this weather?' Even the chief-of-staff C.-in-C. West scoffed: 'Maybe a flock of seagulls?'"

At the end of the first day, Eisenhower and Montgomery were in a position to make the following estimate of their gains and losses:

On the whole, the landing had been successful, but the Americans and the British had nowhere gained their prescribed objectives for the evening of D-Day. North of the Vire the American 82nd and 101st Airborne Divisions, under Major-Generals M. B. Ridgway and M. D. Taylor respectively, which were due to protect VII Corps' right (Lieutenant-General J. L. Collins) and give it access to the right bank of the Merderet, had scattered in small pockets in the night; in addition they lost many men and much

had been completely and devastatingly effective.

"In Ste. Mère-Eglise, as the stunned townspeople watched from behind their shuttered windows, paratroops of the 82nd's 505th Regiment slipped cautiously through the empty streets. The church bell was silent now. On the steeple Private John Steele's empty parachute hung limp . . .

"Passing round the back of the church, P. F. C. William Tucker reached the square and set up his machine-gun behind a tree. Then as he looked out on the moonlit square he saw a parachute and, lying next to him, a dead German. On the far side were the crumpled, sprawled shapes of other bodies. As Tucker sat there in the semi-darkness trying to figure out what happened, he began to feel that

▽ *American landing craft head in towards "Omaha" Beach, which was very nearly a complete disaster when the Germans pinned down the landing forces on the beach.*

matériel in the shallow floods and minefields laid by the Germans. In short, of the 17,262 fighting men of the two divisions who jumped or landed on "the longest day", 2,499, or nearly 15 per cent, were missing.

Nevertheless a regiment from the 82nd Airborne Division had occupied the small town of Sainte Mère-Eglise (because of the panic flight of a service unit of German A.A. defences), maintained its ground, and in the evening had made contact with the American 4th Division which had landed on "Utah" Beach. This unit under Major-General Barton had had a relatively easy task, as the air and naval bombardment on the support points of the German 709th Division (Lieutenant-General von Schlieben) barring its way

he was not alone—that somebody was standing behind him. Grabbing the cumbersome machine-gun, he whirled around. His eyes came level with a pair of boots slowly swaying back and forth. Tucker hastily stepped back. A dead paratrooper was hanging in the tree looking down at him.

"Then (Lt.-Colonel) Krause pulled an American flag from his pocket. It was old and worn—the same flag that the 505th had raised over Naples . . . He walked to the townhall, and on the flagpole by the side of the door, ran up the colours. There was no ceremony. In the square of the dead paratroopers the fighting was over. The Stars and Stripes flew over the first town to be liberated by the Americans in France."

Power of the Allied offensive

Paul Carell, who conducted a careful survey among the German survivors of this campaign, describes the destruction of the defence-works W.5 surrounding the beach near the small village of la Madeleine.

"All the fortifications they had laboriously dug and built through the weeks had been churned up like a children's sand-pit. The 75-millimetre anti-tank gun was a heap of twisted metal. The 88-millimetre gun had taken some bad knocks. Two ammunition bunkers had blown up. The machine-gun nests had

been buried by avalanches of sand.

"Immediately the infernal concert started – rockets. They were firing only at the two corner bunkers with their 50-millimetre armoured carrier-cannon. The rockets slammed against the bunkers. They smacked through the apertures. The left bunker blew up at once, evidently a direct hit, through the aperture, among the stored shells. The bunker on the right was enveloped in smoke and flames. When the attack was over both bunkers and guns were only rubble and scrap metal. The crews had been killed or severely wounded."

A plane appeared and disappeared. "But evidently it delivered its message. The heavy naval bombardment began. Continuous, uninterrupted hell. Blow upon

blow the huge shells crashed into the strongpoint. Trenches were levelled. Barbed wire was torn to shreds. Minefields were blown up. Bunkers were drowned in the loose sand of the dunes. The stone building with the telephone exchange crumbled. The fire-control posts of the flame-throwers received a direct hit."

It is not therefore surprising that the losses of the American 4th Division amounted only to 197 killed, wounded, and missing on June 6. At midnight the whole division had landed (with the exception of one battery), a total of 21,328 men, 1,742 vehicles, and 1,950 tons of *matériel*, munitions, and fuel.

When it landed at "Omaha", the American 1st Division (Major-General C. R. Huebner) had been given the main road N.

△ △ Commandos press inland from the beach area. Note the "funny" bridging tank in the background.
△ The beach area. Only by the most careful planning and training were the schedules so vital for success ensured, and the chaos that could so easily have jeopardised the whole operation avoided.

13, which runs from Caen to Cherbourg, as its objective for the day. This required an advance of three miles from the Vierville beach. It was also to extend its right as far as Isigny and its left as far as the western approach to Bayeux, where it was to make contact with the inner flank of the British 2nd Army. For this purpose Major-General L. T. Gerow, commander of V Corps, had reinforced his corps with a combined regiment drawn from the 29th Division. At nightfall the 1st Division had not got beyond the small villages of Saint Laurent and Colleville.

In addition the air bombardment had missed its target, the majority of the D.D. tanks had sunk before they reached the beaches, and the 1st Division had come up against the newly-arrived, elite 352nd Division. Although U.S. Command knew of this development they had failed to inform their combat troops. At about 1000 hours General Bradley, the commander of the American 1st Army, had sent ashore his chief-of-staff and received a discouraging report from him:

"The 1st Division lay pinned down behind the sea wall while the enemy swept the beaches with small-arms fire. Artillery chased the landing craft where they milled offshore. Much of the difficulty had been caused by the underwater obstructions. Not only had the demolition teams suffered paralysing casualties, but much of their equipment had been swept away. Only six paths had been blown in that barricade before the tide halted their operations. Unable to break through the obstacles that blocked their assigned beaches, craft turned toward Easy Red where the gaps had been blown. Then as successive waves ran in toward the cluttered beach-head they soon found themselves snarled in a jam offshore."

The crisis passes on Omaha beach

Admiral Kirk, however, had no intention of letting his colleagues on land bleed to death; he bunched together his destroyers on the coast, and they fired at the maximum rate on all the German fire-points that showed themselves. At the same time, the German 352nd Division battery positions began running out of shells, and as the Allies' cruisers and their tactical air forces attacked all the crossroads, the Germans were not able to supply their artillery with fresh ammunition. At about 1300 hours, the crisis was over and the infantrymen, after the sappers had blown up the anti-tank dike surrounding the beach, infiltrated the German position through the narrow gullies running up the cliff.

During the night of June 6-7, the remainder of the 29th Division (Major-General C. H. Gerhardt) was landed. But V Corps' losses had been heavy: 3,881 killed, wounded, and missing.

In the American sector: Staff Sergeant Jack Scarborough of Bossier City, Louisiana, with a German corpse outside a captured German bunker.

New breaches in Atlantic Wall

The British 2nd Army (General Miles C. Dempsey) had been assigned Bayeux, Caen, and Troarn (9 miles east of Caen) as its D-Day objectives. It was also ordered to extend its reconnaissance to Villers-Bocage and Evrecy, that is along approximately 18 miles of the Calvados coast. This ambitious programme was not fulfilled.

The British 6th Airborne Division (Major-General Richard N. Gale) was to protect the flanks of the operation. It was ordered:

1. To capture intact the bridges across the Orne and its canal between Bénouville and Ranville;
2. To destroy the Merville battery;
3. To destroy the Dives bridges between Troarn and the coast.

Although the wind prevented the paratroopers from landing accurately on their targets, the division completed these three missions brilliantly. At 0030 hours the British sappers and infantry had jumped from five gliders and captured the Bénouville bridges, clearing them of mines. At about 0400 hours Lieutenant-Colonel Otway had only collected 150 paratroopers from his battalion which was practically without *matériel,* and the gliders which were due to land on the superstructure of the defence works had failed to appear. Nevertheless, he had captured the Merville battery in a fierce fight in which he lost 70 dead and wounded, whilst the garrison of 130 men was left with only 22 survivors. The Dives mission was also completely successful. "All around the battery", according to Georges Blond, "the grass was strewn with corpses, British and German mixed together. Several attackers who had already gone into the defence works ran back:

" 'The guns aren't 6-inch, sir, they're 3-inch.'

" 'Fine,' said Otway, 'Blow them up.'

"The British had lost 5 officers and 65 N.C.O.'s and men, killed and wounded in the attack. It was now nearly dawn. Otway saw one of his officers apparently searching for something in his battle-dress blouse:

" 'What are you doing?'

" 'I'm sending a message to England, sir.'

"The communications officer pulled a pigeon with closed wings from his breast, turning its little head from side to side. It had taken part in the attack too. When it was released, it rose unhesitatingly into the whitening sky."

At dawn, Rear-Admiral Vian's naval forces opened fire on the German defences, and up to nightfall discharged 500 15-inch shells, 3,500 6-inch shells, and 1,380 small calibre missiles. They made

▽ *American reinforcements disembark from a landing craft and remuster before moving up towards the front.*

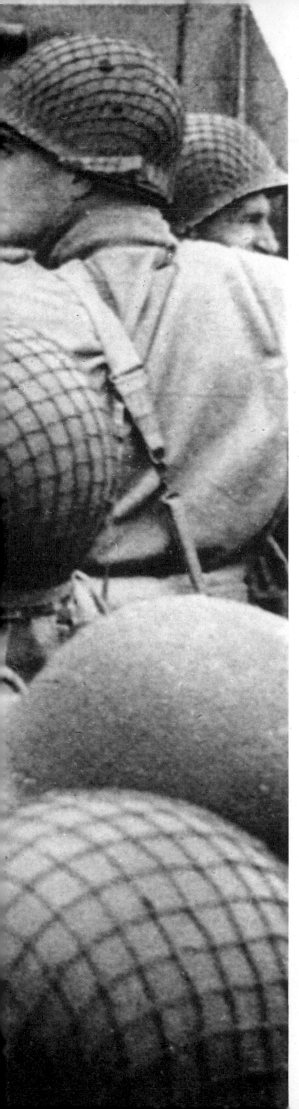

wide breaches in the Atlantic Wall. Two further circumstances favoured the British landing. First, the amphibious tanks were lowered into the water much closer to the shore than at "Omaha", and were sometimes landed directly on the beaches. Secondly, large numbers of the special vehicles designed by Major-General Sir Percy Hobart, commander of the 79th Armoured Division, were used in the first waves of the infantry attack.

In addition to the Crabs, or flail tanks, which cleared the ground of the mines obstructing their tracks and had been used since El Alamein, the British 2nd Army also brought its Crocodiles and its A.V.R.E.s into the line: the Crocodiles were flame-thrower tanks which cast a 360-foot jet of burning oil beyond the range of the enemy's rocket-launchers; these tanks had trailers filled with about 400 gallons of fuel and could sustain prolonged actions; the A.V.R.E.s were mortar tanks carrying a 9-inch mortar on a Churchill tank chassis, and intended for work against armoured strongpoints.

On the other hand, against the British I and XXX Corps (commanded respectively by Lieutenant-Generals J. T. Crocker and G. T. Bucknall) the German 716th Division (Lieutenant-General W. Richter) only had four battalions and their quality

◁ *U.S. infantry await the moment of truth.*
△ *Rudimentary mechanisation: British infantry bring their bicycles ashore.*

was inferior to that of the Allies.

In these conditions, the 50th Division (Major-General D. A. H. Graham), the advance-guard of XXX Corps, proceeded from "Gold" Beach without much difficulty. By the end of the day it had some armour at the approaches of Bayeux and had moved forward about six miles.

In I Corps, the 3rd Canadian Division (Major-General R. F. L. Keller) had a more difficult landing because the Calvados reefs presented a natural obstacle; nevertheless it had advanced eight miles from Bernières ("Juno" Beach) and was near its objective, the Carpiquet airfield. On the other hand the armoured column which it had launched towards Evrecy was driven back with losses above Bretteville-l'Orgueilleuse. The result was that between its left at Saint Aubin-sur-Mer

and the right of the 50th Division, towards Arromanches, the Atlantic Wall had been breached over a front of 12 miles.

Landing at "Sword" Beach in the Riva-Bella area, the British 3rd Division (Major-General G. T. Rennie) had managed to join with the 6th Airborne Division over the Bénouville bridge. In the evening it had advanced to Biéville three miles north of Caen and repelled a counter-attack from the 21st Panzer Division. With its right close up against Lion-sur-Mer it was four or five miles from the Canadian 3rd Division.

D-Day casualties

The British 2nd Army had a total of less than 3,000 killed, wounded, and missing on D-Day.

Allied naval and air losses were insignificant: 114 planes, mainly brought down by A.A. fire; some landing craft and two destroyers—one of these, the *Corry* (U.S. Navy) blew up on a mine in the "Utah" Beach waters; the other, the Norwegian *Svenner*, succumbed to an attack on the Eastern Naval Task Force by three German destroyers from Le Havre commanded by Lieutenant-Commander Hoffmann.

Hitler holds back reinforcements

At 0111 hours (German time) General Erich Marcks, commander of LXXXIV Corps, was at his H.Q. in Saint Lô celebrating his 53rd birthday when he heard from the 716th Division that the paratroopers were coming down between the Orne and the Dives and that the bridges of these two rivers were apparently their objectives. Twenty minutes later the 709th Division signalled the landing of American paratroopers on both sides of the Merderet in the Sainte Mère-Eglise area. Quite correctly, Marcks decided that this was the invasion. He therefore alerted the troops on the coast and informed the 7th Army H.Q. at Le Mans.

The 7th Army quickly transmitted the information to la Roche-Guyon and Saint Germain. Although he hesitated when he received LXXXIV Corps' appreciation, supported by the 7th Army,

The Germans resisted the invasion with great tenacity, but the sheer size of the landing forces alone was almost too much for them. Except where terrain made the Allies' task particularly difficult, all that the Germans could do was to try to contain the invasion. It was a hard, an impossible task. ▷ and ▷▽ Part of the non-stop flood of men, vehicles, and matériel that poured ashore after the beach-head had been consolidated. ▽ Outside Sainte Mère-Eglise.

△ A Sherman Crab anti-mine flail tank moves up. The correct and widespread use of such specialised armour played a very significant part in the Allies' success.

▽ A British Sherman Duplex Drive tank advances towards a Horsa glider. Note the folded flotation screen on top of the hull.

Rundstedt alerted the Panzer-"Lehr" Division and the 12th "Hitlerjugend" Panzer Division and contacted O.K.W., but Hitler forbade him to move them till further orders, which would be given him as soon as the situation was clear.

There was no further news till 0630 hours, when information was received that the Calvados coast defences were being subjected to intensive naval bombardment. At that time, however, the Führer, who had gone to bed as usual two hours earlier, was fast asleep, thanks to Dr. Morell's pills, and no one dared to have him woken. When they finally plucked up the courage, Hitler's reaction was fairly dramatic:

"He was in a dressing-gown when he came out of his bedroom. He listened calmly to the report of his aides and then sent for O.K.W.'s chief, Field-Marshal Wilhelm Keitel, and Jodl. By the time they arrived Hitler was dressed and waiting – and excited.

"The conference that followed was, as Pultkamer recalls, 'extremely agitated'. Information was scanty, but on the basis of what was known Hitler was convinced that this was not the main invasion, and he kept repeating that over and over again. The conference lasted only a few minutes and ended abruptly, as Jodl was later to remember, when Hitler suddenly thundered at him and Keitel, 'Well, is it or isn't it the invasion?'"

Therefore it was only at 1432 that Army Group "B" received the authority, which it had sought for 12 hours, to order the 12th S.S. Panzer Division to support the 7th Army, and at 1507 hours to move the *Waffen*-S.S. I Panzer Corps and the Panzer-*"Lehr"* Division.

But after so much delay, Colonel-General Dollmann now showed excessive haste. Lieutenant-General Bayerlein, commander of the Panzer-*"Lehr"* Division, after leaving his unit to obtain instructions from 7th Army H.Q., was ordered to move towards Caen at 1700 hours. Without success the former chief-of-staff of the *Afrika Korps* (who had had much experience of British air tactics) attempted to persuade Dollmann how foolish it was to set out on the French roads before nightfall. Nevertheless Dollmann kept to his decision, thinking he would thus be able to bring the Panzer-*"Lehr"* Division into action south of Caen at dawn on the following day, June 7. But the first bombs began falling before Bayerlein and his staff had passed Beaumont-sur-Sarthe, south of Alençon.

"For once we were lucky. But the columns were getting farther and farther apart all the time. Since the Army had ordered a radio silence we had to maintain contact by dispatch riders. As if radio silence could have stopped the fighter-bombers and reconnaissance planes from spotting us! All it did was prevent the divisional staff from forming a picture of the state of the advance – if it was moving smoothly or whether there were hold-ups and losses. I was for ever sending off officers or else seeking out units myself.

"We were moving along all five routes of advance. Naturally our move had been spotted by enemy air-reconnaissance. And before long the bombers were hovering above the roads, smashing cross-roads, villages, and towns along our line of advance, and pouncing on the long columns of vehicles. At 2300 we drove through Sées. The place was lit up by

△ *A Panther tank. Despite the Allies' considerable numerical superiority in* matériel, *the Panther was a tank still very much to be feared.*
◁ *Another of Germany's best weapons, the dreaded Nebelwerfer.*
▽ *Another of Britain's specialised armoured vehicles, the Churchill Assault Vehicle Royal Engineers (A.V.R.E.), fitted with a spigot mortar to fire a 40-lb "dustbin" demolition charge up to 230 yards.*

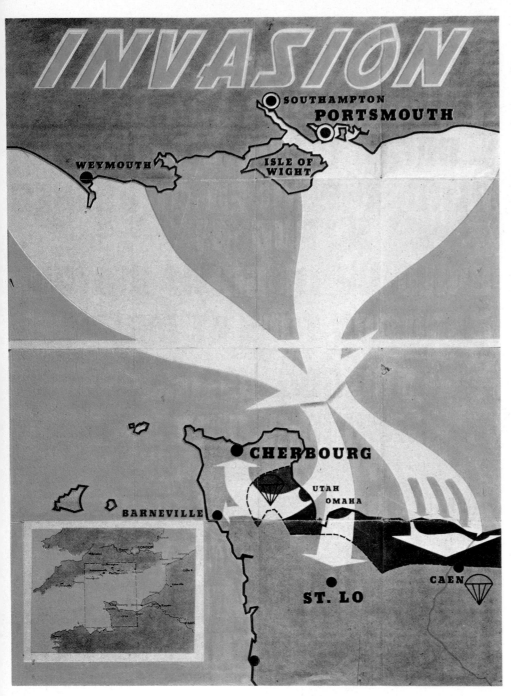

INVASION

SOUTHAMPTON
PORTSMOUTH

WEYMOUTH

ISLE OF
WIGHT

CHERBOURG

UTAH
OMAHA

BARNEVILLE

CAEN

ST. LO

△ *A simplified view of the mounting and primary objectives of Operation "Overlord".*

from la Roche-Guyon, he sent his armoured regiment to follow them. At 0700 hours, he was informed that he was subordinate to the 7th Army; two hours later that he would now take his orders from LXXXIV Corps.

But now General Marcks was becoming more aware of the danger from the sea; for this reason, at 1000 hours, he ordered his new subordinate to abandon the action his armoured regiment was about to take against the enemy paratroopers, and to send it over the Orne to give support to the 716th Division units barring the approach to Caen from the British. This move was completed at 1430 hours and the Germans counter-attacked at 1700 hours. At nightfall the 21st Panzer Division had managed to reach Luc-sur-Mer with its infantry, but its armoured regiment had been engaged by the British 3rd Division and had suffered heavy losses. Moreover it had nearly run out of petrol. Therefore Feuchtinger, who had 146 tanks and 51 assault guns when the engagement commenced, retreated on orders, abandoning the wrecks of 40 tracked vehicles.

The German position

At 1300 hours, a report from LXXXIV Corps to the 7th Army gave an accurate description of the fluctuations of this merciless struggle: "In the Caen area, in the British sector, the enemy is successful. East of the American sector, the landing is more or less repulsed at Vierville. Our counter-attack is in progress in the Sainte Mère-Eglise district; the 8th Regiment of the American 4th Division (Colonel van Fleet) is pinned down there. Where is our air support? Enemy aircraft prevent us from moving or supplying our troops by day."

At midnight, an entry in the 7th Army's signals diary showed the worsening situation in the afternoon in the Caen sector:

"2400 hours. 716 Infantry Division is still defending itself at strongpoints. Communications between division, regimental and battalion headquarters, however, no longer exist, so that nothing is known as to the number of strong-points still holding out or of those liquidated . . . The Chief-of-Staff of Seventh Army gives the order that the counter attack of June 7 must reach the coast without fail, since the strong-point defenders expect it of us."

flares hanging above it like candles on a Christmas-tree, and heavy bombs were crashing down on the houses which were already burning. But we managed to get through."

In the Saint Pierre-sur-Dives region, the 21st Panzer Division (Major-General Feuchtinger) was in a rather different situation: it was Army Group "B"'s reserve, but its commander was authorised to put his infantry into action to support the 716th Division if there was a landing; however, he was not allowed to engage his armour. In accordance with these orders Feuchtinger launched one of his grenadier regiments on the right bank of the Orne to engage the British paratroopers and as he received no orders

CHAPTER 113
The Panzers attack

The Battle of Normandy started very unpromisingly for the Wehrmacht. Nevertheless the Allies took a little more than six weeks to break out of the Avranches bottleneck, although according to plans they should have done so on D+20, June 27; they required another three weeks to complete the defeat of Army Group "B". This delay was due to two different factors:

1. The Normandy *bocage* (mixed woodland and pastureland), where the defenders were undoubtedly favoured by their natural surroundings. The countryside between Troarn and Bayeux, the British 2nd Army sector, was certainly suitable for use by armoured formations, but it assisted the German tanks and anti-tank devices even more; the range of their guns was greater than the Allies'. Moreover in the Norman *bocage* between Bayeux and the western Cotentin coast, the U.S. 1st Army sector, there were fields surrounded by tall, thick hedges with sunken roads between them, very suitable for ambushes, whether by the *Chouans* at the time of the French Revolution, or by the German grenadiers, who spotted enemy tanks and discharged the almost invariably lethal shots from *Panzerfaust* or *Panzerschreck* launchers at very short range. The attackers' task was also complicated by the rivers Vire, Taute, Douve, and Merderet, marshy tracts, and the 7th Army's flooding operations. General Bradley wrote: "Not even

in Tunisia had we found more exasperating defensive terrain. Collins called it no less formidable than the jungles of Guadalcanal."

2. The inferior quality of their armour compared with the Germans' was another very serious handicap for the Allies. The journalist Alan Moorehead, who was a war correspondent at Montgomery's G.H.Q., stated quite frankly after the end of the war: "Our tanks were Shermans, Churchills and Cromwells. None of them was the equal of the German Mark V (the Panther), or the Mark VI (the Tiger) . . .

"The Germans had much thicker armour than we had. Their tanks were effective at a thousand yards or more: ours at ranges around five hundred yards . . . Our tanks were unequal to the job because they were not good enough. There may be various ways of dodging this plain truth, but anyone who wishes to do so will find himself arguing with the crews of more than three British armoured divisions which fought in France."

Admittedly Moorehead was a journalist, but General Bradley is recognised as one of the best brains in the American army. "Originally", he wrote, "the Sherman had come equipped with a 75-mm gun, an almost totally ineffective weapon against the heavy frontal plate of these German tanks. Only by swarming around the panzers to hit them on the flank,

▽ *The first German prisoners taken in Normandy wait in a P.O.W. cage on the beach for transportation to England.*

could our Shermans knock the enemy out. But too often the American tankers complained it cost them a tank or two, with crews, to get the enemy's panzers but only by expending more tanks than we cared to lose. Ordnance thereafter replaced the antedated 75 with a new 76-mm high-velocity gun. But even this new weapon often scuffed rather than penetrated the enemy's armour.

"Eisenhower was angry when he heard of these limitations of the new 76."

We shall not repeat him, as we know that the Pzkw V Panther had an armour thickness of $4\frac{1}{2}$ inches and the Pzkw VI Tiger $5\frac{1}{2}$ inches. The British got their best results when they re-armed their Shermans with the 17-pounder anti-tank guns which they had had since 1943. Firing an armour-piercing shell at an initial velocity of about 2,900 feet per second, it was certainly superior to the American version, but nevertheless it was markedly inferior to the Panther's 7.5-cm, which fired at 3,068 feet per second, and even more to the 8.8-cm of the Tiger II or the *Königstiger* with shells of 20- and 22-lb with a higher velocity, which at 500 yards could penetrate 112 and 182-mm of armour respectively. Even worse, the British and the Americans found that their Shermans were inclined to catch fire suddenly like bowls of flaming punch.

However, the Panzers' undeniable tech-

▽ *Officers at a German command post.*
▽ ▽ *The massive barrel of a Tiger tank points menacingly from its lair in a shattered building.*

◁ *Undisputed master of the first tank battles in Normandy: the Tiger, with all its earlier teething troubles eliminated. In the hands of a master Panzer technician like Hauptsturmführer* Wittmann, *the Tiger was a deadly weapon. In a classic battle Wittmann's solitary Tiger knocked out 25 British tanks within minutes.*

nical superiority was of little help to Rommel, as he was unable to supply them with the required fuel or to defend them against the continuous attacks of the Allied tactical air force, of which they were rightly a priority target.

The word *Jabo* (*Jagdbomber*: fighter-bomber) recurs in all the accounts left by the German combatants after the Normandy battle. In their attacks against enemy armour, the Allies preferred rockets, which were more accurate than bombs and more effective than the 20-mm or 40-mm shell. The R.A.F.'s Hawker Typhoon fighter carried eight 60-pounder rockets, whilst the Republic P-47 Thunderbolt had ten 5-inch anti-tank rockets.

In this ground-air battle, the rôle of the Allied engineers has perhaps not been sufficiently appreciated. They quickly cleared the rubble left in the Normandy towns and villages by the bombardments and restored communications as the troops moved forward. They also had better equipment, notably in machines of American manufacture, and in the Bailey bridge, which had prefabricated components and could be assembled in a great variety of combinations. By May 8 1945, 7,500 Bailey bridges had been built in the Western and Italian war theatres; they certainly contributed not only to the defeat of the Third Reich, but also to the

reconstruction of this part of the continent.

On June 7 and 8 successively the 12th "Hitlerjugend" S.S. Panzer Division and the Panzer-"Lehr" Division failed to drive the British back to the Channel. On June 7 the first of these major units (which under Major-General Witt included 177 tanks and 28 assault guns) should have counter-attacked in the direction of the Douvres operational base (six miles north

△ *Another weapon used in Normandy: a remote-controlled tank, about the size of a Bren gun carrier, designed to deliver a heavy explosive charge into the Allied lines.*

The British Hawker Typhoon IB fighter and ground-attack aircraft

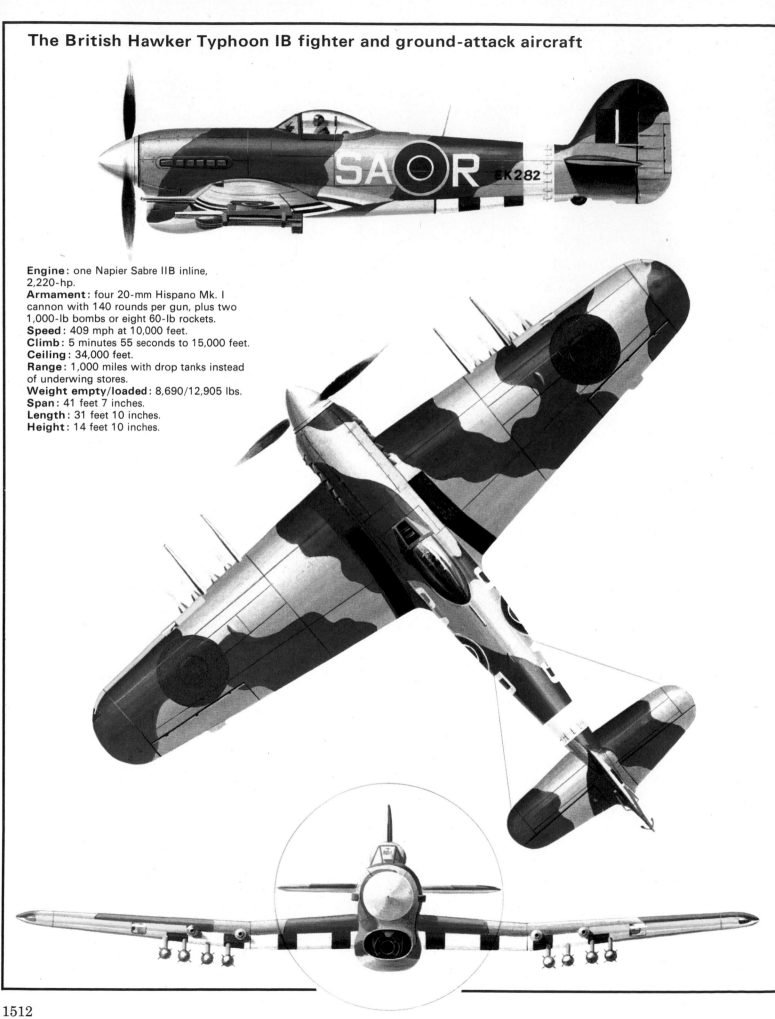

Engine: one Napier Sabre IIB inline, 2,220-hp.
Armament: four 20-mm Hispano Mk. I cannon with 140 rounds per gun, plus two 1,000-lb bombs or eight 60-lb rockets.
Speed: 409 mph at 10,000 feet.
Climb: 5 minutes 55 seconds to 15,000 feet.
Ceiling: 34,000 feet.
Range: 1,000 miles with drop tanks instead of underwing stores.
Weight empty/loaded: 8,690/12,905 lbs.
Span: 41 feet 7 inches.
Length: 31 feet 10 inches.
Height: 14 feet 10 inches.

The American Lockheed P-38J Lightning long range fighter and fighter-bomber

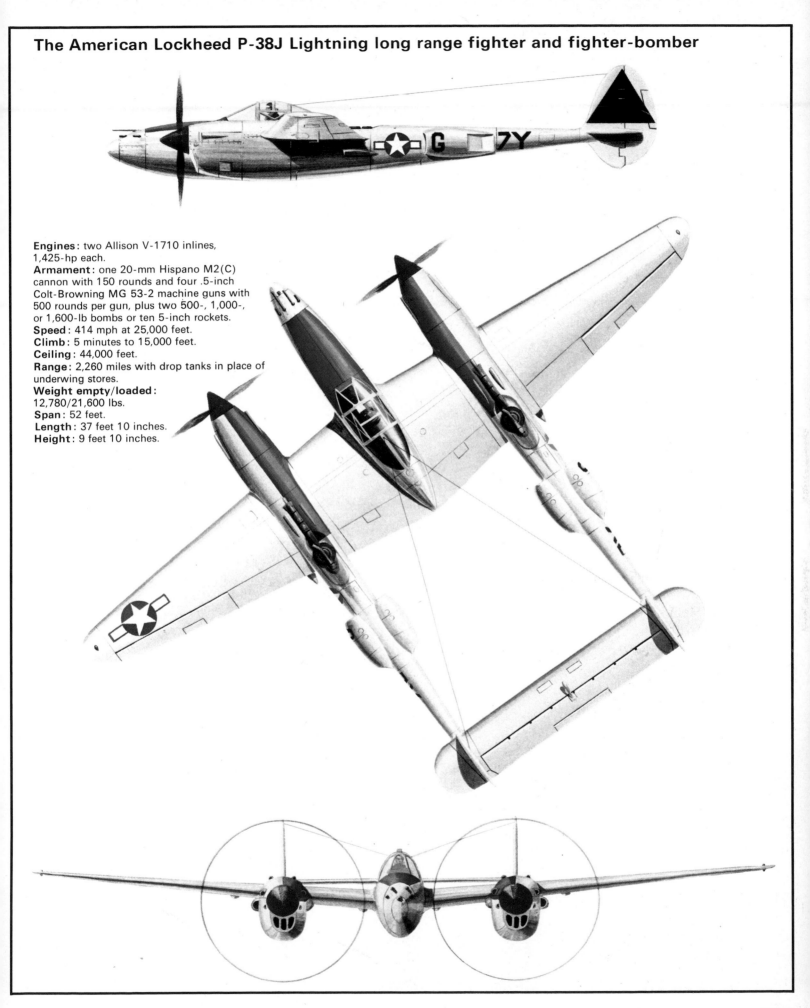

Engines: two Allison V-1710 inlines, 1,425-hp each.
Armament: one 20-mm Hispano M2(C) cannon with 150 rounds and four .5-inch Colt-Browning MG 53-2 machine guns with 500 rounds per gun, plus two 500-, 1,000-, or 1,600-lb bombs or ten 5-inch rockets.
Speed: 414 mph at 25,000 feet.
Climb: 5 minutes to 15,000 feet.
Ceiling: 44,000 feet.
Range: 2,260 miles with drop tanks in place of underwing stores.
Weight empty/loaded: 12,780/21,600 lbs.
Span: 52 feet.
Length: 37 feet 10 inches.
Height: 9 feet 10 inches.

of Caen) with the 21st Panzer Division, which was immediately to its left. It managed to maul a Canadian armoured brigade in the Carpiquet region but when it reached its goal it was halted by massive artillery fire and turned to the left.

The following day the Panzer-*"Lehr"* Division came into the line on the left of the 12th S.S. Panzer Division, but between Sées and Tilly-sur-Seulles it had lost five tanks, 84 all-purpose transport vehicles, 90 cars and lorries, and 40 petrol tankers; these considerable losses caused no less concern to Lieutenant-General Bayerlein than the 12th S.S. Panzer Division's had to his colleague Witt. Moreover Vice-

▽ *Canadian troops move up in the Caen sector.*

Admiral Ruge noted in his personal diary at the la Roche-Guyon H.Q., to which Rommel had returned late in the afternoon on June 6: "The enemy's air superiority is having the effect the Field-Marshal had foreseen: our movements are extremely slow, supplies don't get through, any deployment is becoming impossible, the artillery can't move to its firing positions any more. Precisely the same thing is happening on land here as happened at sea in the Tunisian campaign."

On June 8, when the U.S. 1st Army and the British 2nd Army joined up at Bayeux, Rundstedt put Rommel in charge of *Panzergruppe* "West", which became responsible for the conduct of operations in the sector between the mouth of the Dives and the Tilly-sur-Seulles area, while the 7th Army from now on faced the Americans alone. General Geyr von Schweppenburg, when he assumed this heavy task, was assigned the mission of retaking Bayeux and he proposed that he should break through to the Channel with his three Panzer divisions. But as soon as he set up his headquarters in the Thury–Harcourt region, he was seriously wounded in an air attack which killed many of his staff. Sepp Dietrich took over and ordered his troops to stay on the defensive while they waited for better opportunities to attack.

Intervention of the heavy Panzers

In fact on June 12, with the intervention of the 2nd Panzer Division (Lieutenant-General von Lüttwitz) which had been brought up from the Amiens region, Dietrich managed to halt an assault by the British XXX Corps which had launched the 7th Armoured Division (Major-General G. W. Erskine) against its left wing and its rear. The celebrated Desert Rats got the worst of this chance encounter, which was fought for Villers-Bocage, not for lack of energy and courage but because they were let down by their *matériel*. Chester Wilmot proves this in his description of the episode:

"The troops had dismounted to stretch their legs while the tanks reconnoitred the way ahead, when the crack of a gun split the crisp morning air and the leading half-track burst into flames. Out of the woods to the north lumbered a Tiger tank, which drove on to the road and proceeded right down the line of half-tracks 'brewing up' one vehicle after another. Behind these there was some incidental armour—a dozen tanks belonging to Regimental H.Q., the artillery observers and a reconnaissance troop. The Tiger destroyed them in quick succession, scorning the fire of one Cromwell, which saw its 75-mm shells bounce off the sides of the German tank even at the range of a few yards! Within a matter of minutes the road was an inferno with 25 armoured vehicles blazing—all the victims of this one lone Tiger."

While we do not want to undervalue Captain Wittmann's exploit (he was the tank's commander) we must point out that the Cromwell was very inadequately armed with a 75-mm gun and also had totally inadequate armour protection; for this reason the Desert Rats' morale suffered seriously for several weeks.

The British 2nd Army's defeat was fully compensated for on the same day by the fall of Carentan, whose defenders succumbed to the concentric thrust of the American 29th Division and 101st Airborne Division. The 17th S.S. *Panzergrenadier*

Division *"Götz von Berlichingen"* (Lieutenant-General Ostermann) was alerted on June 7 at its stations at Thouars but arrived too late to prevent General Bradley's V and VII Corps from joining up. When it crossed the Loire it received the same treatment from the fighter-bombers as the Panzer-*"Lehr"* Division. The Anglo-Americans now had a continuous front between the Dives and Saint Marcouf.

Allied reinforcements

During the first days of battle the Germans had already lost 10,000 prisoners and 150 tanks. Even more important, Montgomery and Eisenhower were as aware as Rommel and Rundstedt that, contrary to expectations, the defenders were not getting reinforcements as quickly as the attackers at this stage.

From June 7 to 12 the British and Americans put in their floating reserves, which had sailed on the same day as the first echelon; these consisted of five infantry and three airborne divisions. The American V Corps was joined by the 9th and 20th Divisions; the British XXX

△ *Six days after D-Day and Churchill crosses the Channel to see for himself.*

▽ *Montgomery shows Churchill a map of the beach-head while General Dempsey of 2nd Army looks on.*

△ *Americans in Carentan, the first major town captured in their sector.*

Corps by the 7th Armoured and the 49th Divisions; and the British I Corps by the 51st Highland Division, giving 15 divisions (eight American) out of a total of 37 stationed in the U.K.: 362,547 men, 54,186 vehicles, and about 102,000 tons of supplies landed in a week.

According to S.H.A.E.F.'s estimates, Montgomery was faced by 21 divisions on June 12. In fact, the defence was reinforced at the following rate:

June 6   21st Panzer Division
June 7   12th Panzer Division
June 8   Panzer-*"Lehr"* Division
June 9   353rd Panzer Division
June 11 17th S.S. *Panzergrenadier* Division
June 12 2nd Panzer and 3rd Parachute Divisions

Including the five divisions guarding the area between Cabourg and Mont Saint Michel on D-Day, *Panzergruppe* "West" and the German 7th Army had 12 divisions (including five armoured divisions) in the line; however, the 716th Division was only a cypher and the 352nd and 709th Divisions had been badly mauled. The Panzers went into the attack at random, always behind schedule, and under strength.

German communications disorganised

The air offensive against the French and Belgian railway networks broadly paid the dividends expected of it. This action continued, but from the night of June 5-6 it was made doubly successful by the intervention of the Resistance against the German communications in accordance with the "Green Plan" compiled by French Railways, while the "Tortoise Plan" drawn up by the French Post Office was carried out just as successfully against the occupying forces' telephone communications.

Pierre de Préval has listed 278 acts of sabotage carried out by the French Resistance from June 6 to September 15, 1944 in the department of Meurthe-et-Moselle, and the position was similar in the other departments. On the route from Montauban to the Normandy front, the *Waffen*-S.S. 2nd Panzer Division *"Das Reich"* (Lieutenant-General Lammerding) was harried by the Corrèze *maquis*; the terrible reprisals taken on the in-

habitants of Tulle and Oradour by this division to avenge these ambushes remain unforgotten.

From now on the delay in building up the German defence on the invasion front is perfectly understandable, as the combined action of the Anglo-American forces and the French Resistance networks was effectively assisted by Hitler's personal interference in war operations.

Hitler's error

We have mentioned that when he was expecting the landing, the Führer had an intuition that Normandy might well be the invasion's objective. But he revised his view as soon as Eisenhower had launched Operation "Overlord". Plainly, he thought, he was faced with a diversionary manoeuvre aimed at making him lower his guard in the Pas-de-Calais. If he were to fall into the trap laid for him, the final thrust would be aimed at him in the sector he had unwisely uncovered... but he was not so stupid! Nevertheless on June 8 Major Hayn, LXXXIV Corps' chief Intelligence officer, was brought

△ On June 14 Charles de Gaulle crossed the Channel to tour the narrow strip of liberated France inside the beach-head. Here he gets an enthusiastic welcome from the people of Bayeux.
◁ A smile and a handshake from Montgomery.

American Firefly tanks roll through a Normandy town.
Looking south towards St. Lô —a deceptive vision of the Promised Land. Every hedgerow and ridge crossing the path of the Allied advance was a wasp's nest of German defences.
Mobile fire-power for U.S. armoured divisions: an M7 howitzer motor carriage. The M7 carried a 105-mm howitzer and was known as the "Priest" by the British because of its pulpit-like machine gun position. It had a crew of seven.

a copy of U.S. VII Corps' battle orders which had been discovered on board a barge that had grounded near Isigny after its crew had been killed. This document, which was quite unnecessarily verbose, not only revealed General Collins's intentions, but also listed V Corps' and the British XXX Corps' objectives. The Americans' mission was to reach the Cotentin western coast as soon as possible, and then to change direction to the north and capture Cherbourg. Without delay this battle order was passed through the correct channels; 7th Army, Army Group "B", Supreme Command West, and O.K.W. Hitler, however, obstinately stuck to his opinion that this was a deceptive manoeuvre, and in support of his view he quoted the *Abwehr*'s summaries stating that just before the landing there were 60 or even 67 British and American divisions stationed in Britain. He never asked himself whether the real deception lay in simulating the existence of 30 divisions concentrated in Kent and ready to cross the English Channel at its narrowest point. At the front, on the other hand,

where the Germans saw most of the Allied units they had previously met in Africa and Sicily (U.S. 1st and 9th Divisions, British 7th Armoured Division and 50th and 51st Divisions), they dismissed the idea of a second landing in the north of France. But nothing was done and Rommel was forbidden to use the 18 divisions of the 15th Army which, with the exception of the 346th and 711th Divisions, which were engaged on the right bank of the Orne, remained in reserve until after the breakthrough.

Rommel's plan abandoned

After a week's fighting, Rommel transmitted his appreciation and his intentions to Keitel: "The Army Group is endeavouring to replace the Panzer formations by infantry formations as soon as possible, and re-form mobile reserves with them. The Army Group intends to switch its *Schwerpunkt* in the next few days to the area Carentan–Montebourg to annihilate the enemy there and avert the danger to Cherbourg. Only when this has been done can the enemy between the Orne and the Vire be attacked."

The following conclusions can be drawn from this telephone message:

▽ *An American M7 trundles past a knocked-out* Pzkw IV.

1. Rommel stated he was compelled to give up his first plan to push the enemy back into the sea immediately. Hitler therefore was not able to recover on the Western Front the forces which he hoped to collect for the Eastern Front.
2. In order to release his armoured formations from the front, he would have had to have the same number of infantry formations at his disposal at the appropriate time. For this purpose the veto imposed on him by Hitler on taking troops from the 15th Army did not simplify matters.
3. Even if he had obtained these infantry formations, what he stated in any case shows that Montgomery's idea of free manoeuvre, which he put into practice in Normandy, was soundly and judiciously conceived.
4. Without these formations he could not displace Army Group "B"'s point of main effort from the Caen–Tilly-sur-Seulles area to the Carentan–Montebourg area, and therefore the "strong point" of Cherbourg was from now on virtually written off.

Churchill visits the Normandy front

Georges Blond has written:

"On Monday June 12 shortly after midday a D.U.K.W. landed at Courseulles and drove over the sand. A group of officers who had been looking at the D.U.K.W. through their field glasses for a few moments came forward quickly. A corpulent gentleman was sitting behind the driver, wearing a blue cap and smoking a cigar. As soon as the vehicle had stopped he asked the officers in a loud voice: 'How do I get down?' Just then a soldier hurried up carrying a small ladder. Churchill walked down it with all possible dignity. He shook hands with Montgomery who was standing in front of him in a leather jacket and a black beret, and then with the other officers, Field-Marshal Smuts, Field-Marshal Alan Brooke, and Rear-Admiral Sir Philip Vian, commander of the British Eastern Naval Task Force.

"He then went to his waiting jeep. The jeep started off."

On the following morning, June 13 the first V-1 rockets were fired in the direction of London.

GENERAL DE GAULLE
and the Fighting French

△ De Gaulle inspecting troops in Britain.
◁ "The French Army in combat" by Raoul Auger. For thousands of Frenchmen, de Gaulle's status as the figurehead of French resistance remained inviolate.

1. *Exultant French submariners wave and cheer in Algiers after their dramatic dash from Toulon in 1940.*
2. *With the Free French Navy. General de Gaulle, followed by Admiral Muselier, visits the Free French sloop* La Moqueuse.

De Gaulle's counterblast to Pétain's acceptance of France's defeat in 1940 kept the spirit of French resistance alive, but for a considerable period he had no armies with which to fight. The colonial troops which escaped the disaster in France remained subject to the Vichy régime, and de Gaulle was accordingly obliged to start virtually from scratch – but the men who rallied to the Cross of Lorraine – the symbol of "Free France" – gave him splendid material with which to work towards the rehabilitation of France's honour.

They had a vivid sense of mission. They were ardent patriots. And their desire to hit back and eventually fight their way home made them formidable soldiers.

But de Gaulle had airmen and sailors as well. The former included the Free French "Alsace" Squadron which operated from Biggin Hill and took part in fighter sweeps over their country. Their ranks produced Pierre Clostermann, who ended up commanding a fighter wing in the R.A.F. and wrote *The Big Show*, one of the best books to come out of World War II, which gives a

vivid picture of the life of a fighter pilot. And the Free French Navy was built up from ships which escaped to Britain in 1940: the old battleship *Courbet,* the submarines *Rubis* and *Surcouf,* the destroyers *Le Triomphant* and *Leopard,* and the sloops *Commandant Duboc, Commandant Domine, La Moqueuse, Chevreuil,* and *Savorgnan de Brazza.* Vice-Admiral Muselier, who escaped from Marseilles aboard a British collier and reached England via Gibraltar, was the commander of the Free French Navy. He proved a worthy colleague of de Gaulle.

For the Free French soldiers, the first major turning-point came with the battle of Gazala in May-June 1942. There the Free French troops under General Koenig held the Bir Hakeim box, the southernmost extremity of the 8th Army's defensive front, around which Rommel threw his great encircling move into the rear areas of 8th Army. The Bir Hakeim garrison, completely surrounded, held out from May 27 until June 10, beating off repeated attacks and enduring massive Stuka bombardment, and finally

4

3. *De Gaulle with Air Chief Marshal Leigh-Mallory after visiting Free French pilots serving with the R.A.F., in 1941.*
4. *Shortly after D-Day: de Gaulle in pensive mood.*

5

5. *De Gaulle decorates Colonel Almikvari of the Foreign Legion with the* Croix de la Libération *after the battle for Bir Hakeim in May-June 1942. Bir Hakeim, the southernmost "box" of the Gazala Line, was superbly defended by its French garrison; and the battle earned the Free French combatant troops the title of "Fighting French".*
6. *Legionnaire officers in Bir Hakeim.*
7. *Men of General Leclerc's desert column in Tunisia after their epic march from Lake Chad.*
8. *A briefing for a pilot flying with the "Normandie Niemen" squadron in Russia. This volunteer unit was originally known as the "Normandie Regiment"; it earned the honorific title "Normandie Niemen" after an air battle during the fighting on the East Prussia frontier in October 1944, when 26 German planes were downed by the French pilots with no loss to themselves.*
9. *Triumphant return. Back on French soil after D-Day, de Gaulle addresses an enthusiastic crowd in Bayeux, Normandy.*

6

7

breaking out through the German ring. It was this exploit which earned the Free French the new title of "Fighting French"; and Bir Hakeim was the first battle honour won by de Gaulle's forces.

Later in the desert war came the epic march of General Leclerc's column from Chad in French Equatorial Africa to join up with the Allied forces advancing against Rommel.

The invasion of Vichy France by the Germans in November 1942 radically changed the situation. The split allegiance – Vichy France versus de Gaulle – was eliminated. But personality clashes caused much tension at the top for a while, particularly between de Gaulle and General Giraud, who escaped from prison in Germany but who had strong ideas of his own on how the Allied High Command should be running the war. (Giraud's personal view was that the "Torch" invasion forces, on entering the Mediterranean, should turn left and invade southern France instead of right to land in North Africa.)

The colonial troops in the ranks of the Fighting French won a splendid reputation for themselves. A highlight came during the final Allied push at Cassino in 1944, where General Juin's *goums* swarmed through the mountains and unseamed the strongest part of the German defence line.

Much ink has been spilled over the pros and cons of the "Dragoon" landing in southern France in August 1944, but one fact at least remains clear. When the "Dragoon" force pushed north

and joined hands with the British **8** and American armies advancing eastwards from Normandy, a French army now stood in the line on equal terms with the other component units of "Overlord". This was the 1st Army, commanded by the dashing General de Lattre de Tassigny. It had much hard fighting to do, most notably in the reduction of the "Colmar Pocket", which bulged into the Allied front line on the western bank of the Rhine. But its presence – let alone its performance – gave France the right to join the other Allies at the table when Germany surrendered in May 1945.

The wheel had come full circle from the disaster of 1940. De Gaulle had set the initial spark. From the survivors of Dunkirk and Narvik there had grown a new and determined fighting force, one totally different from the flabby and demoralised army which had gone to war in September 1939. Under de Gaulle's leadership the Fighting French grew into an efficient and confident entity. It won its own battle honours – Bir Hakeim, Cassino, Colmar. It produced dashing generals of Patton's stamp – Leclerc and de Lattre foremost among them – and its own fighter aces.

It was a superb achievement, although painfully attained. De Gaulle's rigid convictions of his duty to France caused constant clashes with his Allies; but he had saved his country's honour in 1940, and the men who rallied to him and carried on the fight upheld that important honour nobly.

9

Aid from the Greeks...

The Greek troops who flung the Italians back into Albania and faced the German invasion of April 1940 were magnificent soldiers, and it was a tragedy for the Allied cause in the Mediterranean that no large-scale evacuation could be mounted to include them. There were two obvious reasons for this: the pace of the German advance and the inadequate resources of the British Mediterranean Fleet. But the German conquest of the mainland made no difference to the fighting spirit of the Greek troops on Crete, many of which carried on the fight with the British in the Western Desert.

Here they served with the 8th Army, organised as a brigade. When Montgomery launched his attack at Alamein in October 1942 the Greeks, under Brigadier Katsotas, were held in initial reserve, together with two Fighting French brigades, a Fighting French flying column, and two British armoured brigades.

Unhappily, one of the strongest influences on the Greek soldiers abroad was the civil strife at home. As in Yugoslavia, so in Greece: the Germans were not the sole enemy of the resistance fighters, who as often as not were locked in battle with rival political groups. In Greece the main internal feud was between loyalists and Communists. By the summer of 1944 the Communist-inspired E.A.M. (National Liberation Front) had set up a provisional government in the Greek mountains—one which owed no allegiance to King George II and his government in exile. As a result of the close attention paid to the conflict by the Greek troops abroad, a mutiny in sympathy broke out among the Greek soldiers in Egypt in April 1944, which had to be suppressed by the British authorities.

The liberation of Greece began in October 1944; but the Greek troops which had been serving abroad were given no part in the proceedings. Churchill was determined to head off the possibility of a total Communist takeover in Greece and he insisted that British troops be sent in from Italy.

2

GREECE FIGHTS ON

3 1. *and* 2. *Posters honouring the "fighting Greeks". As at Dunkirk, the British evacuated as many of their Allies as possible when they pulled out of Greece and Crete, and a Greek brigade fought with the 8th Army in the Western Desert.*
3. *Middle East barbecue: Greek troops prepare for a feast of roast lamb.*
4. *Hospital cases. Greek army, navy, and air force patients on the road to recovery chat with nurses in a Middle East hospital.*

4

...and from the Czechs

1. *Czech pilots hoist their national flag outside their new air base in England.*
2. *Czech volunteer soldiers parade outside their legation in Grosvenor Square before leaving to entrain.*
3. *Irony. An American reminder that the Czechoslovaks were the first real victims of Nazi aggression.*

After the German occupation of Czechoslovakia in March 1939, there was no lack of attempts by Czech soldiers and airmen to escape to the West and fight again. The escape routes were hazardous and extremely roundabout: south through Rumania to the Middle East. France was the first country to offer assistance for the formation of a Free Czech legion, which was formed at Agde in the south. Recruits trickled in not only from Czechoslovakia but from Palestine, and the French Foreign Legion released Czech soldiers who wished to re-enlist in their own unit.

Two Czech regiments, neither fully trained nor fully equipped, were flung into the Battle of France in June 1940. They were immediately swept up in the disastrous retreat from the Marne and fell back to the south. The British sent transports to Sète and Bordeaux to bring off the Czechs, but three-quarters of them failed to arrive at the embarkation ports in time.

In the United Kingdom the Czechs were re-formed as a brigade. A compromise was found which enabled the unit to liaise smoothly with the British while retaining its own internal organisation. For example, each infantry battalion retained its own pioneer platoon for explosive, demolition, and light bridging work.

As with the Poles, the Soviet Union raised Czech formations to operate with the Red Army. This was considerably helped by the sizeable Czech communities inside the Soviet Union–a convenient source of manpower.

Unlike the Poles, the Czech government-in-exile in London warmly approved of the existence of a Czech formation serving with the Russians. This, which in its early days numbered only about 3,000 men under Colonel Svoboda (later War Minister in the Czech Government in Prague), first saw action in March 1943. The unit scored a signal victory on April 2, for which the Soviet press greatly lauded it. On the 10th, warm congratulations from both members of the government-in-exile and Czech communist deputies in Moscow were received. Captain Jaros, killed in action, was posthumously awarded the title of Hero of the Soviet Union while Svoboda was given the Order of Lenin. Another 82 men of the unit that had so distinguished itself in the fighting around the ancient city of Khar'kov were also decorated by the Soviet military authorities.

As the war progressed, the Czech contingent was raised to corps size and this was in the forefront of the battle during the Slovak rising of August-October 1944, fighting its way across the Carpathians through the Dukla Pass to join hands with the insurgents.

A more static rôle lay in store for the Czech troops in the West. Unlike the French and the Poles, they were unable to participate in the eventual liberation of their country. During the Allied advance from the Seine to the German frontier, the Czech brigade was given the unglamorous job of masking off the German garrison which obstinately held out in Dunkirk until the German surrender in the West.

1

2

CZECHOSLOVAKS

YOUR ALLIES

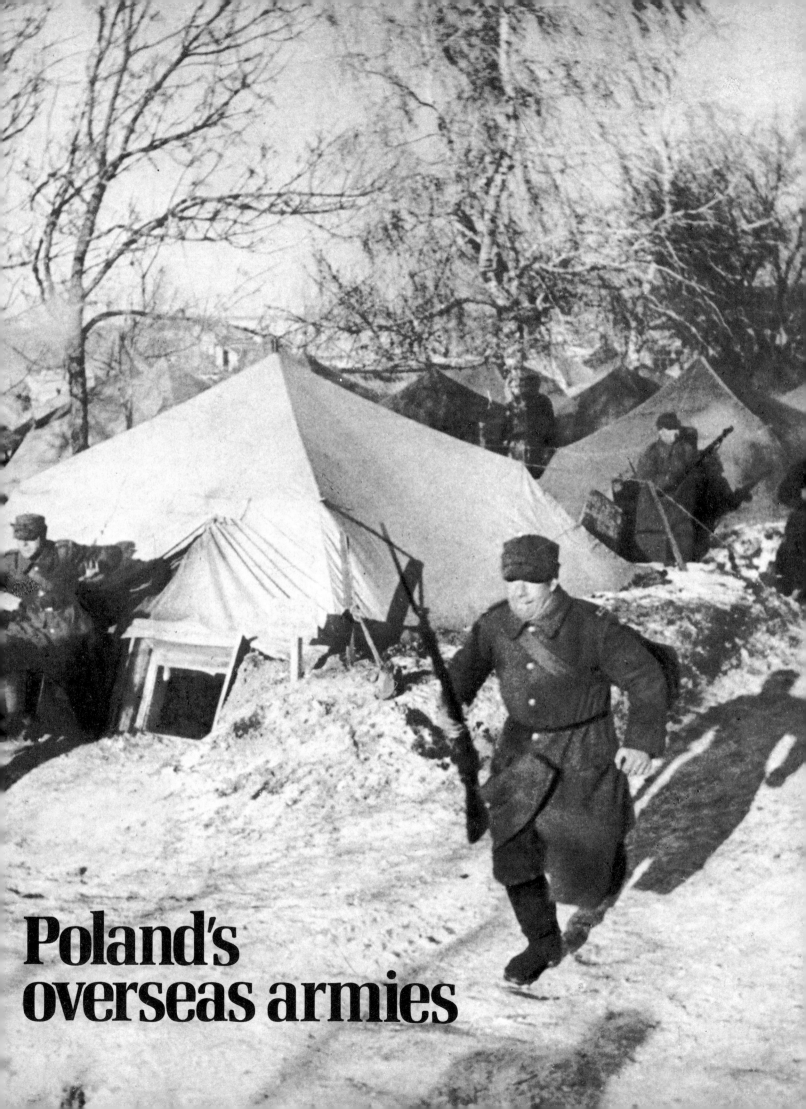

Poland's overseas armies

Despite the total collapse of the Polish Army during the Blitzkrieg campaign of 1939 and the subsequent partition of the country by Germany and the Soviet Union, Poland had by no means been knocked out of the war. Her underground "Home Army" grew in strength and trained against the day when it could rise and fight the invaders; and abroad thousands of Polish soldiers, sailors, and airmen carried on the fight in foreign service.

To start with the only way in which they could do this was to escape to the West via Rumania, a long and hazardous route which some 100,000 Poles managed to cover. The Red Army, during its stab-in-the-back advance into eastern Poland, rounded up about 217,000 Polish prisoners of war. And the first chance that the free Poles had to hit back at the Germans came during the Norwegian campaign of 1940.

As a dramatic curtain-raiser, the Polish submarine *Orzel* torpedoed the German transport

General Władysław Sikorski was born in Poland in 1881. He served with distinction in the Polish Legion during World War I and the struggle against Bolshevism. In 1939 he went to Paris, to take command of a provisional Polish army. When Warsaw fell he became head of the Polish government-in-exile. In 1941, when Hitler attacked Russia, he made an alliance with Stalin, with the intention of forming a new Polish army from the P.O.W.s taken by Russia during the invasion of Poland. Thus his attention was drawn to the disappearance of several thousand Polish officers, who were later found in mass graves near Katyn. He was killed in an air crash in July 1943.

1. *Alert! A stand-to-Arms by Polish troops serving with the Red Army.*
2. *The face of confidence: Polish troops leave for the front in a Red Army truck.*

3

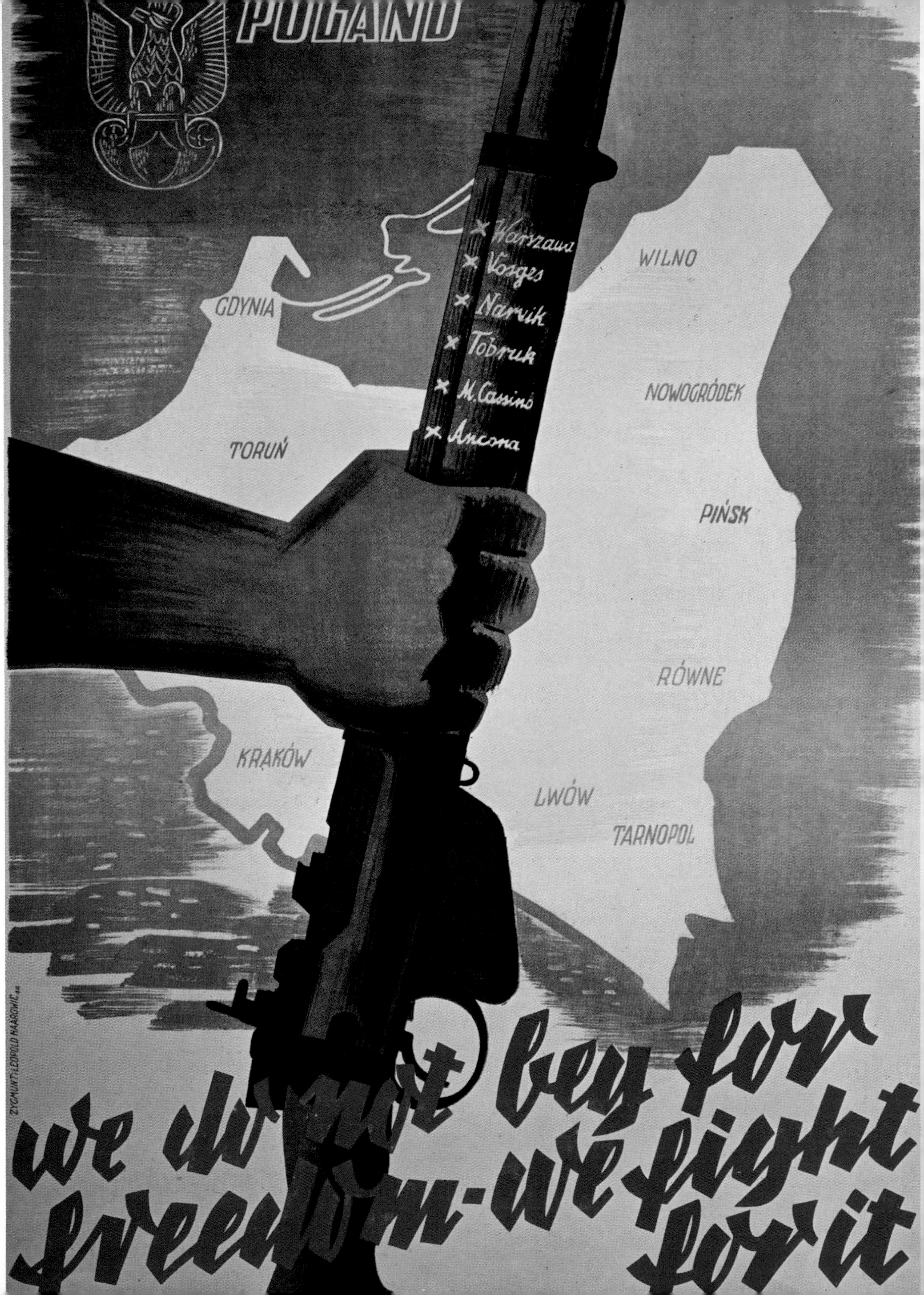
POLAND
Warszawa
Vosges
Narvik
Tobruk
M. Cassino
Ancona
GDYNIA
WILNO
NOWOGRÓDEK
TORUŃ
PIŃSK
RÓWNE
KRAKÓW
LWÓW
TARNOPOL
ZYGMUNT-LEOPOLD HAAROWIC 44
we do not beg for freedom - we fight for it

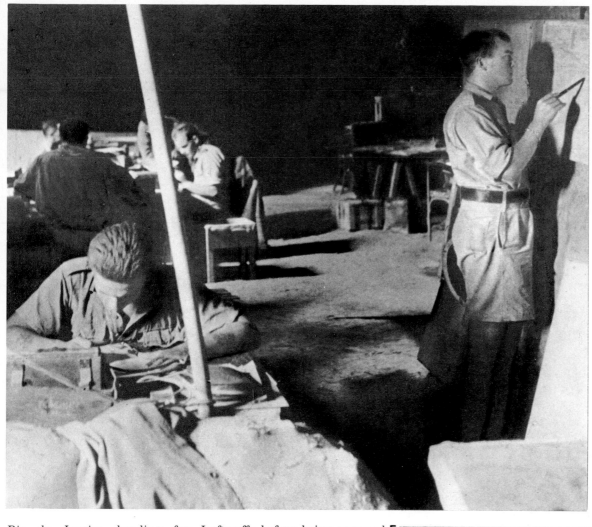

3. *A reminder of why Europe went to war in 1939: Poland's determination to fight for her freedom.*
4. *Polish troops in Tobruk. They took over from the Australians who denied Rommel the fortress in the spring of 1941, and held it until the 8th Army raised the siege in Operation "Crusader".*
5. *Polish regiment heads out to battle in the Western Desert.*
6. *Men of the Polish Carpathian Cavalry Brigade which rode from Syria to join the British after the fall of France in 1940.*

Rio de Janeiro, heading for Norway packed with German troops, in the morning of April 8. This incident should have been instrumental in bringing Norway to a full alert and preventing the German Navy from achieving surprise when it struck at Narvik, Trondheim, and Bergen the following morning. This did not happen; the Germans secured their foothold, and the Allies hastily prepared an expeditionary force to send to Norway. The ensuing fiasco was the first time that British and German forces clashed in World War II – and it was also the first time that free Polish forces saw action. This happened at Narvik, where General Béthouart's 1st *Chasseur* Light Division landed between April 28 and May 7. It included the 1st Carpathian *Chasseur* Demi-Brigade under General Bohusz-Szysko, which played a key rôle in the capture of Narvik – an empty victory, followed almost immediately by the evacuation of the Allied force and its return to Britain.

During the Polish campaign the Polish air force put up a heroic and punishing fight against the Luftwaffe before being removed from the board, and many pilots and aircrew managed to escape to the West. There, re-trained for action in modern fighters, their first big chance for action came with the Battle of Britain. The Polish fighter pilots could not be faulted as far as fighting spirit was concerned, but their discipline in the air often wavered. The R.A.F. ace, Stanford Tuck, found himself obliged to ground Polish pilots for "tearing off on a private war" instead of maintaining formation; but later in the Battle Tuck was touched and honoured when his Polish pilots solemnly presented him with a set of Polish Air Force "wings" to wear on his tunic.

The next theatre in which the free Poles played a prominent rôle was in North Africa. After the Australians under General Morshead had thwarted Rommel's dash on Tobruk and beaten off all his early attacks, they were relieved by General Scobie's 70th Division. This unit, which held Tobruk until the siege was raised by Auchinleck's "Crusader" offensive in November/December 1941, contained

7-9. *Polish pilots of No. 303 Squadron, R.A.F., based at Northolt. Many a R.A.F. fighter commander was forced to take firm action against the fierce, freelance tactics of Polish fighter pilots under his command.*
10. *Formation flying by the fighting Poles: No. 303 Squadron in echelon.*

General Kopa...
brigade. The P...
threw themselve...
of strengthening...
defences and rapi... ...shed
a reputation for aggressive dash
and *panache*. One Polish battalion
commander got into the habit of
strolling across No Man's Land
to the Italian line and haranguing
its troops in good Italian on their
stupidity in remaining allies of
the Germans; and this went on
until one evening he was greeted
with "Three cheers for the Poles!"

But there was nothing light-
hearted about the Polish attitude
to the war. They were grim
and tough fighters and even the
men of Rommel's *Afrika Korps*
did not relish the thought of
falling into their hands. British
Intelligence officers interrogat-
ing German prisoners found it
very useful to have Polish sentries
standing by during the question-
ing. Even recalcitrant prisoners
tended to modify their attitude
on a hint that co-operation would
result in their being placed in
British, rather than Polish,
custody.

By this time the war had been
transformed by the German invasion of the Soviet Union. This
not only brought Russia into the
war, but radically changed the
status of the Polish prisoners of
war taken in September 1939
and imprisoned in Russia. Recruiting of Polish volunteers was
intensified, first as an emergency
measure during the first two years
of German victories in Russia,
and later for political reasons. In
formulating his long-term plans
for Poland, Stalin did not ignore
the value of establishing a Polish
"army in exile", under the aegis
of the Red Army, as well as a
government in exile formed of
sound Communists.

For 4,143 Polish officers, this
new move came much too late.
These were the men exhumed at
Katyn, all of the men captured
in 1939 and taken to Russia. The
Katyn controversy has been
covered elsewhere (see Chapter
98), but the investigations
carried out on the site proved
conclusively that the bodies were
those of the men imprisoned in a
Soviet camp at Kozelsk. When the
other P.O.W.s were released on
the German invasion of Russia
(in many cases after months of
mistreatment in Soviet hands),
urgent enquiries were made as to
the whereabouts of their missing
comrades—enquiries which met
with stubborn silence from Moscow. During these enquiries,

11. *neral Sikorski takes the
ate at a march-past by Polish
roops in Scotland.*

12. *Swearing in new recruits.
Polish volunteers from South
America lay their hands on a
tank and swear the oath of
allegiance as they join an
armoured regiment in England.*

11

12

14

13. *Poles fight with the "Overlord" host: a tank commander gives his orders during the advance from the Seine.*
14. *Polish troops with their wounded at Monte Cassino. When the abbey finally fell, it was the Polish flag that was hoisted over the ruins.*

Lieutenant-Colonel Berling of the Polish General Staff was shocked by a remark from M. Merkulov, the deputy head of the Soviet Secret Police. When Berling mentioned the men in the Kozelsk camp, Merkulov said "No, not those. We made a great mistake with them."

One of the Polish officers who was allowed to go to the West was General Anders. He had been given the job of mustering the nucleus of the new Polish Army at the training camps of Tetskoye and Tatishchevo. Anders gathered some 46,000 ex-P.O.W.s and it was at this time that the extremely small percentage of officers began to sow seeds of doubt in his mind. After much pressure, Stalin agreed to transfer two or three Polish divisions to Persia, where a new Polish corps was to be raised.

This was the origin of the Polish II Corps, to which the British contributed the Polish Narvik veterans and Kopanski's brigade. The II Corps consisted of the 3rd Carpathian Division, the 5th Kresowa Division, and the 2nd Armoured Brigade. It was earmarked for service in Italy under the command of 8th Army; General Anders was to lead it, and the unit landed in Italy in February 1944.

So it was that Anders and the Polish II Corps were given a real baptism of fire: the struggle for Cassino. Its troops attacked with superb dash but suffered murderous losses and Anders was forced to call them off. Before it finally battled its way on to the ruined crest of Monte Cassino, the II Corps lost 3,779 men. It was a heavy price to pay for the glory of being hailed as the "conquerors of Cassino", and for raising the Polish flag over the shattered monastery.

Further hard fighting still lay ahead for Anders and II Corps in Italy during 1944 and the spring of 1945; but in September 1944 came the chance for the Polish troops recruited in Russia. This was the Polish 1st Army, serving under Marshal Rokossovsky's army group. The great Soviet summer offensive carried the Red Army to the gates of Warsaw before it petered out; but the Polish Home Army had already launched its attempt to seize Warsaw. While the Germans ringed off the Poles in Warsaw, the Red Army lay immobile on the eastern bank of the Vistula. Desperate attacks across the Vistula by the Polish 1st Army managed to establish bridgeheads in Warsaw itself and establish tenuous contact with the insurgents, but nothing could be done to prevent their gradual destruction. Apart from the tragedy of the Rising itself, the Poles of the 1st Army were in an agonising position: the official Soviet attitude was that the Rising was the act of "dangerous criminals".

So it was that both in the West and the East, Polish troops fought with honour for Allied victory and their country's freedom.

Volunteers from Holland

Holland was the first of the Western neutral powers to fall under the hammer of the German offensive in May 1940. Five days were sufficient to overrun the country and force the Dutch Army to capitulate–but the Dutch nation was by no means knocked out of the war. The Queen and her government emigrated to England and the Netherlands officially remained in the war, with the resources of the Dutch overseas empire, navy, and mercantile marine at the service of the Allied cause.

The first Dutch troops who refused to accept surrender began to arrive in England on May 15. They had had wildly different adventures. One artillery unit fought its way south through the German lines, crossed Belgium and northern France, and ended up at Cherbourg, whence it was ordered to England by the Dutch government. One Dutch soldier decided quite simply to "go it alone" and set off on foot, lying up by day and marching by night. At one time

he was fired on as a deserter, but he kept walking–across Belgium, across France, over the Pyrenees, and across Spain, ending up at Lisbon, from where he was conveyed to England to join up in the Free Dutch brigade. A steady trickle of escapees managed to cross the Channel in following months. Typical of them were a party of Dutch P.O.W.s who had been fishing off the Dutch coast under armed guards. A sudden mutiny put the Germans over the side and the Dutch P.O.W.s set off for England, where they duly arrived–this incident took place as late as 1942.

The Dutch Legion formed in Britain retained the original Dutch Army uniform until July 1940, when its soldiers were re-equipped with standard British battle-dress. They sported the Dutch lion on the left shoulder with the title "Nederland" below. On June 21 the Dutch government-in-exile called up all Dutch male nationals resident in the United Kingdom, which considerably swelled the numbers of

the Dutch Legion. In July the Legion was given its first operational duties; coastal and airfield defence. A British Military Mission to the Dutch Forces was established on August 12, 1940; and the "Royal Netherlands Brigade 'Princess Irene'" was a going concern by the end of the year.

There had been no Dutch air force as such, the air service being divided into Army and Naval Air Services. Luftwaffe strafing eliminated most of the land-based aircraft but many aircrew of the Naval Air Service managed to escape to England in their Fokker seaplanes. Once in England they were incorporated into the R.A.F., flying Coastal Command patrols; and Ansons with R.A.F. markings and the distinctive Dutch yellow triangle became a familiar and welcome sight on Britain's coastal approaches.

When Japan struck in December 1941 the Royal Dutch Navy in the Far East had a decisive rôle to play. The Dutch Navy had a

fighting tradition second to none. During the 17th and 18th centuries Holland had been a major maritime power. Now it formed an integral part of the hastily-formed Allied naval squadron given the task of defending the Dutch East Indies–"A.B.D.A.", the initials standing for American-British-Dutch-Australian. It never had anything like a fair chance, with the Japanese dominating the skies and keeping touch with every move the Allies made. But under the command of Rear-Admiral Karel Doorman, flying his flag in the Dutch cruiser *De Ruyter,* the A.B.D.A. force made valiant efforts to disrupt the development of the Japanese advance. Doorman's polyglot cruiser/destroyer force was strong enough on paper but it never had the chance to settle down and learn to operate as an integrated unit. Whittled down by torpedo attacks and repeated gunnery engagements, Doorman's squadron gallantly went to its doom in the Battle of the Java sea, its duty done in vain.

1

1. *To fight again. Two Dutch officers arrive in England after crossing the North Sea in a sailing canoe.*
2. *The Christmas spirit, 1940. Free Dutch soldiers at their Christmas dinner in England.*
3. *The Free Dutch versus the Home Guard. In this "invasion" of Birkenhead in August 1941, the Free Dutch swept the Home Guard defenders out of the way and took the town regardless of "casualties".*
4. *Every inch a Tommy–Free Dutch troops drill in British kit.*
5. Overleaf: *Dutch naval cadets on Home Guard duty. About 250 cadets from the Royal Naval College of the Netherlands escaped to England in 1940, and their training continued while in exile. They were a useful supplement to local civil defence units.*

5

CHAPTER 114
Cherbourg falls

Rommel's pessimism in no way tempted him to give up at the military level. Partly, no doubt, this was because of his training as a professional soldier, and his first impulse was to obey the orders he had been given. Nor did his awareness that there was an anti-Hitler conspiracy under way materially alter his views. He probably believed that if Hitler was removed, the argument for territorial bargaining counters gained more force. Otherwise, the new German representatives would be empty-handed, and would have to accept any conditions the victors chose to impose.

The attack on Cherbourg

According to the plan worked out by General Montgomery, the port of Cherbourg was the first objective of the American 1st Army, and especially of VII Corps, which, with the landing of the 90th and 91st Divisions, and the 2nd Armoured Division, had gradually been brought up to six divisions. On the German side, LXXXIV Panzer Corps had been taken over by General von Choltitz, following the death of General Marcks, killed by a fighter-bomber on leaving his command post at Saint Lô. "May I respectfully request you not to take too many risks. A change of command now would be most unfortunate." This remonstrance on the part of his chief-of-staff, just as Marcks was getting into his car to visit the front, brought forth the following reply: "You and your existence! *We* can die honourably, like soldiers; but our poor Fatherland . . ." A few seconds later he was dead, struck by a shell which cut through the femoral artery of the one leg left to him since the retreat in Russia in the winter of 1941-42.

To defend the Cotentin area, Choltitz had five divisions (the 77th, 91st, 243rd, 353rd, and 709th); however, in their ranks was a certain number of Soviet volunteers, recruited mainly in the Ukraine, in the Crimea, and in the valleys of the Caucasus, from a dozen different nationalities, and this incredible hotch-potch had scarcely made them better fighting units. As Lieutenant-General von Schlieben, commander of the 709th Division, who was fully aware of this, said: "How do you expect Russians, in German uniform, to fight well against Americans, in

Previous page: After four years of German occupation, the Tricolour flies again in Cherbourg.

△ and ▽ *Huge explosions wreck the harbour installations at Cherbourg. The extensive German demolitions effectively denied the Allies the use of the port; the main stream of supplies and reinforcements would still have to come in through the Mulberry port and over the beaches.*

Back on the defensive as the result of the failure of his counter-attacks, Rommel now had no illusions about the fate awaiting his forces, and on June 11 he spoke quite openly about it to Vice-Admiral Ruge, in whom, quite justifiably, he had full confidence. In his view, the best thing that Germany could do, given her situation, was to end the war now, before the territorial bargaining counters she still held were prised from her grasp. But Hitler did not see things that way, and in any case, none of Germany's enemies was willing to enter into any negotiations.

France?" His own division was made up of rather elderly troops (30- to 35-year-olds), and some of the artillerymen of the coastal batteries were over 40.

American successes under General Eddy

The first part of General Bradley's plan to capture his objective was to advance to the west coast of the Cotentin, and then turn north, making his columns converge on Cherbourg. The 90th Division, however, in its first engagement, got into such trouble in crossing the Douve that at one time the Allied command thought seriously of breaking it up, and distributing it amongst the other divisions. Finally, General Bradley merely replaced its commander with Major-General Landrum, who, however, was quite incapable of infusing any life into it, so badly had its morale been affected by its baptism of fire.

In happy contrast, on June 14 the American 9th Division, which had already distinguished itself in Tunisia, crushed

◁ Safety first. Lobbing a brace of grenades over a wall to cope with possible snipers.
▽ Infantry and armour push deeper into Cherbourg.

enemy resistance, which had been favoured by the marshy terrain. Commanded by a resolute and skilful soldier, Major-General Manton Eddy, it advanced quickly along a line Pont l'Abbé–Saint Sauveur-le-Vicomte–Barneville, reaching the western coast of the Cotentin at dawn on June 15, and thus isolating to the north the 77th, 243rd, and 709th Divisions – or what was left of them. Then Lieutenant-General Collins's VII Corps, covered in the south by his two airborne divisions and his 91st Division, launched an assault on Cherbourg. On the right was the 4th Division, commanded by Major-General Barton, and on the left, the 79th Division (Major-General Ira Wyche), which had just landed, and the 9th Division. The latter had less than a day to wheel from west to north, with all its supplies and arms – a difficult military exercise which General Eddy accomplished brilliantly.

"Within 22 hours", wrote General Bradley, "he was expected to turn a force of 20,000 troops a full 90 degrees toward Cherbourg, evacuate his sick and wounded, lay wire, reconnoitre the ground, establish his boundaries, issue orders, relocate his ammunition and supply

dumps, and then jump off in a fresh attack on a front nine miles wide. Eddy never even raised his eyebrows and when H-hour struck, he jumped off on time."

It is true that the German LXXXIV Corps had been very badly mauled, and that under the incessant attacks of the Anglo-American air force, Generals Hellmich and Stegmann, commanding the 77th and 243rd Divisions respectively, had been killed. However, the speed with which the 9th Division switched fronts enabled the remnants of the 77th Division, now under the command of Colonel Bacherer, to slip through the American forward posts and regain the German lines, having captured on the way 250 prisoners, 11 jeeps, and thousands of yards of telephone cable.

Meanwhile, on either side of Carentan, the American XIX Corps had entered the line, between the left wing of VII Corps and the right wing of V Corps. On the whole, General Bradley could consider himself satisfied with the situation, until, on June 19, a storm destroyed the artificial port being set up on "Omaha" Beach, and hundreds of landing craft and thousands of tons of supplies were lost; this, in turn, created a very difficult weapons shortage for the 1st Army, and delayed the entry into the line of General Middleton's VIII Corps.

Schlieben rejects ultimatum

In spite of these difficulties, VII Corps succeeded in overcoming the resistance that Schlieben, with forces much too slender for the wide front he was holding, tried to put up, on Hitler's own orders, at Cherbourg. However, he refused to reply to General Collins's first call to surrender, couched in the following terms: "You and your troops have resisted stubbornly and gallantly, but you are in a hopeless situation. The moment has come for you to capitulate. Send your reply by radio, on a frequency of 1520 kilocycles, and show a white flag or fire white signal flares from the naval hospital or the Pasteur clinic. After that, send a staff officer under a flag of truce to the farmhouse on the road to Fort-du-Roule, to accept the terms of surrender."

Fort Roule, the key to this great port, had indeed just fallen to the Americans, and Fort Octeville, where Schlieben and Rear-Admiral Hennecke had taken

refuge, was being subjected to such an intense bombardment that clouds of poisonous fumes were seeping into the galleries where more than 300 wounded lay sheltering. This being so, Schlieben sent his negotiators to General Eddy on June 26, at 1400 hours, specifying that only Fort Octeville was to be discussed.

The time thus gained by the Germans enabled their pioneers to carry out the destruction of the port installations, and mine the ruins of the town, making the clearing up of the roads a longer and more costly process. In actual fact, only a month was needed before the Americans were able to bring in their first ships to Cherbourg; a few weeks later, an immense drum, 36 feet in diameter, was towed into Cherbourg harbour; around it were strung the last few yards of "Pluto" (Pipe Line Under The Ocean), the latest development by those Allied planners who had been responsible for the artificial port of Arromanches, which had resisted the storm of June 19 better than "Omaha". Starting at Sandown, on the Isle of Wight, Pluto's four tubes, each three inches in diameter and about 170 miles long, enabled 250,000 gallons of petrol a day to be pumped to the Allied armies.

The Allies occupy Cherbourg

The last strongholds of the town did not fall until July 3. On June 27, receiving the surrender of Major Küppers, Osteck fortress commander, General Barton, com-

△ △ *The "Battle of the Hedgerows"—a typical scene. Troops dash across a lane to reach cover on the far side. The tank in the foreground is a Panther.*
△ *Shermans squeeze past "killed" Panzers.*

manding the 4th Division, showed Küppers his map of the situation; later Küppers told Paul Carell:

"The entire network of the German positions was shown on the map with absolute accuracy, and in far greater detail than our own maps. On the back were listed precise data about the types of weapons and ammunition at each emplacement and bunker, as well as the names of all strongpoint commanders, and of the battalion and regimental commanders to whom they were responsible. The adjoining sheet covered the former defence sector 'East' in the Saint-Pierre-Eglise area outside the Cherbourg fortified zone . . . All command-posts showed the names of their principal officers. True, the entry for 11th Battery, 1709th Artillery Regiment still listed its commander Lieutenant Ralf Neste, who had lost his life in an accident with a *Panzerfaust* on May 5, 1944–but that seemed to be the only mistake.

"Their success had been tremendous. The full story of this gigantic espionage and Intelligence operation still remains to be written. It is the story of the Alliance of Animals, that most important secret Intelligence organization of the Allies in France; the story of 'Panther', the French Colonel Alamichel who set up the organisation; the story of Colonel Fay, who was known as 'Lion', and of Marie-Madeleine Merrie, that young, pretty, and courageous French woman who oddly enough bore the code-name of *Hérisson* ('Hedgehog').

▽ *Instant cavalry. Men of the U.S. 4th Division patrol Cherbourg on "liberated" horses.*

▷ *The shattered approaches to Cherbourg.*
▷ ▷ *"After the fight . . ." Amid a litter of abandoned German equipment, Sergeant Vernon Pickrell of Los Angeles samples a bottle of cognac found in a bunker.*

"The chief of the Alliance had three headquarters in Paris for the staff of officers and for his British chief radio-operator, 'Magpie'. One of these headquarters was the contact point for couriers, the second was an alternative headquarters for emergencies, and the third, in the Rue Charles Laffitte, was headed by 'Odette', the famous Odette. At these headquarters all information converged. Here it was sorted according to Army, Navy, Air Force, political or economic."

Germans stand firm

But Bradley had no intention of resting on his laurels. He quickly brought his VII Corps into the line, in between the left wing of VIII Corps and the right wing of XIX Corps, such was his impatience to begin phase two of the Normandy campaign, which meant breaking up the German front between Saint Lô and Coutances, and then exploiting this breakthrough in the direction of Avranches. The operation had to be carried out quickly, so as to prevent the enemy digging in and returning to the techniques of trench warfare which had caused such bloody losses in 1914-18.

On June 24, Bradley's 1st Army consisted of VIII, VII, XIX and V Corps (nine infantry divisions, two armoured divisions, and the 82nd and 101st Airborne Divisions, although these latter were badly in need of a rest). His resources were thus greater than those of the enemy's 7th Army, but the Germans were tough, well commanded, and in good heart, as is shown by this letter, written by a German sergeant who had been taken prisoner: "The R.A.F. rules the skies. I have not yet seen a single plane with a 'swastika', and despite the material superiority of the enemy we Germans hold firm. The front at Caen holds. Every soldier on this front is hoping for a miracle and waits for the secret weapons which have been discussed so much."

In particular, between the sea and the Vire, in the sector where the American VII and VIII Corps were in action, the nature of the terrain favoured the defence, since both towards Coutances and Saint Lô marshy land alternated with woodland. If the tanks took to the main roads, they fell victims to the redoubtable German 8.8-cm, which pounded them whilst

difficult; bad weather made air sorties, if not impossible, at least very dangerous, not least for the troops they were intended to support.

These different factors explain the slowness of the American advance across the swollen rivers and the flooded meadows of this neck of the Cotentin which extends between the Channel and the estuary of the River Vire. VIII Corps only took la Haye-du-Puits at the cost of exhausting combat; whilst VII Corps, despite the nickname "Lightning Joe" which they had bestowed on their dynamic General Collins, only became masters of what was left of the ruins of Saint Lô on July 20, 44 days later than laid down in the plan drawn up the April before . . . And not without quite considerable losses.

General Bradley, referring to this fierce resistance which halted his advance and cost so many lives, has given the following description of the ordeals his men had to undergo as they fought through Nor-

▲ Tearing down the sign from the H.Q. of the hated Organisation Todt at Cherbourg.
▷ The German P.O.W. column moves out.

▽ On the Cherbourg battlefield: a captured German mortar.

remaining safely out of range; if they took to the little-used country roads, they got in everybody's way and at the same time exposed themselves to the risk of being shot at by a *Panzerschreck* or a *Panzerfaust* fired through a neighbouring hedge. Furthermore, the wet weather of the second half of June and the whole of July reduced to a minimum those air force sorties which could have helped the American 1st Army; even in fine weather the rolling green woodlands of the region would have made air support

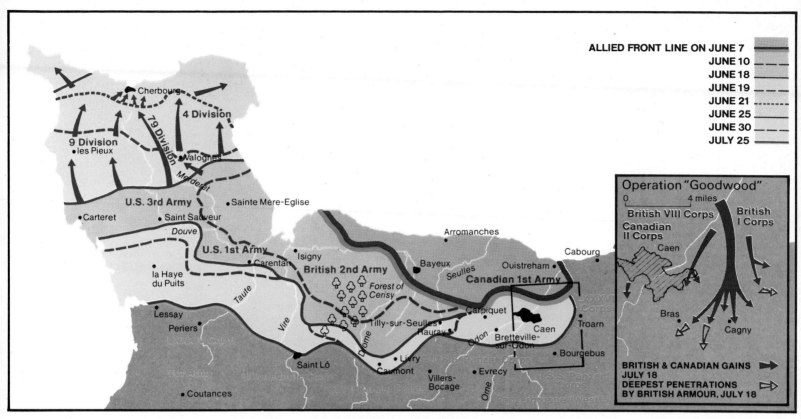

Operation "Goodwood"

0   4 miles

British VIII Corps
Canadian II Corps
British I Corps
Caen
Bras
Cagny

BRITISH & CANADIAN GAINS JULY 18
DEEPEST PENETRATIONS BY BRITISH ARMOUR, JULY 18

Cherbourg
4 Division
79 Division
9 Division
les Pieux
Valognes
Merderet
U.S. 3rd Army
Sainte Mère-Eglise
Carteret
Saint Sauveur
Douve
U.S. 1st Army
Isigny
Arromanches
la Haye du Puits
Carentan
Bayeux
Cabourg
Taute
British 2nd Army
Seulles
Ouistreham
Forest of Cerisy
Canadian 1st Army
Vire
Dôme
Tilly-sur-Seulles
Rauray
Carpiquet
Odon
Bretteville-sur-Odon
Caen
Troarn
Lessay
Saint Lô
Livry
Caumont
Villers-Bocage
Evrecy
Bourgebus
Periers
Orne
Coutances

mandy, Lorraine, the Ardennes, the Sieg-fried Line, and then into the very heart of Germany:

"The rifleman trudges into battle knowing that statistics are stacked against his survival. He fights without promise of either reward or relief. Behind every river, there's another hill–and behind that hill, another river. After weeks or months in the line only a wound can offer him the comfort of safety, shelter, and a bed. Those who are left to fight, fight on, evading death but knowing that with each day of evasion they have exhausted one more chance for survival. Sooner or later, unless victory comes, the chase must end on the litter or in the grave."

And indeed, between June 22, the seventeenth day of the invasion, and July 19, American losses had leapt from 18,374 (including 3,012 dead), to 62,000, more precisely 10,641 dead and 51,387 wounded, two-thirds of whom, if not more, were as usual the long-suffering infantrymen.

These mounting losses and the very slow progress being made by the American 1st Army provoked a fair amount of criticism from the host of correspondents accredited to S.H.A.E.F., especially as from June 22 the Russian summer offensive, with its almost daily victories, allowed unflattering comparisons to be made on Eisenhower and Bradley: compared with Vitebsk, Orcha, Mogilev, Bob-

ENTRE LE MARTEAU ...

... ET L'ENCLUME !..

ruysk, and Minsk, la Haye-du-Puits, Pont-Hébert, Tribehou, and even Saint Lô were but puny things. Some even went so far as to say that the "halting" of operations on the Western Front was part of some concerted plan, drawn up at the highest level, and intended to bleed the long-suffering Russians white with a view to the future.

△ *How the Allies consolidated the Normandy beach-head.*
◁ *Proud acknowledgment of the co-operation between the Anglo-American invasion forces and the work of the Resistance.*

CHAPTER 115
The tension grows

△ The British advance—past the grave of a German soldier.

The unsavoury gossip about Bradley was nothing to the criticisms made of Montgomery regarding the mediocre victories which the British 2nd Army could claim at that time. It had in fact to attack three times, and it was not until July 9, 1944 that it was able to announce the capture of Caen, its D-Day objective.

Of course, Montgomery could hardly reveal to the journalists whom he gathered round him for periodical press conferences that he had no intention of opening up the route to Paris. Still less could he tell them that his plan aimed first and foremost at forcing Rommel to concentrate his Panzers against the British 2nd Army, and wearing them down on this front by a series of purely local actions. Having said this, however, it may be said that in this battle of equipment, Montgomery the master-tactician did not sufficiently bear in mind the

enormous technical superiority that German armour enjoyed over the British and American tanks. If we look again at accounts of the furious battles fought out in the Caen sector in June and July, 1944, all we seem to read about is Sherman tanks burning like torches, Cromwell tanks riddled like sieves, and Churchill tanks, whose armour was considered sufficiently thick, never surviving a direct hit. Here, for example, is part of Major-General Roberts's description of Operation "Goodwood" on July 19 and 20.

"But 3 R.T.R. were through. They had started with 52 tanks, been given 11 replacements, making 63 tanks in all. With Bras now in their hands, they had nine tanks left. Major Close's A Squadron had lost 17 tanks in two days, seven being completely destroyed, the others recoverable; all Troop officers had been killed or wounded, and only one troop Sergeant was

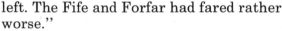

left. The Fife and Forfar had fared rather worse.''

In the circumstances it is not surprising that the famous units that had formed part of the 8th Army in North Africa (the 50th and 51st Infantry Divisions, and the 7th Armoured Division) did not have the success expected of them in this new theatre of operations. Writing of these veterans of Bir Hakeim, Tobruk, and El Alamein, Belfield and Essame remind us of the old saying current in the British Army–"An old soldier is a cautious soldier, that is why he is an old soldier.'' Quite probably. But perhaps the hiding the Desert Rats received at Villers-Bocage on July 12, when they first came into contact with the 2nd Panzer Division, was such as to make even the most reckless prudent.

As for the 12 British divisions which came under fire for the very first time in Normandy, however realistic their training may have been, however keen they may have been to fight, the real thing was very different, and the conditions they were called upon to face in real combat sometimes took away some of their aggressiveness.

It is also possible to criticise the British High Command for the tendency in its instructions to try to foresee everything, even the unforeseeable. Having seen orders issued by the main American commanders, we know that they subscribed to the same theory as the Germans, that the order should contain all that the lesser commander needs to know to carry out his task but nothing more; whereas British orders tended to go into further detail, limiting the initiative of the tactical commanders, because of theoretical situations that did not always arise. For in war, it is said, it is the unexpected that happens.

In this list of Montgomery's resources, an honourable mention must be made of the artillery, for which Rommel's grenadiers had a special dislike, for it fired quickly and accurately. In particular, the 25-pounder "gun-howitzer'' fired so rapidly that the Germans thought it must have been fitted with a system of automatic loading. And this fact goes a long way to explain the form which the fighting took in the Caen sector, for if the British tanks

△ *British Shermans in open country. By maintaining the strongest possible pressure on the Caen front, Montgomery planned to pull the bulk of the German armour away from the American sector of the front.*

The North American P-51D Mustang long range fighter and fighter-bomber

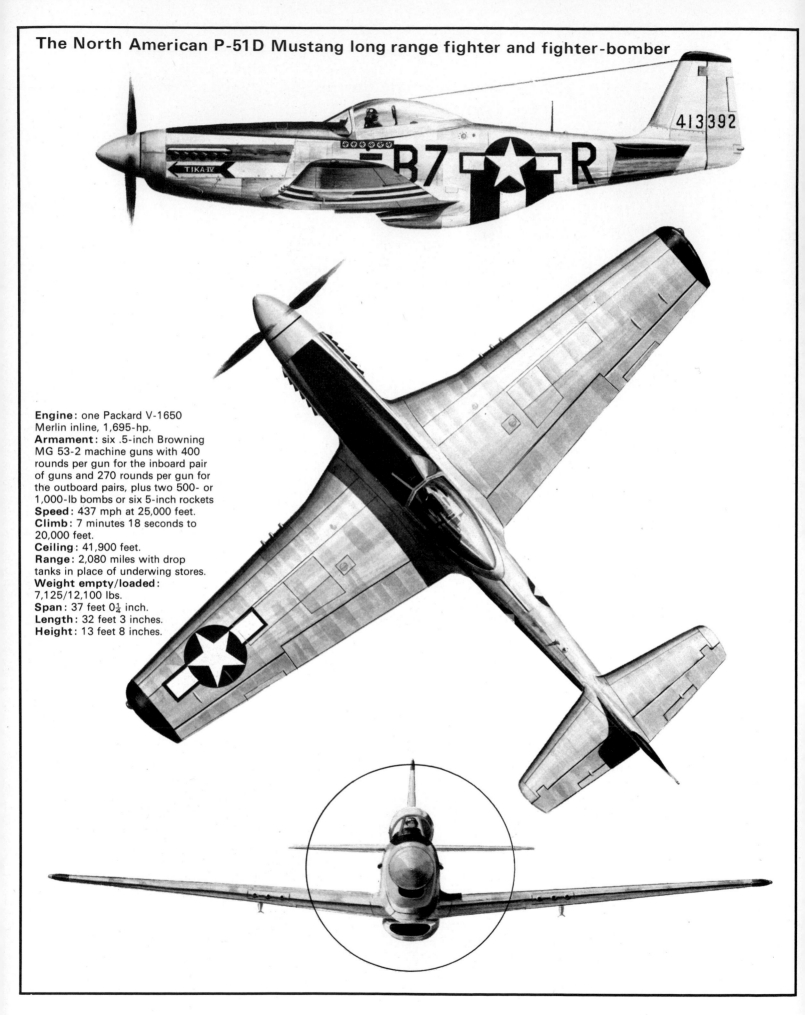

Engine: one Packard V-1650 Merlin inline, 1,695-hp.
Armament: six .5-inch Browning MG 53-2 machine guns with 400 rounds per gun for the inboard pair of guns and 270 rounds per gun for the outboard pairs, plus two 500- or 1,000-lb bombs or six 5-inch rockets
Speed: 437 mph at 25,000 feet.
Climb: 7 minutes 18 seconds to 20,000 feet.
Ceiling: 41,900 feet.
Range: 2,080 miles with drop tanks in place of underwing stores.
Weight empty/loaded: 7,125/12,100 lbs.
Span: 37 feet 0¼ inch.
Length: 32 feet 3 inches.
Height: 13 feet 8 inches.

◁ *A British patrol pushes into the ruins of Caen.*
▽ *The Cassino of France. What was left of Caen.*

failed in all their attempts at breakthrough whenever they came up against the German Panthers, Tigers, and the 8.8-cm anti-tank guns of *Panzergruppe* "West", the German counter-attacks collapsed under the murderous fire of the British artillery concentrations whenever they went beyond purely local engagements. All the more so since at that distance from the coast the big guns of the Royal Navy were able to take a hand. So it was that on June 16 in the region of Thury-Harcourt, about 20 miles from Riva-Bella, a 16-inch shell from the *Rodney* or the *Nelson* killed Lieutenant-General Witt, commanding the 12th S.S. Panzer Division *"Hitlerjugend"*.

The failure of British XXX Armoured Corps and the 7th Armoured Division to turn the front of *Panzergruppe* "West" at Villers-Bocage seems to have caused Montgomery to shift the centre of gravity of his attack to the countryside around Caen, where his armour would find a more suitable terrain.

Operation "Epsom", begun on June 25, brought into action VIII Corps, just landed in Normandy and commanded by Sir Richard O'Connor, released from captivity by the signing of the Italian armistice. Covered on his right by XXX Corps' 49th Division, O'Connor was to cross the Caen–Bayeux road to the west of the Carpiquet aerodrome, push on past the Fossé de l' Odon, then switching the direction of his attack from south to south-west, he would finally reach Brette-ville-sur-Laize, ten miles south of Caen, near the Caen–Falaise road. This would give the British 2nd Army not only the capital of Normandy, but also the Car-piquet air base, upon which Air-Marshals Coningham and Leigh-Mallory had long been casting envious eyes.

VIII Corps had 60,000 men, 600 tanks, and 700 guns. The 15th and 43rd Divi-sions, each reinforced by a brigade of Churchill tanks, provided O'Connor with his shock troops, whilst the 11th Armoured Division would then exploit the situa-tion. For all three divisions it was their first taste of combat.

Whilst the left wing of XXX Corps attacked the Panzer-*"Lehr"* Division, VIII Corps' attack brought it into contact with the 12th S.S. Panzer Division *"Hitler-jugend"*, commanded, since the death of General Witt, by General Kurt Meyer, a leader of extreme resolution, of rapid and correct decisions, whom his men had nicknamed "Panzer-Meyer". By nightfall, at the price of fierce combat and despite incessant counter-attacks, the British infantry was able to bed down near the Caen–Villers-Bocage road, three miles from their starting point. On June 27, the 15th Division managed to capture a sound bridge over the Odon, and the 11th Ar-moured Division advanced and began the switching movement mentioned earlier: the first objective was Hill 112, the summit of the ridge which separates the Odon and Orne Valleys.

German counter-attack fails

The VIII Corps, however, was now behind schedule, and some very trouble-some bottlenecks were building up at its rear. These difficulties enabled Sepp Die-trich, commanding I S.S. Panzer Corps, to avoid the worst by bringing in General Paul Hausser's II S.S. Panzer Corps, which had just come back from the Gali-cian front. He even tried to take the 11th Armoured Division in a pincer movement between the 9th S.S. Panzer Division *"Hohenstaufen"* and the 10th S.S. Panzer Division *"Frundsberg"* and only failed because O'Connor evacuated his troops from a salient that had become too exposed.

On the other hand the *Panzergruppe* "West" failed in its efforts to turn this defensive success into a general offensive,

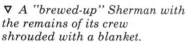
▽ *A "brewed-up" Sherman with the remains of its crew shrouded with a blanket.*

for II S.S. Panzer Corps was literally pinned down by artillery fire and tactical air bombardment whenever it made the slightest move. In this connection General Harzer, Chief Operations Staff Officer of the 9th S.S. *Panzergrenadier* Division said later: "Now, if the Luftwaffe had been able to deal with the Allied navies and also stop the accurate bombing of certain targets, I think that the British-Canadian landings would once again have 'fallen in the ditch', as they say. As it was, our counter-offensive broke down under air attack and artillery fire, particularly the heavy guns of the battleships. They were devastating. When one of these shells dropped near a Panther, the 56-ton *(sic)* tank was blown over on its side, just from the blast. It was these broadsides from the warships, more than the defensive fighting of the enemy's troops, which halted our division's Panzer Regiment." At all events, after this sharp lesson, the Germans gave up any further idea of throwing the enemy back into the sea. Instead, they had been forced to feed into a defensive battle the reserves they needed for a major counter-strike.

Montgomery, in his June 30 directive to Generals Bradley and Dempsey, declared himself to be quite satisfied

with the results obtained, although Operation "Epsom" had only dented the enemy line.

"All this is good . . . by forcing the enemy to place the bulk of his strength in front of the Second Army, we have made easier the acquisition of territory on the western flank.

"Our policy has been so successful that the Second Army is now opposed by a formidable array of German Panzer Divisions—eight definitely identified, and possibly more to come . . .

"To hold the maximum number of enemy divisions on our eastern flank between Caen and Villers Bocage, and to swing the western or right flank of the Army Group southwards and eastwards in a wide sweep so as to threaten the line of withdrawal of such enemy divisions to the south of Paris."

△ *American combat team: rifles, sub-machine gun, and a mortar.*

Caen occupied

The carrying out of this plan meant continuing to place the main weight of this battle of attrition on the shoulders of General Dempsey, for the slightest

△ *When a ditch becomes an improvised trench. An American section prepares to break cover.*

The British attack again: Operation "Goodwood"

Because of a delay by the U.S. 1st Army out on the Allied right flank, in preparing Operation "Cobra", the attack which was to crush German resistance, Montgomery asked Dempsey for one more effort to engage and tie down the Panzers on his front, and, if possible, to advance the armoured units of his 2nd Army into the region around Falaise. To this end, Operation "Goodwood" had moved the centre of gravity of the attack back to the right bank of the Orne, where the British 1st and 8th Armies were massed, whilst the Canadian II Corps, two divisions strong, was concentrated within the ruins of Caen. To it fell the task of capturing the suburbs of the town to the south of the river, and of developing an attack towards Falaise. The enemy's front, tied down in the centre, would be by-passed and rolled back from left to right by the three armoured divisions (the 7th and 11th, and the Guards Armoured Divisions), breaking out from the narrow bridgehead between the Orne and the Dives, which General Gale's parachute troops had captured on the night of June 5-6. VIII Corps possessed 1100 tanks, 720 guns and a stockpile of 250,000 shells. But above all, the Allied air forces would support and prepare the attack on a scale hitherto undreamed of: 1,600 four-engined planes, and 600 two-engined planes and fighter-bombers would drop more than 7,000 tons of explosives on enemy positions, and then support VIII Corps' armour as it advanced.

However, the Germans had seen through the Allies' intentions, and had organised themselves to a depth of ten miles; it is true that they only had in the line one division, the 16th Luftwaffe Field Division, and what was left of the 21st Panzer Division, but they still possessed considerable fire-power, in the shape of 272 6-tube rocket launchers and a hundred or so 8.8-cm anti-aircraft guns operating as anti-tank guns. So the Allies were to find difficulty in making their overall superiority tell.

On July 18, at 0530 hours, the thunder of 720 guns signalled the beginning of Operation "Goodwood". Then, as one member of VIII Corps put it, the aircraft "came lounging across the sky,

slackening of pressure would mean that Rommel would be able to reorganise and re-form.

On July 9, Caen and Carpiquet aerodrome fell to Lieutenant-General J. T. Crocker's British I Corps. The old Norman town, already badly bombed by the R.A.F. on the night of June 5-6, was now reduced to rubble by the dropping of 2,500 tons of bombs. The only part more or less spared was the area around the majestic Abbaye-aux-Hommes, which was protected by the Geneva Convention and was a refuge for many thousands of homeless. Although this pitiless bombing forced the *"Hitlerjugend"* Division to retreat, it also created such ruin, and slowed down the advance of the Canadian 3rd Division so much, that when it arrived at the river Orne it found all the bridges blown.

The American/British Sherman Tankdozer

This was the basic Sherman gun tank fitted with an M1 or M1A1 dozer blade, for use in clearing rubble and filling in craters in the face of opposition and knocking down enemy emplacements. The need for such vehicles had been realised at Cassino, and Tankdozers proved invaluable in such operations as the clearing of Caen. Other bulldozer-type modifications were developed for cutting through the high hedgerows in which Normandy abounds.

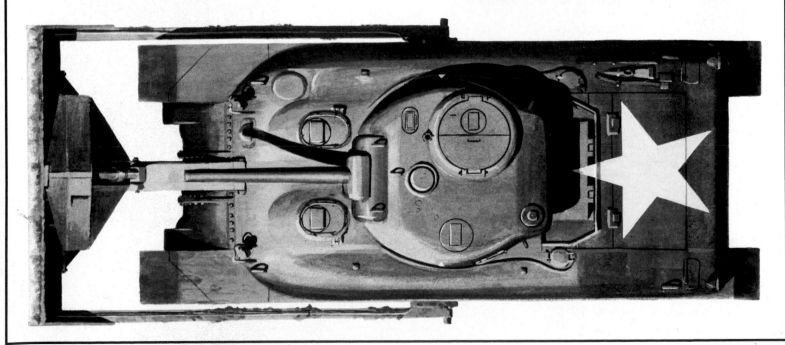

scattered, leisurely, indifferent. The first ones crossed our lines, and the earth began to shake to a continuous rumble which lasted for three-quarters of an hour; and at no time during that period were fewer than fifty 'planes visible. The din was tremendous. We could see the bombs leaving the 'planes and drifting down almost gently, like milt from a salmon, and as they disappeared behind the trees the rumble rose a little and then sunk to its old level again. The Jocks were all standing grinning at the sky. After weeks of skulking in trenches, here was action; action on a bigger scale than any of them had dreamed was possible."

At 0745 hours the 11th Armoured Division, preceded by a continuous barrage of an intensity never before experienced, began to advance, and quickly got through the first position, defended by troops still groggy from the pounding

△ British Bren-gunner on the Caen – Falaise front, where every ruined house was a nest of resistance by the hard-pressed German forces.
▷ An American paratroop patrol encounters German corpses.
▷ △ Tired German prisoners limp through the British lines to the rear.
▷ ▷ A negro artillery team digs in its "Long Tom" 155-mm gun.

nflicted by Bomber Command. But towards mid-day the attack came up against he railway line running from Caen to Paris, where it stopped.

Meagre success for the British

This was due, first, to the fact that the British artillery, which had stayed on the left bank of the Orne, no longer had the enemy within range; and second, that on the bridges which the Guards and the 7th Armoured Division had to take to get across to the right bank and link up with the 11th Division, there were tremendous bottlenecks. Above all, however, was the fact that 8.8-cm guns and *Nebelwerfers* were firing from the many villages on the outskirts of the town. At nightfall the 1st S.S. Panzer Division *"Leibstandarte"*, which formed Sepp Dietrich's reserve, surprised the 11th Armoured Division, just when it was about to bed down, and according to its commander, Major-General Wisch, destroyed about 40 tanks.

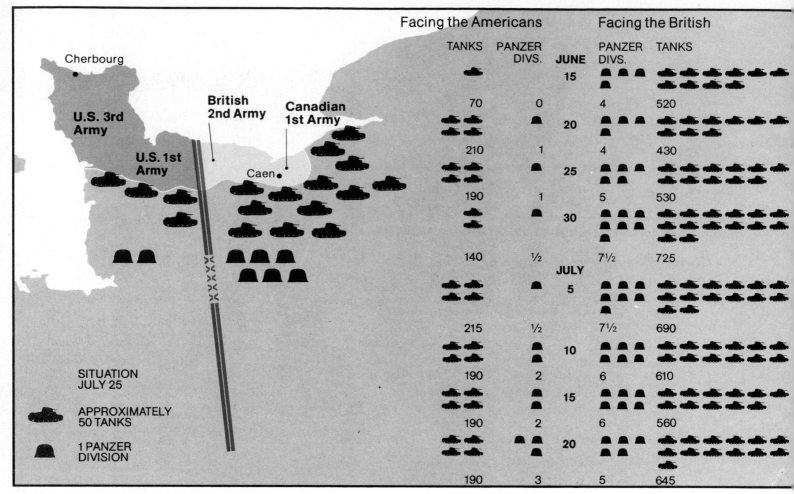

On July 19, with the rain taking a hand, the terrain got into such a state owing to the bombing the day before, that operations had to stop. South and south-west of Caen, the British and Canadians had advanced about five miles into the enemy's defensive positions, but had not succeeded in overrunning them. All in all it was rather a meagre success, especially as it had been paid for at the enormous price of 413 tanks, but there was a certain strategic compensation, as the 116th Panzer Division of the German 15th Army, stationed up till then near Amiens, was ordered to move towards Caen; and then Kluge, Rundstedt's successor at the head of Army Group "B", afraid of a British breakthrough in the direction of Falaise, thought it advisable to move his 2nd Panzer Division from Saint Lô to Caen, less than a week before the beginning of Operation "Cobra".

By this same day of July 19, the losses of the British 2nd Army since June 6 had amounted to 34,700 officers and men, of whom 6,010 were killed, and 28,690 were missing. They were therefore far less severe than those suffered during the same period by the American 1st Army (62,028 men). Of course, on D-Day the American 1st Division, on "Omaha" Beach, and the 82nd and 101st Airborne Divisions, around Sainte Mère-Eglise, had had a harder time of it. But in the Normandy woodlands the infantry-based American attacks had also been more expensive, in terms of men, than the British tank-based attacks in the Caen area— which seemed to prove once more Guderian's theory that tanks are a weapon that saves lives.

Montgomery's tactics

Basing his calculations on the figures supplied by Brigadier Williams, head of his Intelligence staff, Montgomery saw a situation arising in which, in spite of the apparent failures of the British 2nd Army, he would in a few days be able to send in the American 1st Army. Between June 6 and July 25, German strength had shifted away from the American front to that of their Allies, the British, as can be seen from the chart at left, based on figures culled from Montgomery's Memoirs. The moment for the final break-through was approaching.

CHAPTER 116
Montgomery's new plan

Although, of course, Montgomery's superiors, General Eisenhower and the Combined Chiefs-of-Staff Committee, as well as his most important subordinates, were aware of the strategic objective hidden by his apparently slow manoeuvres, S.H.A.E.F. was beginning to show some signs of impatience. Writing ten years after the event, Montgomery thought he saw personal reasons, unconnected with the military situation, behind many of the criticisms made of his methods within the Allied High Command.

"One of the reasons for this in my belief was that the original COSSAC plan had been, in fact, to break out from the Caen–Falaise area, on our eastern flank. I had refused to accept this plan and had changed it. General Morgan who had made the COSSAC plan was now at Supreme Headquarters as Deputy Chief of Staff. He considered Eisenhower was a god; since I had discarded many of his plans, he placed me at the other end of the celestial ladder. So here were the

seeds of discord. Morgan and those around him (the displaced strategists) lost no opportunity of trying to persuade Eisenhower that I was defensively minded and that we were unlikely to break out anywhere!"

As far as Sir Frederick Morgan is concerned, Montgomery may have been right, but he is surely on more dangerous ground when he goes on to assert that Air-Marshal Coningham, commander of the Tactical Air Force, associated himself with these criticisms for similar reasons. Coningham, he wrote, "was particularly interested in getting his airfields south-west of Caen. They were mentioned in the plan and to him they were all-important. I don't blame him. But they were not all-important to me. If we won the battle of Normandy, everything else would follow, airfields and all. I wasn't fighting to capture airfields; I was fighting to defeat Rommel in Normandy. This Coningham could scarcely appreciate: and for two reasons. First, we were not seeing each

▽ *American sappers probe for mines on one of the approach-roads to St. Lô. The wreckage of a jeep trailer, recent victim of a mine, litters the ditch to the left.*

other daily as in the desert days, for at this stage I was working direct to Leigh-Mallory. Secondly, Coningham wanted the airfields in order to defeat Rommel, whereas I wanted to defeat Rommel in order, only incidentally, to capture the airfields."

And events were to show that in order to defeat Army Group "B", it was not necessary to be in possession of the airfields that Coningham would have liked. It is still true, however, that by remaining in the Caen area, instead of wearing the enemy down in the Falaise area, 15 miles further south, as the original project had planned, the British 2nd Army asked its air force for a great deal of support, and yet placed it in a difficult position.

In the Normandy beach-head airfields were scarce, and their runways were so short that for the pilots getting fighter-bombers loaded with a ton of bombs or rockets into the air was a real problem. And landing posed similar problems; as Belfield and Essame have noted, "anyone who flew over the bridgehead in Normandy must have retained vivid memories of fighter aircraft, twin engined Dakotas (used as ambulances) and the small Austers all milling about in a horribly confined airspace. The perpetual risk of collisions greatly increased the strain on the pilots who had to fly from the bridgehead".

It may be that the commander of the 2nd Tactical Air Force did not like being treated as a subordinate by the man with whom he had been on equal terms in North Africa, but his criticisms did not all spring from personal ill-feeling. And it should be noted that at S.H.A.E.F. Air-Marshals Leigh-Mallory and Tedder both approved Coningham's attitude.

As for Eisenhower, it may fairly be said that his memoirs are marked with a calm philosophy that he was far from feeling when Operation "Goodwood" was breaking down on the Bourguébus ridge. For after all, according to the plan worked out by Montgomery, Bradley's enveloping movement ought to have begun on D-Day plus seventeen, June 23, when the Allies would be firmly established on a front extending from Granville to Caen, passing through Vire, Argentan, and Falaise. "This meant", he wrote, "that Falaise would be in our possession before the great wheel began. The line that we actually held when the breakout began on D plus 50 was approximately that planned for D plus 5.

"This was a far different story, but one which had to be accepted. Battle is not a one-sided affair. It is a case of action and reciprocal action repeated over and over again as contestants seek to gain position and other advantage by which they may inflict the greatest possible damage upon their respective opponents."

Be that as it may, in his opinion Montgomery needed a touch not of the brake, but of the accelerator, and Eisenhower's repeated efforts to get Montgomery to show more aggression could not have failed to annoy his troublesome subordinate.

In this argument, which went as far as Winston Churchill, Montgomery had a faithful defender in Brooke, who did all he could to prevent this potential conflict from becoming too bitter. At the time Montgomery was also on the best of terms with Bradley, who wrote that "Montgomery exercised his Allied authority with wisdom, forbearance, and restraint. While coordinating our movements with those of Dempsey's Monty carefully avoided getting mixed up in U.S. command decisions, but instead granted us the latitude to operate as freely and as independently as we chose. At no time did he probe into First Army with the indulgent manner he sometimes displayed among those subordinates who were also his countrymen. I could not have wanted a more tolerant or judicious commander. Not once did he confront us with an arbitrary directive and not once did he reject any plan that we had devised."

There is no doubt therefore that Bradley, who enjoyed Eisenhower's full confidence, tried to influence him the same way as Brooke. The differences over strategy that arose between Bradley and Montgomery from the autumn of 1944, and the coolness that affected their relations afterwards, right up to the end of the war, are very well known, which makes Bradley's comments on Montgomery's handling of this initial phase of the Battle of Normandy all the more valuable. "Whilst Collins was hoisting the flag of VII Corps above Cherbourg, Montgomery was losing his reputation in the long and arduous siege of the old university town of Caen. For three weeks he had been engaging his troops against those armoured divisions that he had deliberately lured towards Caen, in accordance with our diversionary strategy. The town was an important communications centre which he would eventually

need, but for the moment the taking of the town was an end in itself, for his task, first and foremost, was to commit German troops against the British front, so that we could capture Cherbourg that much easier, and prepare a further attack.

"In this diversionary mission Monty was more than successful, for the harder he hammered toward Caen, the more German troops he drew into that sector. Too many correspondents, however, had overrated the importance of Caen itself, and when Monty failed to take it, they

◁ ◁ △ *Montgomery and Bradley confer with Patton, whose 3rd Army would spearhead the breakout operation.*
◁ ◁ ▽ *"Better roll up your map, Herr General—I don't think your counter-attack's going to come off"—a sardonic comment by Giles of the* Daily Express.
△ *Eisenhower takes a snack lunch while visiting the U.S. 79th Division.*

▽ *De Gaulle makes a point to Eisenhower.*

The British A.E.C. Mark III armoured car

Weight: 12.7 tons.
Crew: 4.
Armament: one 75-mm gun and one 7.92-mm Besa machine gun.
Armour: 30-mm maximum.
Engine: one A.E.C. 6-cylinder Diesel, 158-hp.
Speed: 41 mph.
Range: 250 miles.
Length: 18 feet 5 inches.
Width: 8 feet 10½ inches.
Height: 8 feet 10 inches.

The American Chevrolet T17E1 Staghound I armoured car

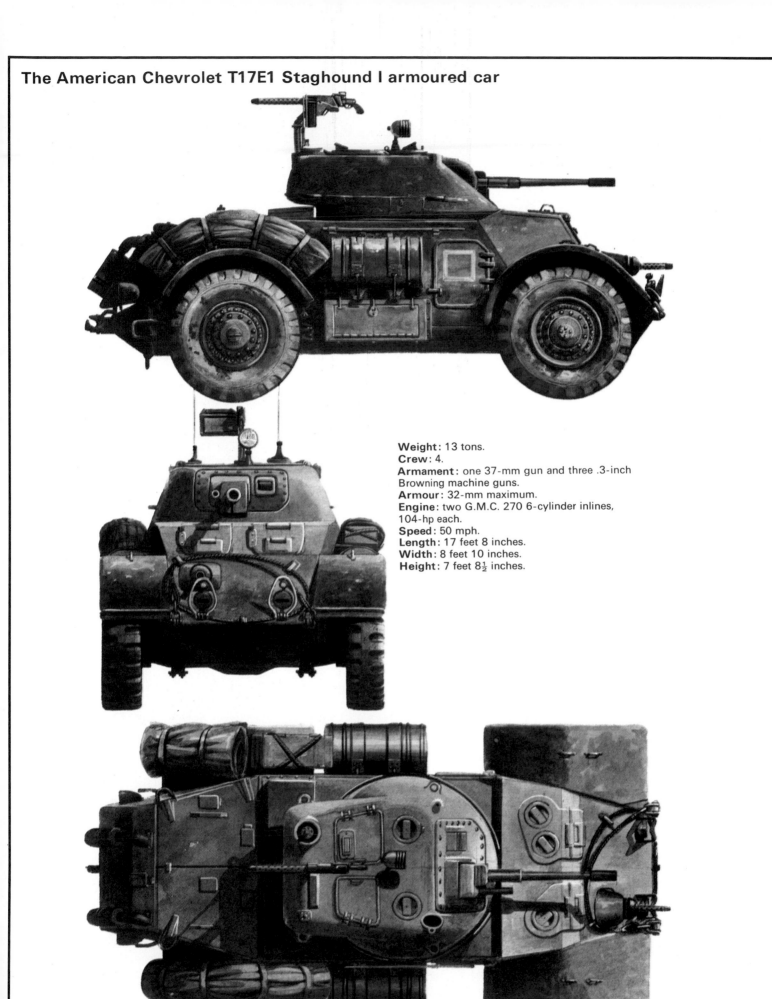

Weight: 13 tons.
Crew: 4.
Armament: one 37-mm gun and three .3-inch Browning machine guns.
Armour: 32-mm maximum.
Engine: two G.M.C. 270 6-cylinder inlines, 104-hp each.
Speed: 50 mph.
Length: 17 feet 8 inches.
Width: 8 feet 10 inches.
Height: 7 feet $8\frac{1}{2}$ inches.

△ *A picture vividly expressive of the strain of the fighting for St. Lô.*

blamed him for the delay. But had we attempted to exonerate Montgomery by explaining how successfully he had hood-winked the German by diverting him toward Caen from Cotentin, we would have also given our strategy away. We desperately wanted the Germans to believe this attack on Caen was the main Allied effort." It seems pretty clear that Montgomery was right. During World War I, Joffre had been severely criticised for his phrase "I'm nibbling away at them". Thirty years later, it must be admitted that Montgomery, though paying a heavy price, "nibbled" his opponent's armoured units, which were technically superior and on the whole very well trained, to excellent effect.

Caen may also be compared with Verdun, in World War I, where Colonel-General Falkenhayn intended to bleed the French Army white. But where the head of the Kaiser's General Staff failed against Joffre, Montgomery succeeded against Rommel, and with the American 1st Army and Patton behind Bradley, he had at his disposal a force ready to exploit the situation such as Falkenhayn never had.

At all events, the accredited pressmen at S.H.A.E.F. did not spare Montgomery, and above him Eisenhower, whom they criticised for tolerating the inefficiency of his second-in-command. It was even insinuated in the American press that with typical British cunning, Montgomery was trying to save his troops at the expense of the Americans, and that, most careful of English lives, he preferred to expend American soldiers, without the naïve Eisenhower realising what was happening.

However far-fetched such quarrels may seem, they continued long after the war, but under a different guise. For after the brilliant success of Operation "Cobra", which took Bradley almost in one fell swoop from Avranches, in Normandy, to Commercy and Maastricht on the Meuse, it would have been both indecent and ridiculous to accuse Montgomery of having kept the best things for the Anglo-Canadian troops, and given the Americans nothing but the scraps. Critics now tried to show that his attempts to tie down the enemy's mobile reserves with General Dempsey's troops failed. Thus, in 1946, Ralph Ingersoll, a war correspondent with Bradley's forces, portrayed the "Master" as being impatient to fight it out with Rommel: "The blow . . . could be struck with British forces under a British headquarters, for British credit and prestige". This would have confirmed Montgomery's domination of the American armies. "The result of Montgomery's decision was the battle of Caen—which was really two battles, two successive all-out attacks, continuing after Caen itself had fallen. Beginning in mid-June and ending nearly a month later, it was a defeat from which British arms on the continent never recovered. It was the first and last all-British battle fought in Europe. As he had feared, Montgomery was never again able to fight alone but thereafter had always to borrow troops and supplies to gain the superiority without which he would not even plan an attack."

What does this mean? That the 2nd British Army's attacks did not reach their geographical objectives is beyond question, but when one realises the tactical and material advantages gained over the enemy, it is impossible to join with Ingersoll and talk of "defeat". This can be seen in the cries of alarm, and later of despair, which German O.B. West sent to O.K.W. Of course, Ingersoll wrote his book in 1946, and was not in a position to appreciate all this.

Mistakes of the German strategists

Colonel-General Count von Schlieffen, the old Chief-of-Staff of the Imperial German Army, used to say to his students at the Military Academy, that when analysing a campaign, due allowance was never given to the way in which the vanquished

◁ Once the Germans built dummy tanks to conceal their strength; now the dummies were desperately offered to the swarming Allied fighter-bombers. ▽ and ▽▽ Two typical scenes from the tank battles of July.

positively helped the victor. It will therefore be instructive to see how Rommel, Rundstedt, and Hitler smoothed the path of Montgomery and Eisenhower.

◁ and △ *This was St. Lô. The Americans finally cleared the town on July 18.*

Hitler's blindness

In all this Rundstedt played a very secondary rôle. The great strategist whose Army Group "A" had conquered Poland, and who had played such a big part in the defeat of France, no longer dominated, nor did he seem to want to do so; Lieutenant-General Speidel, Chief-of-Staff of Army Group "B", paints him as having adopted an attitude of "sarcastic resignation", considering the "representations" and "despatches full of gravity" sent to Hitler as being the height of wisdom. He did, however, loyally support Rommel

they had reached by June 12, it would have been necessary to disengage the armoured units that Rommel had thrown in against Montgomery in the Caen sector, but this would only have been possible by drawing upon the 15th Army, stationed between the Seine and the Escaut, and the best placed to intervene. But Hitler expressly forbade Army Group "B" to do this. The Germans were therefore obliged, after scouring Brittany, to seek reinforcements at the very opposite end of France, and on June 12, the 276th Division received orders to leave Bayonne and get to the front: "The broken railways, the destroyed bridges and the French Maquis so delayed them that the last elements of the division finally arrived at Hottot in Normandy on July 4. In other words, to make a journey of some 400 miles, which could normally be completed by rail in seventy-two hours, required no less than twenty-two days. The main body of the division had to march at least one-third of the distance on foot, averaging approximately twenty miles each night."

△ Two nuns and a housewife give directions to a party of G.I.s. ▷ ▷ Searchlights and muzzle-flashes make a colourful display at an American A.A. battery.

in his discussions with Hitler—nothing more, nothing less.

Responsibility for the German defeat in the West therefore has to be shared between Rommel and Hitler. On D-Day, both wondered if this attack was not rather a diversion, covering a second landing aimed at the Pas-de-Calais. And due to the successful Allied deception measures, Hitler remained true to this idea until the end of July, whilst Rommel abandoned it when the American VII Corps' orders fell into his hands. The results of such blindness were catastrophic. To stop the Allies on the front

Similar misfortunes befell the 272nd Division, drawn from Perpignan, and the 274th Division, hastily organised in the Narbonne area; whilst, in order to reach the Caen sector, the 16th L.F.D., on watch over the coast at IJmuiden, had first to follow the Rhine as far as Koblenz. All this makes it easy to understand why Army Group "B" was confined to a series of piecemeal tactical operations, devoid of any overall strategy.

Hitler meets his Field-Marshals

At Rundstedt's urgent request Hitler agreed to meet him and Rommel together at the command post he had installed in 1940, at Margival, near Soissons, when Operation *"Seelöwe"* had been planned to conquer Great Britain. According to Lieutenant-General Speidel's account: "Hitler had arrived with Colonel-General Jodl and staff on the morning of June 17. He had travelled in an armoured car from Metz, where he had flown from Berchtesgaden. He looked pale and worn for lack of sleep. His fingers played nervously with his spectacles and the pencils before him. Hunched on a stool, with his marshals standing before him,

▽ Alfresco meal for American paratroops in a Normandy farmyard.

Captured while he slept, a German soldier hurriedly hauls on his boots under the gaze of his captor.

his former magnetism seemed to have vanished.

"After a few cold words of greeting, Hitler, in a high, bitter voice, railed on about the success of the Allied landing, and tried to blame the local commanders. He ordered that Cherbourg be held at all costs."

Rommel, who also spoke for Rundstedt, defended his officers from these attacks. When they began to discuss future action, the gulf between the two commanders and their garrulous leader became even more pronounced.

In Hitler's view, the use of flying bombs would soon bring the Third Reich victory, provided that they were concentrated against London; whereas, logically, it was suggested that he ought to use them against the embarkation ports which were sending over reinforcements to Normandy. Hitler did not deny the shortcomings of the Luftwaffe, but asserted that within a short time the coming into service of jet fighters would wrest from the Allies their present supremacy, and thus allow the Wehrmacht's land forces to resume the initiative. But without Hitler's earlier obstruction, the jets would have already entered service . . .

Objective Falaise–a Canadian column on the move.

Hitler intervenes . . .

Above all, however, was the fact that Rommel, backed by Rundstedt, categorically rejected the possibility of a second Allied landing north of the Seine, and demanded complete freedom of action, for it was now to be expected that the enemy would "break out of the Caen and Bayeux areas, and also from the Cotentin, towards the south, aiming for Paris, with a secondary attack upon Avranches to isolate Brittany". To cancel out this threat, they would have to bring into action the infantry divisions stationed in the Orne sector, then carry out "a limited withdrawal to be made southwards, with the object of launching an armoured thrust into the flank of the enemy and fighting the battle outside the range of the enemy's naval artillery . . ."

Hitler vetoed this plan absolutely: it was to be total resistance, no retreat, as at the time of the Battle of Moscow. Events have shown that this policy condemned the German forces in Normandy to disaster. But whether Rommel's plan would have been possible, given the

enormous Allied superiority and the dilapidated state of his troops, is doubtful, to say the least.

. . . and changes the High Command

As was to be expected, the fall of Cherbourg and the Cotentin operations increased even further the tension between those at the front and Hitler.

Furious at the way things were going, the Führer, despite Rommel's and Rundstedt's objections, ordered Colonel-General Dollman to be the subject of a judicial enquiry. On hearing this news, Dollman suffered a heart attack at Le Mans on June 29, and was replaced at the head of the 7th Army by General Hausser, who handed over command of II *Waffen-S.S.* Panzer Corps to his colleague Bittrich. On the same day *Panzergruppe* "West" was re-christened the 5th *Panzerarmee,* but General Geyr von Schweppenburg, only just recovered from the wounds he had sustained on June 12, having resumed command, had been dismissed and

replaced by General Eberbach, because he had had the temerity to point out the strategic patching-up of the Supreme Command.

The same day also, Rommel and Rundstedt were called to the Berghof by Hitler, who, however, refused to speak to them in private, and added nothing new to the rantings with which he had assailed their ears at Margival, about the decisive effect which the new weapons would have upon the course of the war. As for the two marshals, they emphasised the urgent necessity of ending the war on the west, so as to enable the Reich to fight on in the east. On seeing the indignant way in which their suggestion was greeted, they both thought they were going to be sacked on the spot. In fact the Führer's wrath fell only on Rundstedt, and even then it was somewhat mitigated by the award of the Oak Leaves to his Knight's Cross. He was replaced by Kluge, who had now recovered from the winter car accident which had obliged him to give up his command on the Eastern Front. At the Berghof, the new Supreme Commander in the West was duly spoken to by Hitler, Keitel, and Jodl, who impressed upon him the necessity of making his subordinate, Rommel, see reason. Hence the violent incident which took place at la Roche-Guyon, when the hero of Tobruk was told in no uncertain terms by his new chief that "he would now have to get accustomed to carrying out orders".

Kluge changes his views

Rommel reacted to these remarks with a written protest on July 3, to which he added a long aide-mémoire in justification, whose reasoning, both honest and full of good sense, led Kluge, an intelligent man, completely to revise his opinion.

In any case, the developing situation in Normandy allowed no other conclusion than Rommel's. The 5th *Panzerarmee* and the 7th Army were still containing the Allied advance, but with more and more difficulty. Despite their losses, Allied numbers and supplies were increasing daily, whereas the German forces' losses could not be made up. Between June 6 and July 15 it had only received 6,000 men to replace 97,000 killed, missing, and wounded, amongst whom there were 2,360 officers, including 28 generals and 354 lieutenant-generals. Its supply position

△ *Moment of humour during Churchill's visit to the beach-head: a Cherbourg worker offers the Prime Minister a light.*

△ *A drink of water and a cigarette for a wounded German.*

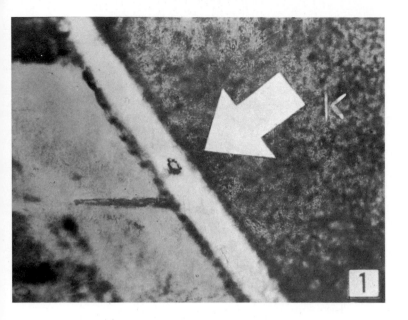

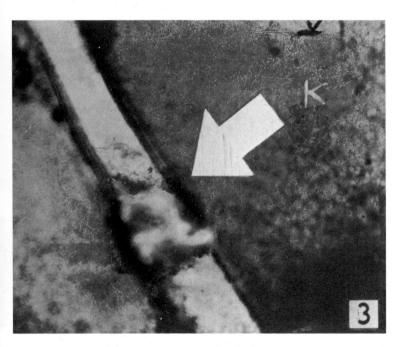

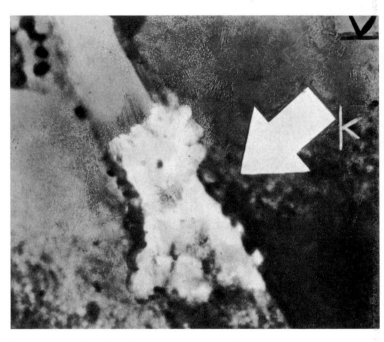

△ *Was this the attack that knocked Rommel out of the battle for Normandy? These pictures are "stills" from the camera-gun film exposed during a strafing run by Lieutenant Harold O. Miller of the U.S. 8th Air Force. For a while it was believed that Rommel had been killed in the attack – but he survived. There was a grimmer fate in store for him . . .*
▷ ▷ *False alarm. A Frenchman nervously "surrenders" to a bespectacled American rifleman.*

had become so precarious because of enemy bombing that the most drastic economies were imposed.

Such were the facts that Rommel, with the approval of Kluge, pointed out in his last report to Hitler on July 15 1944 – a sad catalogue leading to the following conclusions:

"It must therefore be expected that within the next two to three weeks, the enemy will break through our weakened front, and advance in depth through France, an action which will have the gravest consequences.

"Everywhere our troops are fighting heroically, but this unequal struggle is inevitably drawing to a close. I am forced to ask you to draw the necessary conclusions from this situation, without delay. As leader of your Western forces,

I felt it my duty to explain it to you as clearly as possible."

What would have happened if Rommel had not been badly wounded on the Livarot–Vimoutiers road, the very day after dispatching this strong message? Hitler would almost certainly have refused, told him that he must not surrender, and would probably even have dismissed him. In that event, would Rommel have sent officers to parley with Montgomery? He would have been able to count on all his general staff, and certain field-commanders, such as Lüttwitz and Schwerin, at the head of the 2nd and 116th Panzer Divisions respectively. But would he have taken this enormous step after the shattering news came through of the bomb attempt on Hitler's life and the collapse of the "July Plot"?

CHAPTER 117
The July Plot
Jaques Nobécourt

8 GERMAN OFFICERS HANGED BY HITLER

INTO OCCUPIED FRANCE—AND OUT

The Exclusive Story of the American Girl Who Did It!

Start It Today! On Page 7

New York *Journal American*

7TH SPORTS

WALL ST. SPECIAL

from

5¢

100

Biddle

Pro

DAILY NEWS

New York

GENERALS REBEL, TRY TO KILL HITLER

Fuehrer, Hurt by Bomb

Himmler to

News Chronicle

ONE PENNY

FRIDAY, JULY 21, 1944

HITLER: ASSASSINATION ATTEMPTED AT HIS HEADQUARTERS

The Fuehrer escaped with slight burns and concussion, says Berlin

AIDE-DE-CAMP WAS HURT

Denis Weaver, who before the war represented the News Chronicle in Berlin, has spent the past three years in Stockholm, on Hitler's doorstep. This message he dispatched from Sweden four hours before the Germans reported the attempt to assassinate Hitler.

13 HIGH-RANKING OFFICERS INJURED IN EXPLOSION

THE German News Agency announced last night that an attempt on the life of Hitler was made yesterday at his headquarters, but that he escaped with slight burns and concussion.

Thirteen high-ranking officers who were with him, including General Jodl, his chief military adviser, were injured, four of them seriously.

This is the text of the statement issued from Hitler's H.Q. shortly before a o'clock last night:

An attempt on the life of the Fuehrer was made today.

The following persons in his entourage were severely injured: Lieut.-Gen. Schmundt, Col. Brandt, Lieut.-Col. Borgmann and

Himmler is now the Dictator in Germany

STOCKHOLM, Thursday.
HEINRICH HIMMLER, S.S. and the Gestapo, is today in practice dictator of Germany.

Allies storm through 9 Normandy villages

FROM DOON CAMPBELL
ORNE FRONT, Thursday.

ALLIED troops are fighting in the streets of Troarn and Bourguébus

NAZI HAD NO DOUBT WAR WAS LOST

From MICHAEL MOYNIHAN
News Chronicle War Correspondent
NORMANDY, Wednesday.

STALIN ISSUES TWO ORDERS OF DAY:

Lwow outflanked and 30-mile advance on 90-mile front

Gen. Jodl among the injured

"Thankfulness"

Guarded from air attack

LATE NEWS

OSTROV GAINS

HUNGARIAN VICE-PREMIER RESIGNS

BLACK-OUT TIMES

Japan faces her crisis

1,200 heavies hit at heav

ballito STOCKINGS

RELY ON THE QUALITY

On April 7, 1943, Lieutenant-Colonel Claus von Stauffenberg, head of the Operations Staff of the 10th Panzer Division, was severely wounded by a strafing American aircraft while his unit was withdrawing in southern Tunisia. He lost his right hand, two fingers of his left hand, and his left eye. In August, when barely recovered from his wounds, he was appointed to the General Staff of the Reserve Army in Berlin; and there he began to make contact with the leaders of the anti-Hitler movement.

On July 20, 1944, Stauffenberg placed within a few feet of Hitler a bomb which should not have failed to kill him, and afterwards flew back to the offices of the War Ministry in Berlin, where he tried in vain to organise a takeover of power by the Wehrmacht. That night, under the glare of truck headlights, he was shot with three other officers. General Beck, former Chief of the Army General Staff and figurehead of the resistance movement in the Army, had committed suicide shortly before. Beck was 64 years old, Stauffenberg 38. They represented two generations of German officers—two totally different men, both symbolising the dilemma of an army powerless in the face of a doctrinaire dictatorship which was dragging its country to ruin.

These dramatic scenes did not have their origin in the war; for that one must go back some ten years. The basic conflict which resulted in the "July Plot" –the National Socialist conception of the state versus the opposition elements summed up by the phrase "German resistance"–had its roots in the conditions behind Hitler's accession to power on January 30, 1933. This event had been greeted with cautious relief by the small officer corps of the professional Army. Party anarchy ceased. Order returned to the streets. Social measures put an end to strikes and unemployment. And the new Chancellor pledged himself to the full restoration of Germany's national honour. More than any other man, Hitler seemed capable of "breaking the shackles of Versailles" at last.

Under the official aegis of the elderly Field-Marshal von Hindenburg, President of the Republic, Hitler's régime seemed to be a satisfactory compromise. Sponsored by leading conservatives, it was supported by tightly-controlled militants. It appeared to stand halfway between the Imperial monarchy which still inspired nostalgia in many soldiers, and the Republic which they served without genuine enthusiasm. Hitler, after all, had given every assurance that the constitution of the armed forces would ensure the restoration of Germany's political power. But what was to come next? The conquest of new *Lebensraum* in the East. But when this was put to the Army and Navy commanders on February 3, 1933, the programme caused deep mistrust. No active opposition ensued, however, and Hitler was able to begin consolidating the position of the Nazi party—a process which was to have dire consequences for the armed forces.

▽ *This view of Hitler's triumphal visit to Memel in 1939 shows the three main layers of his power: well-drilled Party officials, rapturous civilians –and the troops of the Wermacht, every man of them bound to the Führer by oath.*

Col. von Stauffenberg

Gen. Olbricht

Gen. Tresckow

Gen. Beck

F. M. von Kluge

Col. Mertz von Quirnheim

F. M. von Witzleber

Gen. von Stülpnagel

Col. von Haeften

Gen. Hoeppner

Adm. Canaris

Gen. Oster

CONSPIRATORS

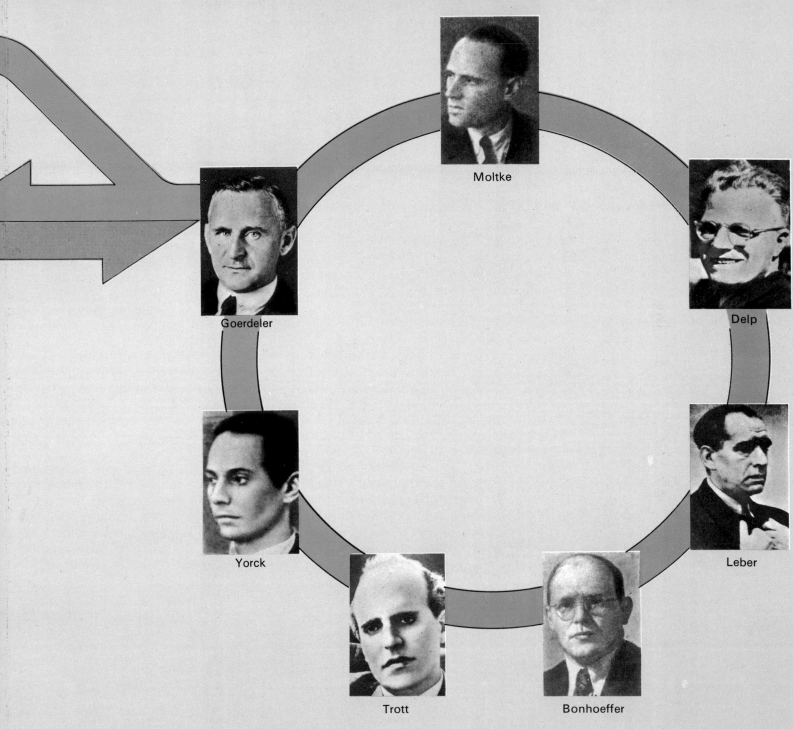

Moltke

Delp

Goerdeler

Yorck

Leber

Trott

Bonhoeffer

This chart shows the inter-relation of the leading members of the German resistance and the men they hoped to involve. At bottom left are Canaris and Oster, the conspirators of the Abwehr or German Military Intelligence. General Beck and Field-Marshal von Witzleben, together with ex-Panzer General Hoeppner, form the right-hand column. To their left are Olbricht, Haeften, and Mertz von Quirnheim from Reserve Army H.Q. in Berlin's Bendlerstrasse, and General von Tresckow, who made repeated efforts to organise attempts on Hitler's life from Army Group "Centre" in Russia. General von Stülpnagel, Military Governor of France, was to direct operations from Paris once the news of Hitler's death came in. Finally there is the elusive figure of Field-Marshal von Kluge, who refused to act in the few brief hours when the conspiracy could have succeeded, and committed suicide afterwards. The civilian conspirators at right included Carl Goerdeler, former Mayor of Leipzig; the courageous priests Bonhoeffer and Delp; the Socialist Julius Leber—all members of Count von Moltke's "Kreisau Circle". This was a resistance group of young idealists formed before the war, which included Adam von Trott zu Solz and Count Peter Yorck von Wartenburg.

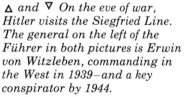
△ and ▽ *On the eve of war,*
Hitler visits the Siegfried Line.
The general on the left of the
Führer in both pictures is Erwin
von Witzleben, commanding in
the West in 1939 – and a key
conspirator by 1944.

While Hindenburg was still alive, the German officer corps followed his lead and did not bother itself too much with the doings of the Nazi régime. But Hindenburg's death changed all that. The young Colonel Guderian – still, at the time, dreaming of massive armoured divisions – was moved to write the following lines to his wife when he heard of the old Field-Marshal's death on August 1, 1934:

"The old gentleman is no more. We are all saddened by this irreplaceable loss. He was like a father to the whole nation and particularly to the armed forces, and it will be a long and hard time before the great gap that he leaves in our national life can be filled. His existence alone meant more to foreign powers than any numbers of written agreements and fine words. He possessed the confidence of the world. We, who loved and honoured him, have become much poorer for his death. Tomorrow we swear the oath to Hitler. An oath heavy with consequences. Pray God that both sides may abide by it equally for the welfare of Germany. The Army is accustomed to keep its oaths. May the Army be able, in honour, to do so this time."

On August 2 not a single German officer refused to take the oath which bound him explicitly to the person of Adolf Hitler. But all the questions raised by the oath, all the worries which it created, even the diversity of meanings in "the welfare of Germany", can be read between the lines of Guderian's letter.

The Army stood apart from the liquidation of all political opposition, not lifting a finger to stop the Socialist, Catholic, and Communist leaders from being thrown into concentration camps. Its policy of benevolent neutrality was confirmed by the plebiscite of August 19, 1934. It was reassured by the subsequent liquidation of Röhm and the left wing of the Nazi Party. But all too soon the Army found itself on the defensive. In its rôle as an instrument of foreign policy the Army understood that that policy must be reasonable, suited to military resources, and vaguely based on the idea of German sovereignty. But none of the Army leaders of the time saw the real, long-term explosive power of ideology backed by totalitarian power.

This failure to face the facts characterised the members of the German resistance movement until late into the war. Their sincere nationalism lacked the one thing which would have given them victory in the civil war which they were prepared to risk: ruthless fanaticism.

Caution the watchword

From the official birthday of the new Wehrmacht on May 16, 1935, to the French campaign of 1940, the German generals, in their relations with Hitler, were primarily concerned with preventing the military machine from being used before it was ready. The vast majority of Germany's ranking officers buried themselves in the work of building up a national army. Shaken by the excessive tempo which Hitler imposed on them, the top commanders laid it down that the Reich was still too weak to risk a head-on clash with a hostile coalition. The generals were still haunted by memories of 1918. But Hitler, taking the gamble, overcame them. The only man to sense that the Rhineland venture of March 7, 1936, was a viable one, he went ahead. And on November 5, 1937 he revealed his long-term plans to the Wehrmacht commanders: "It is my irrevocable decision to settle the problem of German living-space by 1943-45 at the latest." If, before this time, France suffered an internal crisis or went to war with Italy, the Reich could seize Czechoslovakia and Austria with impunity.

Here, clearly revealed, was Hitler's programme. And it drove the Army Chief-of-Staff, who still suffered sharp pangs of conscience which had bedevilled him since taking the oath to Hitler in August 1934 (when he had toyed with the idea of resigning), to stand out in opposition to Hitler's policy.

Born in 1880 and a general staff officer since 1911, Ludwig Beck had built up his prestige by qualities which were more those of an intellectual than of a soldier. He was the complete opposite of the traditional idea of a soldier or even of a military commander, but his intelligence, his insight, and his shrewdness impressed themselves on all who knew him.

But his later career revealed the reverse sides of these fine qualities. He was too much of an analyst to back daring or risky moves. He was too meticulous to go ahead without having first amassed all the information and covered all possibilities. He saw things too clearly to be able to cope with the consequences of a setback. In all these ways Beck was very similar to his opposite number, General Gamelin, whom he met during a trip to Paris in 1937. "Significant of his way of thinking was his much-vaunted method of fighting which he called 'delaying defence'," noted Guderian.

Was it likely that such a dyed-in-the-

▽ *Claus Schenk von Stauffenberg, the "iron man" of the conspiracy, whose will led to the attempt on July 20. He is seen here earlier in his career as a young cavalry officer.*
▽▽ *Stauffenberg, still recovering from the severe wounds he suffered in Tunisia, seen with his children.*

DIE WEHRMACHT

AUSGABE A
Berlin, 3 März 1943
7. Jahrgang Nr. 5
Belg. 2 Fr., Bulg. 8 Lewa, Dänemark 40 Öre, Finnl. 4,50 mk,
Frankr. 4 Fr., Griechenl. 30 Dr.,
Ital. 2 Lire, Kroatien 5 Kuna,
Niederld. 20 Cts., Norwegen
40 Öre, Portugal 2,— Esc.,
Rumän. 20 Lei, Serb. 4 Dinar,
Spanien 1,25 Pts., Schweden
45 Öre, Schweiz 40 Rappen,
Slowakei 2,50 Ks., Türkei
12,50 Kurus, Ungarn 36 fillér.

HERAUSGEGEBEN VOM OBERKOMMANDO DER WEHRMACHT

1582

wool procrastinator and arch-priest of caution could have headed a conspiracy or an opposition movement? The fact remains that Beck was the only general to risk his career and reputation by so doing. Yet his revolt was motivated more than by anything else by his philosophy of the rôle of the German officer in the state. It was said of Beck that he made the German land forces the brain and instrument of German policy, and the German general staff the "conscience of the Army". German commanders should define limited situations in the light of precise data and proceed according to the resources at their disposal. Nothing was more alien to this idea of Beck's than the Nazi myth of race and of blood, and the notion of spreading the German master race through the great land spaces of the East. Beck, however, ruled out these ideas on account of their lack of proportion and balance before he condemned them on ethical grounds.

Right to the end, the officers of the anti-Hitler movement were inspired by the image of the German officer corps. "Their ideology stems from the fact that the Wehrmacht is an autonomous body within the Reich, an entity which exists in its own right and according to its own laws," commented one of the reports on the interrogation of the conspirators in the plot of July 20.

More power for Hitler

After Hitler's address on November 5, 1937. Beck countered by urging the Army Commander-in-Chief, von Fritsch, to tell Hitler to stick to possibilities and not to be side-tracked by desirabilities. Beck's uneasiness mirrored that felt by other Army commanders; but once again Hitler reacted too fast for the Army. He assessed the internal divisions of the general staff. He took into account the natural rivalry between the generations in the officer corps. He estimated that the national character of the armed forces, swelled as they were by compulsory service, would cancel out the resistance of the "Prussian technocrats". Step by step Hitler eliminated the War Minister, Field-Marshal von Blomberg – although the latter opposed the malcontents of the Army – and General von Fritsch, himself. Then, as the crowning move, on February 4, 1938 Hitler became Commander-in-Chief of the Wehrmacht. Promotions and postings advanced many generals who would make their names in the war.

Army malcontents gather around Beck

Retained as Chief-of-Staff of the Army, command of which went to General von Brauchitsch, Beck refused to modify his opinions. Hitler said of him at this time, speaking to his Minister of Justice: "Beck is the only man I fear. That man would be able to undertake anything against me." Moreover, Beck remained in contact with several leading personalities who did not conceal their hostility to the régime – Admiral Canaris, chief of the *Abwehr,* German counterespionage; Carl Goerdeler, former mayor of Leipzig, who contributed much confused activity to the embryo opposition movement; and the diplomat Ulrich von Hassel, German Ambassador at Rome.

Without doubt this was basically nothing more than a loose net of malcontents with neither leaders nor programme. Hitler had just added still more to his powers by bringing the Army under his sway. And yet it was in this spring of 1938 that Beck began to add to the conspiracy the following officers whom he deemed reliable: Colonel Hans Oster, A.D.C. to Canaris in the *Abwehr*; Generals Erwin von Witzleben, Erich Hoeppner, Karl-Heinrich von Stülpnagel, Eduard Wagner, Franz Halder and Kurt von Hammerstein-Equord. The civilians included the magistrates Hans von Dohnanyi and Justus Delbrück, Pastor Dietrich Bonhoeffer, and the land-owner Carl Ludwig von Guttenberg.

These formed the hard core, and nearly all of them died after July 20, 1944. Some of their stories make sad telling. Too many of them continued to serve the régime they were attempting to overthrow. Oster, for example, had pushed his personal convictions into the realms of high treason by warning Norway and Holland of the date of the imminent German attacks. (He hoped in so doing to force the victims to react in time and shorten the war.) But Witzleben and Hoeppner commanded in France and Russia until the end of 1941. In 1942 Stülpnagel became Military Governor of France, and his record

△ *Himmler, whom the conspirators hoped to eliminate with Hitler, and Göring as well. Neither were in the conference room when the bomb went off, and Himmler was packed off to Berlin to crush the last elements of resistance in the capital.*
◁ *Cover of* Wehrmacht *at the time of Stalingrad, idolising the heroism of the troops at the front.*

▽ *Stülpnagel, key man in Paris. He took the courageous step of rounding up the S.S. and Gestapo on July 20, but failed to induce Kluge to take over the Putsch in the West. He failed to commit suicide, merely succeeding in blinding himself. He too, died by strangulation in Berlin's Plötzensee Prison.*

there was so forbidding that it was not cancelled out by his rôle in the July Plot, followed though this was by his abortive suicide attempt on the battlefield of Verdun. Halder, who succeeded Beck as Army Chief-of-Staff, and Wagner, Army Quartermaster-General, worked simultaneously on their plans for an Army *coup* and on the technical details of the offensives in the West and in Russia.

In the summer of 1938, General Hoeppner commanded the new 1st Light Division at Wuppertal. (The 1st Light was redesignated 6th Panzer Division on the outbreak of war.) At this time he had posted to his staff as head of the logistic services (Department 1b) the young Captain von Stauffenberg, fresh from the War Academy. It was to be many years before their destinies combined. In 1938 Hoeppner would certainly not have sympathised with the deep-rooted opinions of his new staff officer. But Stauffenberg himself was like other officers of his own generation. They felt themselves to be men apart, as technicians of the military arm, and certainly not as rebels. "Certainly, we tended to criticise heavily certain aspects of the Party in our daily talk," one of Stauffenberg's colleagues was to say. "But I would not pretend for one moment that Stauffenberg showed any opposition to Hitler or to the Party. For Stauffenberg as for ourselves, Hitler was the Reich Chancellor, and it was to Hitler that we had sworn allegiance on the flag."

Beck resigns

Beck's renewed warnings on May 5 and July 16, 1938, stressed his belief that the Führer's grandiose schemes would lead to prolonged global war. He argued to Brauchitsch that the Army leaders should resign *en bloc* and shoulder "their responsibility towards the majority of their people", for, as he added, "exceptional times demand exceptional measures". But the young officers remained deaf to Beck's arguments.

By advocating "exceptional measures" Beck was on the verge of preaching a *coup d'état*, to be carried out in legal

One unequivocal belief motivated Beck: "A soldier's duty of obedience ends as soon as he is given an order which is incompatible with his conscience, his knowledge, and his sense of responsibility." As the war progressed the stakes involved would be increased more and more, in such a way as to make the problem vital for those who remained loyal until the last possible minute. To have laid this principle down so precisely as early as 1938 was to Beck's credit. From 1938 his activity in the anti-Nazi field continued to develop and to grow more heated – but without becoming any more organised or disciplined, and he was always putting off the decision until a favourable moment should arrive.

It is, therefore, obvious that the story of the German resistance had deep roots. The outbreak of war in 1939 was only a minor milestone, and the development of the war had only partial effects on the real problem. The basic issues at stake were already established: the restlessness of the long tradition of the "military state" and its relations with the sovereign power, a tradition which was founded as much on genuine values as on political expediency.

"In ridding Germany of Hitler, the generals seem to be looking to the Führer for orders," noted Hassel in his diary. Sarcastic, certainly, but not without truth. The fact that the head of state was also Hitler, the trouble-maker, troubled many a conscience. Forcible resistance would lead Germany to civil war and expose the Reich to the same "stab in the back" which, according to Hindenburg, the "civilians" of 1918 had dealt the Imperial Army. And what would resistance achieve, in concrete terms? Better, surely, to end the war with an honourable peace, which would leave the fruits of victory secure. The problem of doing away with a régime which was dishonouring Germany remained unresolved until as late as 1943.

An occasion which the conspirators hoped to exploit – Hitler is shown new uniforms for the Wehrmacht. On three occasions, Army volunteers in the resistance movement proposed to blow up Hitler – and themselves – by time-bombs concealed in their pockets. These men were Colonel Freiherr von Gersdorff, Captain von dem Bussche, and Captain von Kleist – son of the general. All these attempts were frustrated by Hitler's habit of suddenly changing his schedule. In this photograph the small, smiling officer at centre is General Helmuth Stieff, guardian of the conspirators' bombs later arrested and executed.

fashion, which would add power to a strike by the generals. He put his cards on the table to Brauchitsch: he wanted not only to avoid war, but to restore "normal judicial conditions" by smashing the Party and the S.S. by force.

"Let there be no doubt that our actions are not directed against Hitler but against the evil gang which is leading him to ruin ... nothing we do should give the impression of a plot. It is also essential that all the generals support us and support us to the end, whatever the consequences ... Our watchwords must be brief and clear: for the Führer – against war – against the Party favourites – freedom of expression – the end of police-state methods – restoration of justice in the Reich – Prussian decency and simplicity."

But the generals did not offer their support. Hitler secured their obedience. And Beck offered his resignation, which was accepted. He retired on September 1, becoming a passive and increasingly impatient spectator of a chain of events which he had forecast long before – but without defining any practical short-term remedies.

First stirrings of active resistance

The different streams of resistance at the same time chimed in with movements which were as organised as could be, given the need for secrecy, in the occupied countries. The aim of the latter movements

△ Wolfsschanze–"Wolf's Lair"
–Hitler's headquarters in the
pine forests of Rastenburg in
East Prussia. Two concentric
defence perimeters screened the
wooden huts and bunkers. On
July 20 it was known that the
Führer conference which
Stauffenberg was to attend
would not be held in the
command bunker but in the
conference hut. Although this
would disperse the force of the
explosion, the plotters knew
that the bomb should still be
powerful enough to kill Hitler.

was unequivocal: to bring an end to German occupation. Eventually this aim was expanded: to emerge from the war with far-reaching political changes in the liberated nations. There it was easy, however. The enemy was the foreigner, not the compatriot. It was a practical problem, too: the resistance leaders knew where to recruit their soldiers and their forces. Even if the actual number of men was small, the underlying cause was clear-cut and good. Everything in wartime Europe helped to justify the spirit of resistance and to trigger it into activity.

Resistance, in short, was part and parcel of the war. The underground fighters knew that the peace won by the Allies abroad would be their peace–a victorious conclusion to their own efforts in the field.

But resistance in Germany could never achieve any durable or encouraging link-up between the enemies of Hitler and the Anglo-American bloc, let alone with the Soviet bloc. This was not because no overtures were made, but because each tentative approach was rejected, for the Allied high command could not count on its orders being obeyed. Moscow formed the "Committee of Free Germany", to which belonged the generals taken at Stalingrad and the old German Communist émigrés. But neither London nor Washington would agree to treaties which would affect the post-war scene.

This decision of the Allies not to listen to any spokesmen from Germany discouraged many responsible Germans from taking solitary action. At the Casablanca Conference in January 1943, the Allies laid it down that the elimination of Hitler would not determine the conditions of peace. Until Casablanca, the post-war political programmes of the German opposition had all been based on the results of Germany's initial victories. Goerdeler and his friends clung to the idea that the inevitable chaos caused by Hitler's overthrow must be kept to the minimum. The basic structure of the régime would be preserved; the Party and its machine would be dismantled, but only step by step. The main ideal was not so much to reconstruct the state as to abolish the authority of the Party, together with its excesses–in other words, to cancel out the misdealt hand of 1933, when both nationalists and conservatives had been cheated. No excessive "change for the sake of change" was the watchword. In their innumerable talks Goerdeler, Beck, and their friends persuaded themselves that all they would have to do was to extend their network of loyal German malcontents, and all the loose ends would be tied up with the greatest of ease.

Dynamic leadership

At the time when Claus von Stauffenberg entered the German resistance movement, its leaders had reached an all-time low of despair and empty gestures. It was the period when the students Hans and Sophie Scholl, and their teacher, were executed at Munich for having launched an appeal for a revolt of conscience.

When Stauffenberg joined the conspirators, the idea of an attempt on Hitler's person had only just been accepted by Beck and Goerdeler. The success of such an attempt was to be followed by the entry of the Reserve Army, which would carry out the actual coup d'état. Of all the top-ranking commanders, Field-Marshal von Kluge seemed to be the only man willing to support the attempt. Two assassination attempts in 1943, organised by General von Tresckow, Chief-of-Staff of Army Group "Centre", had failed. And it was Tresckow who now gave Stauffenberg the relevant details.

They intended to use Plan "Valkyrie", drawn up in 1942 to mobilise the Reserve Army in the event of an insurrection by the foreign prisoners-of-war in Germany. Promoted joint Chief-of-Staff of Army Group "Centre" and stationed in Berlin, Stauffenberg spent the autumn issuing detailed orders for the coup. The executive order would go out from the War Ministry

continued on page 1591

▷ *The conference hut before the explosion, looking towards the end of the room from the position of the long map table.*

▽ *After the explosion. The circular table shown above has been hurled to the far end of the room. An arrow marks the spot where the bomb went off.*

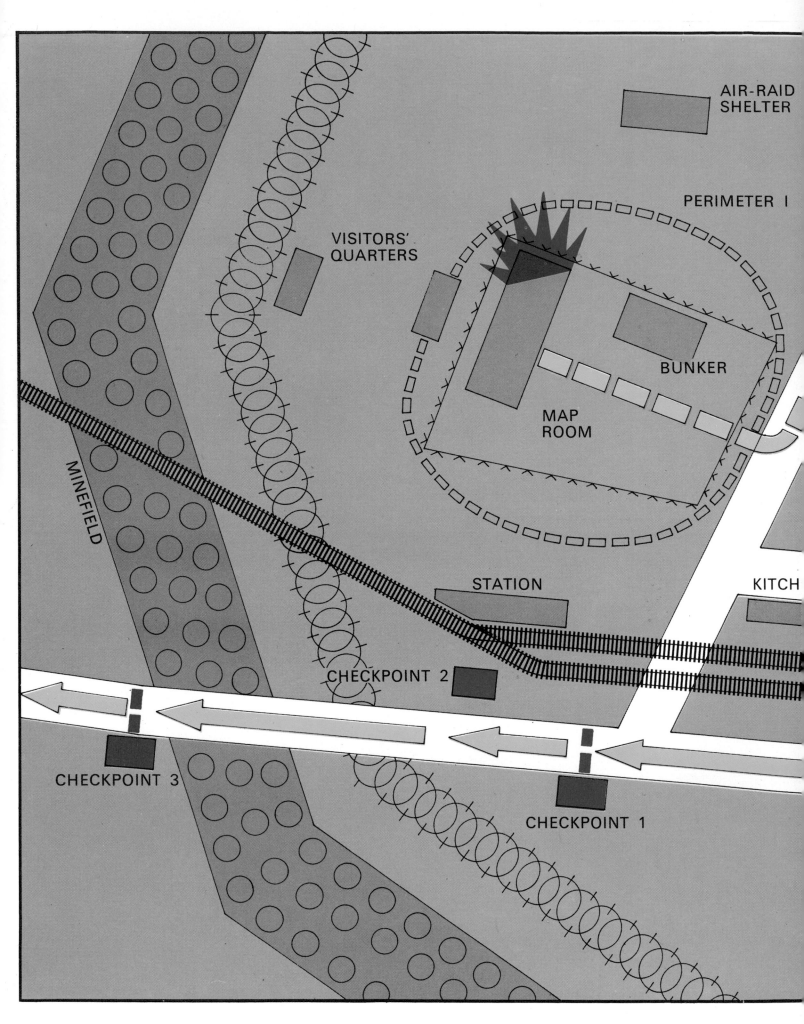

AIR-RAID
SHELTER

PERIMETER I

VISITORS'
QUARTERS

BUNKER

MAP
ROOM

MINEFIELD

STATION

KITCH

CHECKPOINT 2

CHECKPOINT 3

CHECKPOINT 1

1588

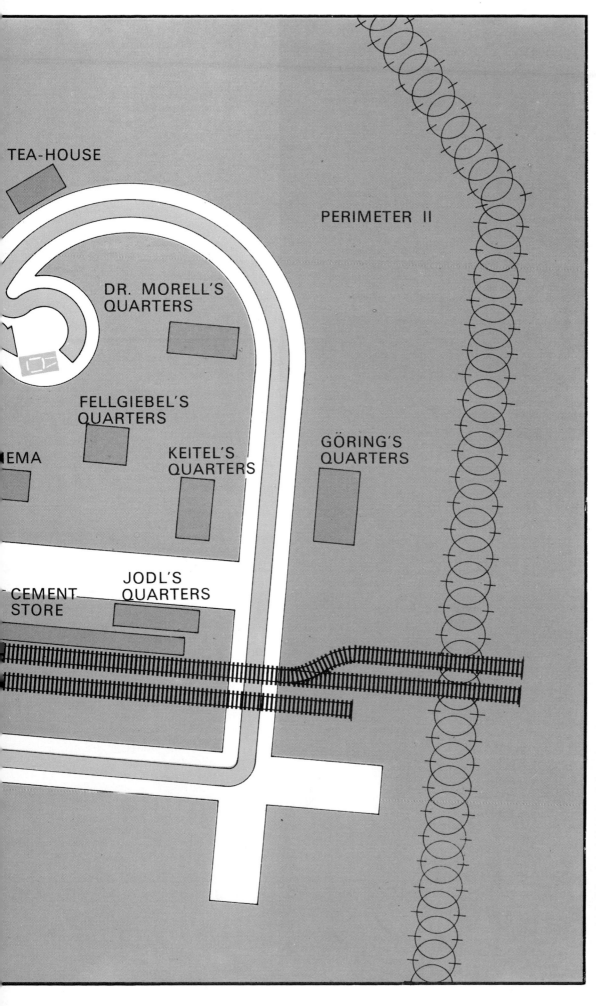

TEA-HOUSE

DR. MORELL'S
QUARTERS

FELLGIEBEL'S
QUARTERS

EMA

KEITEL'S
QUARTERS

GÖRING'S
QUARTERS

PERIMETER II

JODL'S
QUARTERS

CEMENT
STORE

How Stauffenberg and his adjutant, Lieutenant Werner von Haeften, escaped from the "Wolf's Lair" after the attempt on Hitler's life on July 20, 1944. The diagram shows the concentric security perimeters and the checkpoints through which they had to pass to make a safe get-away.

Stauffenberg's plane touched down at Rastenburg after a 3-hour flight from Berlin. A 9-mile drive lay ahead, and Stauffenberg left his pilot with instructions to be ready to take off any time after noon—the Führer conference was scheduled for 1300 hours. On arriving at the "Wolf's Lair" Stauffenberg found that the conference had been brought forward by 30 minutes, for Mussolini was arriving that afternoon and all reports at the conference were to be kept short.

While Keitel fussed at the delay, Stauffenberg returned to the ante-room to collect his cap and belt. There, using the three surviving fingers of his "good" hand, he activated the bomb.

It had a 10-minute fuse. A 3-minute walk to the conference room. Up to the big map table. Slip the briefcase under the table, as close to Hitler's feet as possible. Then a murmured excuse: a telephone call from Berlin. Out of the room, through the inner-most checkpoint of "Perimeter I", and across to where Haeften was waiting.

Then, at 1242 hours by their watches, came a monstrous explosion from the hut. The two officers jumped into their car and tore round to the first check-point out of "Perimeter II", where Stauffenberg phoned the Duty Officer direct and obtained clearance to leave. He had no trouble at the second check-point, but by the time he reached the third the "Wolf's Lair" had been brought to full alert and the car was stopped. By great good luck Stauffenberg was able to persuade the Duty Officer to let him through—and the car set off at full speed for the air-field. On the way Haeften dis-mantled the reserve bomb and threw the pieces to the side of the road. At 1315 they were air-borne for Berlin, confident not only that Hitler was dead at last but that the plotters in Berlin knew and that the *coup d'état* was in full swing.

But it was not.

Mussolini: "What has happened here today gives me new courage. After this miracle it is inconceivable that our cause should meet with misfortune."

Hitler: "It is obvious that nothing is going to happen to me; undoubtedly it is my fate to continue on my way and bring my task to completion."

continued from page 1586

once the definite news of Hitler's death had been received. The key centres of the capital would be occupied and the S.S. put under Army control, voluntarily or by force. The chain of command would be reorganised.

Precise, far-sighted, and quick-thinking, Stauffenberg introduced into the conspiracy a dynamism which no officer before him had shown. Level-headed, impatient of political theories, and flexible in his approach both to men and events, he gradually became the rallying-point for the resistance elements which had hitherto remained at loggerheads. Weighing the problems, always trying to find a balance, he insisted on "possible compromises and points of joint agreement, without contradictions". But Stauffenberg's flexibility of spirit and his optimism could and did lead him astray. He was hardly being realistic, for example, when on May 25, 1944 he drew up a list of topics to be discussed with the Allied high command. These included the following:

1. The Eastern Front to be held; all occupied areas in the North, West, and South to be evacuated;
2. The Allies to abandon all projects for the occupation of Germany; and
3. Eastern European frontiers to be restored to the *status quo* of 1914, Austria and the Sudetenland to remain part of the Reich, but autonomy for Alsace-Lorraine.

The conspirators clung to the hope of an alliance between the Western Allies and the Reich against the Soviet Union. "To save what remains of our military power to allow Germany to continue to play a part in the international power balance"—such was Stauffenberg's intention until the Allies landed on D-Day.

Since autumn 1943 several more assassination attempts had failed. The plans had been reworked and the conspirators extended their contacts throughout the Reich and the occupied territories. At the end of May 1944, Stauffenberg was appointed chief-of-staff at the high command of the Reserve Army in Berlin—a post which kept him in the capital, but which nevertheless permitted him to take part in certain discussions at Hitler's headquarters.

The Allied landings in Normandy on June 6, 1944, wrecked Stauffenberg's hopes that his country would be left at least some freedom of manoeuvre. The assassination attempt must take place,

◁ *and* ◁▽ *Hitler greets Mussolini at Rastenburg—the Duce arrived within hours of the explosion—and shows him the scene of the "miracle". This was the last time the two dictators met.*

▽ *Göring visits the shattered hut and congratulates Hitler on his "providential" escape.*

Tresckow urged. Every day that passed would make it more complicated. There was no more time in which to look for the right man. Stauffenberg decided to act himself.

July 20

July 11. July 13. Two more postponements. And then, on July 20, Stauffenberg at last managed to leave his briefcase, containing a time-bomb, within feet of Hitler in the conference-room at O.K.H. headquarters in East Prussia. After hearing the explosion from outside, he flew back to Berlin. The order went out. "Valkyrie" was in force. Or so Stauffenberg believed.

At 1600 hours Beck finally arrived at the War Ministry at the *Bendlerstrasse* in Berlin. It was still not certain that Hitler was dead–but no matter. Prompt action was needed to take over Berlin.

The last hours of the 20th passed in total confusion, of which Hitler and his supporters took full advantage. The commander of the battalion on guard duty, uncertain as to which orders he should obey, was put directly in touch with Hitler by Goebbels. He was told to restore order.

As night fell the conspirators saw their hesitant allies abandon them, one by one. Stauffenberg, unshaken, ordered all the plans to be carried out. But at 2300 hours Fromm, C.-in-C. of the Reserve Army, surrounded by officers of the guard, arrested the last conspirators: Colonel Mertz von Quirnheim, General Olbricht, Stauffenberg, and Lieutenant Haeften.

They were hurried outside and shot.

But this was only the beginning. Hitler's revenge was immediate. Some 200 suspects, closely or remotely implicated in the plot, were hideously executed – hanged from meathooks on piano-wire nooses, their death agonies being filmed for Hitler–mostly at Plötzensee Prison in Berlin.

A few days before July 20, Stauffenberg had declared to one of his friends: "The time has come to do something. But whoever has the courage to do it must realise that he will probably be branded as a traitor in future German histories. Yet if he declines to act he will only be a traitor in his own conscience."

When all is said and done, every verdict on the political and military intentions of the conspirators, and on their chances of success, must give place to this comment, which Stauffenberg justified by his death.

CHAPTER 118

Aftermath

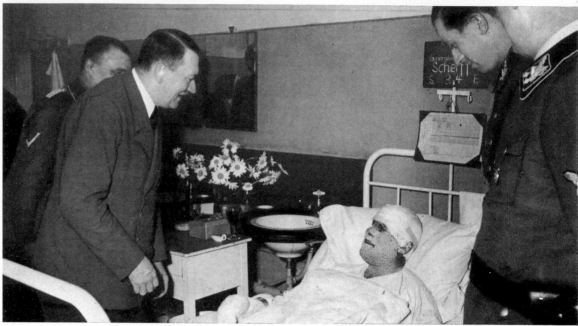

△ △ ▷ *Hitler at the bedside of General Scherff.*
△ △ *and* △ *Shredded uniforms of bomb plot victims, displayed with grim relish for the Nazi records.*

Was the attempt on Hitler's life on July 20, 1944, based on any genuine national desire to rid the German nation of the man who was leading it to ruin? Or was it, as the Nazi propagandists maintained, merely the work of foresworn malcontents and traitors to whom their solemn oath of allegiance meant nothing?

The first point to note is that the civil and military personnel who took part in the plot operated largely in isolation not only from the mass of the German people, but also from their fellow-officers in the Army. The plot had its roots in the German aristocracy, especially in the Prussian nobility, in the upper middle classes, and in certain intellectual, university, and religious circles which had little to do with the ordinary people, and the savage repression of the uprising aroused no feeling of reprobation or even of sympathy in the majority of the nation.

Was this silent disavowal of the conspirators by a majority of the German people the result of Goebbels's propaganda and the terror caused by Himmler's police? It must have been. But Anglo-Saxon propaganda also played its part by implying as it did that workers and peasants would unite in punishing Hitler and his accomplices, whereas the systematic destruction of the cities of the Third Reich, causing thousands of civilian casualties every day, only strengthened the régime's grip on the people, both morally and materially.

The officers concerned in the plot came solely from the Army. Göring controlled all promotions in the Luftwaffe and therefore had all his officers on a tight rein. The Navy, like most navies throughout the world, was apolitical, and its personnel, whether at sea or in harbour in Norway, France, or Italy, had no idea of the atrocities perpetrated by the régime and only a vague suspicion of the catastrophe about to break on the Eastern Front.

The conspirators

No general with a command on the Eastern Front seems to have been implicated. General Carl Heinrich von Stülpnagel, the military commander in France, and Lieutenant-General Speidel, chief-of-staff of Army Group "B", had both taken part at least in the plot aimed at the overthrow of the régime if not in the attempt on Hitler's life engineered by Lieutenant-Colonel Claus Schenk von Stauffenberg. In Paris, at a given signal, Stülpnagel was supposed to facilitate the *coup* by neutralising the Gestapo. Rommel had known of the plot, but disapproved. Instead, he was proposing to contact

Montgomery, to sign an armistice in the West.

At O.K.H. the two front-rank men were Generals Wagner and Fellgiebel. The former was Quartermaster-General and the latter head of communications and, as such, had the job, once the explosion was heard, of putting out of action the Rastenburg telephone exchange and radio station. In Berlin Field-Marshal von Witzleben, Rundstedt's predecessor at Saint Germain-en-Laye, Colonel-General Ludwig Beck, former Army Chief-of-Staff who resigned over the Sudeten crisis, Colonel-General Hoeppner, relieved of his command of the 4th *Panzerarmee* in January 1942 for completely specious reasons, Colonel-General Fromm, commanding the *Ersatzheer* (units in the process of formation within the Reich), and General von Hase, the military commander of the capital, were all to exploit immediately a success.

We know that Hitler escaped by a miracle when the time-bomb, left in a brief-case by Stauffenberg, went off at his feet. Goebbels's determination and Major Remer's discipline, together with a battalion of infantry, were then enough to put an end to the Berlin conspirators. This shows how little this plot, hatched by a handful of generals and general staff officers, scarcely known to the soldiery and even less to the country, had taken root in the Army.

Criticism from all sides

Not only the fanatics of the régime and Hitler's toadies, but also Manstein, Dönitz, and Guderian openly criticised the plot. They did so for moral and patriotic reasons, the value of which might be questioned given the situation of the moment, but which must be admitted as well-founded in principle.

Apropos of the attempt to overthrow the government by force, Field-Marshal von Manstein, even though unjustly disgraced by Hitler, was not afraid to say:

"I will merely say that I did not think that, in my position as a responsible military leader, I had to envisage the idea of a *coup d'état* which, in my opinion, would have led to a rapid collapse of the front and brought Germany to chaos. Not to mention, of course, the question of the oath or the legitimacy and the right of committing murder for political reasons.

As I stated at my trial: 'One cannot, as a military leader, for years call upon soldiers to sacrifice their lives for victory and then bring about defeat by one's own actions.' On the other hand it was already clear that a *coup d'état* would not have changed in any way the Allies' determination to demand unconditional surrender from Germany."

Grand-Admiral Dönitz, though he did not refuse to recognise that the July 20 conspirators had a "moral justification" for what they did, "particularly if they were privy to the mass murders ordered by the Hitler régime", nevertheless criticised their actions as follows:

"The mass of the people was behind Hitler. It did not know the facts which had determined the plotters to act. The elimination of Hitler in itself was not enough to destroy the National Socialist state. Its organisms could be expected to rise against any new government. There would be internal chaos. The front would be severely weakened. It would receive no more reinforcements or supplies. Under these conditions the soldiers could only repudiate any overthrow of authority. Their officers were constantly being called upon to ask them to sacrifice their lives. Could they then support an act which, by weakening the front, would make conditions more difficult for their hard-pressed men?"

△ *Rommel, Germany's most famous general, had known of the plot and was fatally implicated when it failed. The man who had once commanded Hitler's bodyguard, seen above as Hitler congratulated him for the capture of Tobruk, must die — but it was hoped that the embarrassment of a People's Court trial could be avoided. Rommel, still convalescing at home from his wounds suffered in Normandy, was visited by two O.K.H. officers. They gave him the choice between a cyanide capsule, a "heart attack", a state funeral, and generous care for his wife and son — or the humiliation of public disgrace. He chose the former, told his wife and son that he would be dead in 15 minutes, and drove off with the officers. The whole ghastly charade was carried out as promised, with wreaths from Hitler, Goebbels and Göring, and Rundstedt pronouncing the funeral oration.*

BEFORE THE PEOPLE'S COURT

ACCUSED: I thought of the many murders—

FREISLER: Murders?

ACCUSED: At home and abroad—

FREISLER: You really are a low scoundrel. Are you breaking down under this rottenness? Yes or no—are you breaking down under it?

ACCUSED: Herr President!

FREISLER: Yes or no, a clear answer!

ACCUSED: No.

FREISLER: Nor can you break down any more. For you are nothing but a small heap of misery that has no respect for itself any longer.

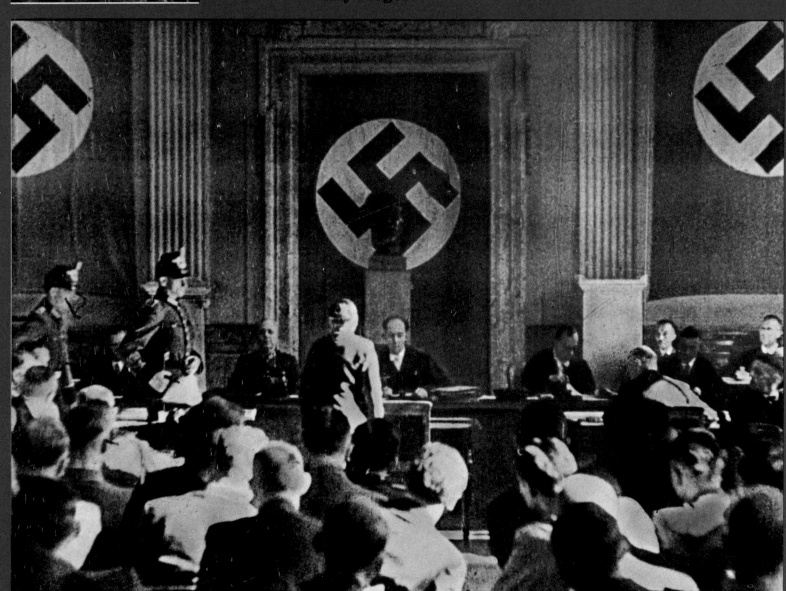

◁ ◁ and ◁ *Two of the civilian conspirators in court: Delp (left) and Goerdeler.*
◁ ◁ ◁ *Freisler, President of the People's Court, promised Hitler "Draconian justice". The Führer called him "our Vishinsky".*
◁ ◁ ◁▽ *A session of the court. Under glaring lights (the hearings were filmed) the accused stood alone against the torrent of abuse pouring from Freisler. Technicians grumbled that Freisler's yelling made a decent recording job almost impossible.*

◁ *Witzleben takes the stand, struggling with the baggy suit (minus belt) which he had been given to make him look ridiculous. "You disgusting old man!" bellowed Freisler. "Stop fiddling about with your trousers!"*

◁ *Hoeppner, disgraced by Hitler after the battle of Moscow and forbidden to wear uniform. Like Witzleben, he was hanged.*

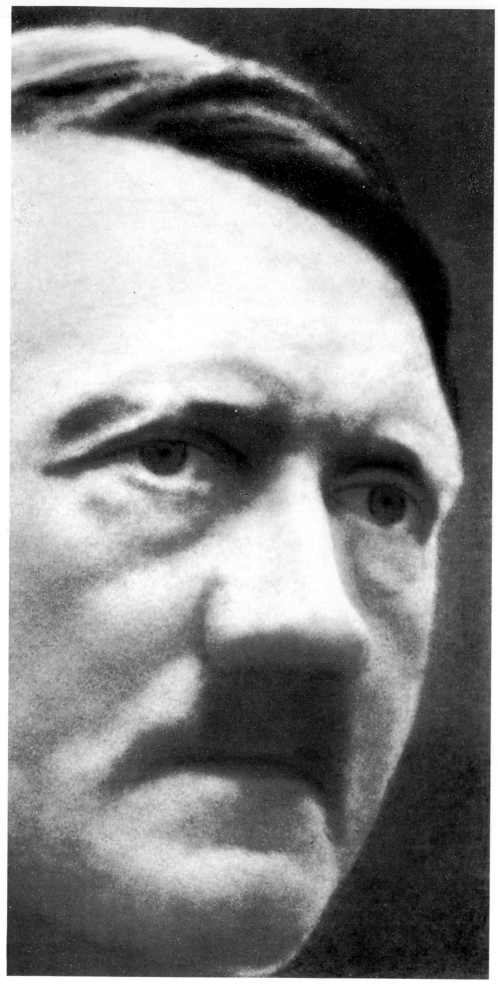

He added: "There is no doubt that the authors of the attempt were grievously wrong in their concept of what was to be expected from abroad. It would not have altered in any way the enemy's determination to obtain 'unconditional surrender'. Hitler's death would not have stopped the flow of blood as many thought."

This is also in line with Colonel-General Guderian's thinking. "Evidently," he wrote, "the question is still being asked: 'What would have happened if the attempt had succeeded?' No one can say. One thing seems certain, however: at the time a great majority of the German people still believed in Adolf Hitler; they would have been convinced that the authors of the plot had removed the only man perhaps capable of bringing the war to an honourable conclusion. The whole odium would have fallen on the officer corps in the first place, on the generals and the general staff, both during the war and after. The hatred and the scorn of the people would have been turned against the soldiers who, in the midst of a life and death struggle, would have been thought to have broken their oath to the flag and to have removed the pilot of the ship of state in peril by assassinating the supreme leader of the Reich. For this reason it is improbable that our enemies would have treated us any better than they did after we were defeated."

These criticisms of the July conspirators, men of honour and integrity, take us back to the arguments about the legitimacy of tyrannicide so common in the Middle Ages and during the Renaissance.

"Providence has protected me so well from all harm that I can continue to labour on the great task of victory." It was in these terms that Hitler announced to the German people that he had emerged practically unharmed from the attempt on his life which killed General Schmundt, his A.D.C., General Korten, Chief-of-Staff of the Luftwaffe, and several other people in his entourage.

But what paths would the aforesaid Providence take to bring the Third Reich to final victory through the instrument of its miraculously-saved leader? During the first half of this year it had been the *matériel* and moral action of his missiles which Hitler had used to give heart to his generals. The liberation of Normandy, then Picardy, the Pas-de-Calais and Flanders, had then put London out of range of the V-1 flying bombs, so now

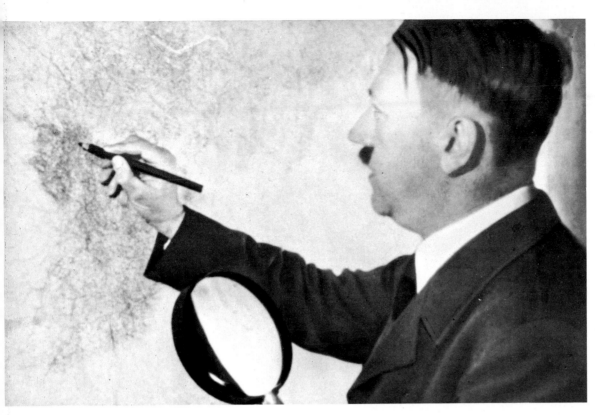

"It is a gang of criminal elements which will be destroyed without mercy . . . This time we shall settle accounts with them in the manner to which we National Socialists are accustomed."

he called upon the ghost of Frederick the Great when he summoned his generals around him or received one of them in his office.

At the end of 1761 everyone thought that Frederick's cause was hopelessly lost, in spite of the King's military genius, as six years of the vicissitudes of war and the eventual enormous superiority of the coalition of Austria, France, and Russia had brought the little Prussian kingdom to its knees. By December 26 it all seemed over when Providence disposed of the Tsarina Elizabeth and brought to the throne of Russia the Prussophile Peter III, who came to terms with Frederick behind the backs of his allies on May 5 and June 19, 1762. Discouraged by this defection, Louis XV and Maria Theresa threw their hand in and on February 15, 1763 recognised Frederick's occupation of Silesia.

Frederick, by holding on in spite of all appearances to the contrary had, by his genius, prevailed over those of his counsellors who had advised him to give in and thus reaped the reward of his perseverance. Exactly the same point had been reached in 1944. The unnatural

coalition between the Soviet Union and the Anglo-Saxons could dissolve at any moment. The Red Army's enormous daily successes could only accelerate the process as Stalin would be unable to resist the temptation of Constantinople and the Straits, which would inevitably arouse the hostility of Great Britain.

Improbable as it may seem, this was the way Hitler's thoughts ran during the night of September 12-13 in conversations with Colonel-General Friessner, who was striving to keep the Russians out of the Hungarian plain after the "defection" of Rumania and Bulgaria. To his utter amazement, Friessner was told by Hitler that *"Germany was no longer the political objective of the Soviets, but the Bosporus.* That was how things stood now. The U.S.S.R. was going to put the Balkans and the Bosporus first. Within a fortnight, or at the latest within six weeks, there would be a major clash of Allied interests in these areas. Germany must therefore expect the war *to take a decisive turn to her advantage.* England had clearly no interest in seeing Germany razed to the ground; on the contrary she needed *Germany as a buffer state.* But Germany

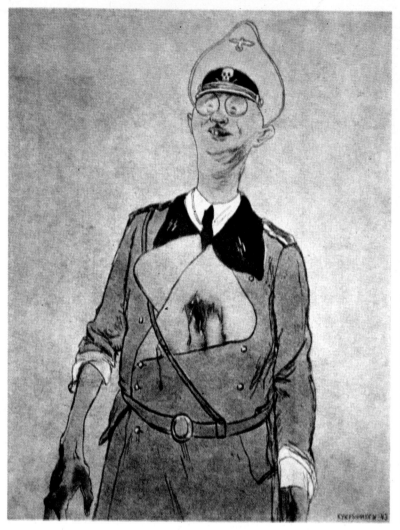

△ *Savage Russian caricatures of the two Nazi leaders who did most to crush the July Plot and defame its adherents: Himmler and Goebbels.*

had to gain time: every effort should be made to hold the Balkan fronts."

Hitler's conclusions were evidently based on two hypotheses at which he had arrived arbitrarily, as was his custom:
1. that Stalin would march on Constantinople without more ado, and
2. that Britain which, in his opinion, was the dominant partner in the Anglo-Saxon alliance, would try to stop him by force.

But Stalin was to wait for the liquidation of Germany before turning to the Turkish narrows. And everybody knew that between Roosevelt and Churchill the British Prime Minister did not have the last word.

Hitler's vengeance

At this juncture, however, no one dared to contradict Hitler. The failure of the July 20 plot allowed him to wreak terrible vengeance on the German Army. Seventeen generals were executed, the luckiest of them shot, the others hanged with atrocious refinements of cruelty and publicity. Field-Marshals von Kluge and Rommel, Colonel-General Beck, General Wagner, Major-General von Tresckow, chief-of-staff of the 2nd Army, took poison or shot themselves.

A wave of terror swept through the Army. To keep a tighter rein on his generals, Hitler took their families as hostages, returning to the principle of collective responsibility, a throwback to the ancient German custom. *Reichsführer* Heinrich Himmler was appointed head of the *Ersatzheer* in place of Colonel-General Fromm, whilst the faithful Dr. Goebbels was given the job of organising total mobilisation. The military salute was replaced by the Hitler salute and the party appointed political commissars in units and headquarters, to be responsible for the supervision and National Socialist indoctrination of the fighting troops.

And so the Führer controlled all the means of pressure which would allow him to change a military defeat, 1918 style, into a national catastrophe in which not a single inch of the soil of the Fatherland would be spared.

THE PROPAGANDA WAR

GOEBBELS:
The arch-priest

The name of Joseph Goebbels will always be firmly linked with the theory and practice of propaganda. His brilliant use of the German language to "sell" National Socialism to the German people cannot be denied. A fanatically faithful Nazi, he remained loyal to Hitler until the end; his task, of implanting that loyalty in every citizen of the Third Reich, was faithfully and effectively carried out.

Goebbels was in one sense a rarity in the Nazi Party; he had a university education behind him. In point of fact he had attended eight universities –all of them in the first rank of German learning–by the time he had graduated from Heidelberg in 1921 with a Ph.D., at the age of 24. He was a devoted and impassioned nationalist, with superimposed bitterness due to his crippled left leg, the result of osteomyelitis at the age of seven followed by an unsuccessful operation. In 1922, having heard Hitler speak at Munich, Goebbels joined the Nazi Party.

Despite a succession of rabble-rousing speeches against the French occupation of the Ruhr (he was a Rhinelander himself, born at Rheydt in 1897), it took some three years for Goebbels to make his mark in the Party. And when he did it was as a protégé of Gregor Strasser, leading Nazi radical who put far too much emphasis on the socialist part of National Socialism for Hitler's liking. Matters came to a head when the Strasser-Goebbels faction of the Party pressed for a link-up with the Communists in a programme to deprive the surviving royalty and nobility of their hereditary possessions.

Hitler, however, won back Goebbels at Munich in April 1926. He turned the full blast of his personality on Goebbels, inspiring the latter to flights of near-hysterical hero-worship from which he never departed again.

Master-speaker though he was, with a fine voice and razor-keen sense of timing, Goebbels was no mere tub-thumper for the Party. He played a key rôle in unsavoury but crucial operations such as the firing of the Reichstag and the anti-Röhm "Blood Purge", not to mention taking decisive action to contain and round up the Army plotters in Berlin after the failure of the 1944 "July Plot".

He kept faith until the end, killing his family and committing suicide with his wife in the Berlin *Führerbunker* in 1945.

◁ ◁ *At the microphone: the master in action.*
◁ *The Minister at his desk.*
▽ ◁ *Public relations work, standard for Nazi leaders: beaming over a small child.*
▽ *Party official on parade, radiating devotion to the Führer.*

This page: *The distinctive Kukryniksy style compared with similar efforts abroad.*
◁ *Stockholm's* Sondagnisse Strix *shows Himmler and Goebbels keeping a tight hold on "General Scapegoat"–keeping him in reserve for when the Führer's intuition results in a defeat.*
▽ ◁ *Kukryniksy par excellence. Goebbels shrilly claims more smashing victories in Russia. And a wooden echo from the row of coffined Wehrmacht troops adds: "We hope for more successes in the future . . ."*
▽ *Bance Russell of the* New York Post *adopts the simian look for his version of Goebbels.*

▷ *Before the Non-Aggression Pact: capitalism, fond godfathers of Nazism–France, Britain, Wall Street, and the industrial magnates of the Ruhr.*
▷▽ *Munich time, 1938: the dictators and the appeasers.*

1604

RUSSIA: savage and hard-hitting

When Germany invaded the Soviet Union in June 1941, Russian propagandists had to make a swift about-turn. Ever since the Non-Aggression Pact of 1939 they had been following the Molotov line: war with Germany was contrary to the mutual interests of the two countries. Operation "Barbarossa" put an abrupt end to that.

The savagery with which the Russian propagandists fell upon the invading "Hitlerite hordes" was a faithful by-product of the Russo-German war; but in many ways the Russian technique had been foreshadowed. One of the most obvious examples was the caricaturists' treatment of the Nazi leaders – Hitler the villain of the piece, the wolf in sheep's clothing with dripping fangs; Himmler with his headsman's axe; Goebbels wizened, monkey-like (with or without tail, according to choice). There are two fair examples of this general similarity on the opposite page, one from Stockholm and one from America.

One of the key principles of modern propaganda was summed up by Lewis Carroll's Humpty Dumpty in *Alice*: "When *I* use a word it means exactly what I intend it to mean; neither more nor less." And nowhere was this more true than in the original Soviet propaganda before the Ribbentrop pact of 1939. Russian propaganda in the 1930s screamed of the growing menace of Nazidom and the cowardice of the Western democracies in failing to tackle the Axis dictators head-on.

In the first months of the German invasion there was all too little for Russian propagandists to cheer about. Bedrock appeals to Russian nationalism – "The Motherland Calls!" – were ranged beside hard-hitting criticism of Nazi brutality. An early theme to emerge from the Kukryniksy team of caricaturists was "the training of Fritz" – a Nazi boyhood, from torturing cats as a young boy, beating up old folk in the Hitler Youth, and finally emerging with his blood-spattered ceremonial axe, all ready for service in Russia.

Then came Moscow in December 1941, and a clear-cut victory. At once a theme emerged which would remain a constant stand-by: the theme of Russian might, represented by a gigantic pair of pincers carving deep into the emaciated German lines, or a massive, monolithic tank.

After Stalingrad came another new style. This was the personification of the Red Army soldier: a young giant with a stern and vengeful expression, sweeping the Germans before him with a broom made of bayonets. It was a fair reflection of the deliberate glorification of the Red Army in the post-Stalingrad era, when the long chain of victories began.

Stalin's propagandists were also quick to exploit the many sieges of Russian capitals and provincial centres – Odessa, Leningrad, Moscow, Stalingrad, Sevastopol'. As with the British victims of the Blitz, this identified the urban population with the front-line troops, with battle honours of their own of which they could be proud.

△ *Kukryniksy jeer at Hitler after Moscow: the* Blitzkrieg *drum bursts.*
◁ *Past enemies of "Mother Russia" preserved as a warning. From left to right: Charles XII of Sweden, defeated by Peter the Great; Napoleon; Hitler; and a Japanese soldier, the last being a reference to the brisk frontier war with Japan fought in 1938-39.*
▷ *Decline of the Axis, 1941-44.*

The German recovery after Stalingrad inspired a natural note of caution among the Russian propagandists; but then came Kursk, the turning-point on the Eastern Front, and the era of the massed "victory salutes" in Moscow began. But the image of the "Nazi beast" remained, and there were two obvious reasons for this. The first was the discovery of German atrocities in the territories liberated by the Red Army; the second was the tenacity of the Wehrmacht in defence, which grew ever more ferocious as it fell back on the frontiers of the Reich.

These two factors inspired the notorious "hate propaganda" of Ilya Ehrenburg. "We cannot live as long as these grey-green slugs are alive. Today there are no books; today there are no stars in the sky; today there is only one thought: Kill the Germans. Kill them all and dig them into the earth." And again: "We are remembering everything. Now we know. The Germans are not human. Now the word 'German' has become the most terrible swear-word. Let us not speak. Let us not be indignant. Let us kill . . . If you have killed one German, kill another. There is nothing jollier than German corpses."

Ehrenburg's "hate propaganda" was maintained at red-hot intensity right through to the spring of 1945. As the invasion of the Reich proceeded he was writing: "The Fritzes are still running, but not lying dead. Who can stop us now? General Model? The Oder? The Volkssturm? No, it's too late. Germany, you can now whirl round in circles, and burn, and howl in your deathly agony; the hour of revenge has struck!" But by April 1945 it was increasingly obvious that "hate propaganda" was out of date in view of Germany's imminent collapse and the post-war problems of administering the occupied sectors of the Reich; and Ehrenburg was abruptly muzzled. His "hate propaganda" had served its turn; now it was not only outdated but a positive embarrassment.

As the string of Russian victories lengthened, ridicule began to emerge more and more in Russian posters and cartoons. The Nazi beast tended to give place to the tattered scarecrow, emaciated, ridiculous, but never quite pathetic.

Being as it was the product of a totalitarian state, Russian propaganda was manipulated with stone-faced cynicism and little scope was given to individual viewpoints. The "official line" remained all-important. Yet Russian propaganda never lost its edge. Right to the end it remained ruthless and hard-hitting, with a style all its own. From the months of defeat to final victory, these characteristics remained.

△ △ *"The Nazi beast aboard his tank"—standard Kukryniksy view of the German invaders down to Stalingrad.*
△ *"The tired old organ-grinder takes to the road"—ridicule takes over. Hitler shambles from the scene with Mussolini and Rumania's Antonescu as his performing monkeys.*
▷ *Moscow, 1941—and the first genuine note of confidence. Russia's field army is portrayed as an invincible pair of pincers. The same motif would be repeated many times when other sieges were raised—most notably in the case of Leningrad, with vengeful swords slicing through the shrinking German arms encircling the city.*
▷ ▷ *"The Führer is beside himself"—derisive Kukryniksy jibe at the shaky relations between the Führer and his commanding generals. The surrenders at Stalingrad gave the Russians plenty of opportunities to weigh up these weaknesses for themselves.*

CASTLES OF THE AIR

Man the walls!

Join a BALLOON BARRAGE SQUADRON

AUXILIARY AIR FORCE

MILITARY NOTICE

FOR TALKING OF TROOP AND SHIP MOVEMENTS

PENALTY

DEATH

FOR YOUR COMRADES

It all depends on YOU – *GO TO IT!*

THE GLORIOUS END OF THE "GLOWWORM." This destroyer, one YOU helped to build, engaged a force of enemy cruisers and destroyers in Norwegian waters and went down fighting.
SHIPS, TANKS and LORRIES are the FORCES' URGENT NEED
CARRY ON AT TOP SPEED!

THORNYCROFT

◁ ◁ *When the war came home to the British: the bogey of the Blitz.*

△ ◁ *Attractive and comforting, but hardly aggressive: an appeal for balloon barrage volunteers.*

△ *"Careless talk" posters were ubiquitous. This is a particularly strong variant.*

◁ *Supply minister Herbert Morrison coined one of the best home front slogans of the war: "Go to it!" This exhortation was extended to almost every facet of the British war effort.*

Entente cordiale!

However, as the war progressed the British developed considerable skill in the field of "black" propaganda. As opposed to "white" propaganda–the traditional medium–"black" propaganda had a subtlety which often bordered on the fiendish. One form was the "*Kreisleiter* letter". German parents would receive a fake document regretfully informing them that their son had been killed in action on such and such a day, and that his personal effects had been forwarded home to his local *Kreisleiter*. Naturally the *Kreisleiter,* when approached, would know nothing about the dead soldier's possessions. It was an ingenious way of using enemy battle casualties to undermine faith in the Nazi régime.

Then there was *Soldatensender Calais,* a broadcasting station aimed at the German troops in Western Europe. This was put to good use before and after D-Day, undermining German morale with grim warnings of what was coming and depressing news of what the continuation of the war was doing to their homes. *Soldatensender Calais* used tough

The Mediterranean Invasion. British troops, tanks guns pouring ashore from landing craft.

VICTORY OF THE ALLIES IS ASSURED

THE RED ARMY's Fight is YOUR Fight!

The Communist Party says **ACT NOW!**

★ *Remove Pro-fascists from high places*
★ *End Employers' Mismanagement and Waste*
★ *Restore T.U. Rights and "Daily Worker"*

AID SOVIET—SMASH HITLER!

soldier's jargon and pulled no punches. It was obviously a foreign station—that was the point.

It must be concluded that the "black" approaches proved to be the most skilful refinement of British propaganda. In the more conventional media, the British technique always seems to have been too polite.

△ *Axis subtlety: the "Big Three" alliance corroded by the American dollar, for the benefit of the occupied French.*
△ ▷ *British sobriety: once again, the direct approach.*
▷ *A blast from the British Communist Party—with the Red Army coming off second best to trades union rights and the Daily Worker.*

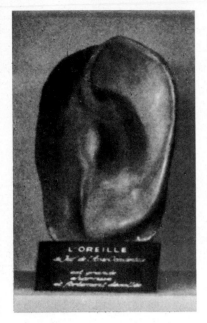

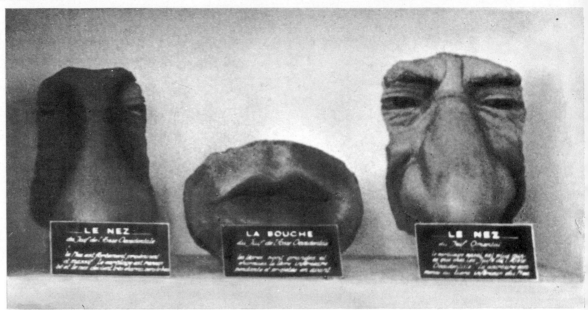

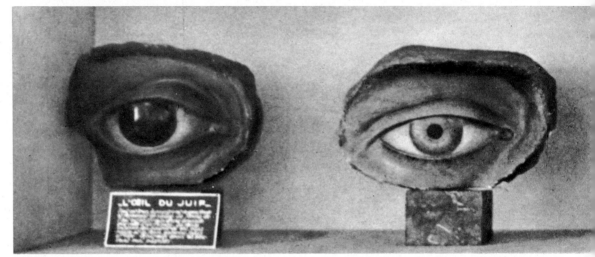

△ and ▷ *"Every Frenchman who is determined to combat the Hebrew menace must learn how to recognise the Jew." These so-called "Jewish features" were put on public display as part of the anti-Semitic programme in France.* ▷▷ *Poster for a public exhibition: "The Jew and France."*

THE JEWS: prime victims

Anti-Semitism had always been a classic Nazi platform, and it necessarily motivated a great deal of propaganda. From the earliest day of the German Nazi Party's career Jew-hating was urged on all "good Germans" by the Party's propagandists. The most notorious was the bullying Julius Streicher, "Jew-baiter No. 1", and his illustrated paper *Der Stürmer*. This nauseating publication was tireless in churning out the worst in anti-Semitism, vacillating between the incredibly childish and the brutally obscene.

But the crudity of *Der Stürmer* was only a very small part of the anti-Jewish programme. Behind the street-corner roaring and bullying lay the horror of the pseudo-scientific attempts to prove for ever that

"Aryans" were the master-race and Jews the source of all corruption and degeneracy. What Churchill referred to as "the lights of perverted science" applied precisely to this aspect of the anti-Jewish programme; and the display casts of so-called "typically Jewish features" shown above are an excellent example.

Playing on anti-Semitic instincts was an inevitable part of the Nazi policy towards occupied countries. In France, for example, a mass of anti-Jewish material appeared, fit to gladden the heart of Streicher himself.

It is a curious fact that very little propaganda appeared as a counter-blast to the Nazi anti-Semitic programme. After all, there is little that can be said

to refute the vicious generalisations which were the Nazis' stock-in-trade than to quote and condemn them. It has to be admitted that "Save the Jews" never emerged as a dominant Allied propaganda line. Appeals to patriotism; exhortations to enlist, to work harder; condemnations of certified enemy atrocities –these carried more weight and predominated in public propaganda during World War II. It should also be remembered that the tangible evidence of the full extent of the "Final Solution" –the death camps–was not brought to the public eye until the closing months of the war. So it was that one of the grimmest aspects of the war remained largely an Axis prerogative in the powerful sphere of propaganda.

E NAZI THREAT
HE MODERN WORLD
USED ANTISEMITISM AS ONE OF ITS WEAPONS F

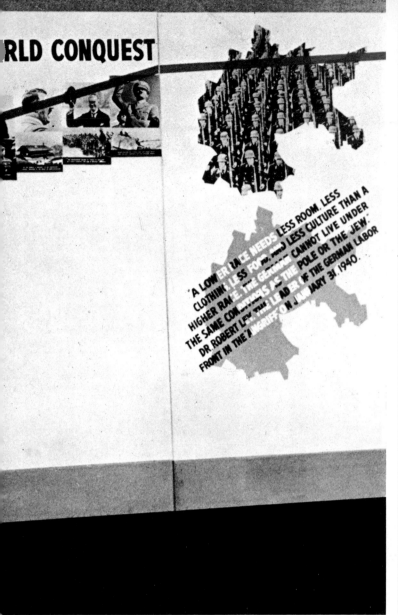

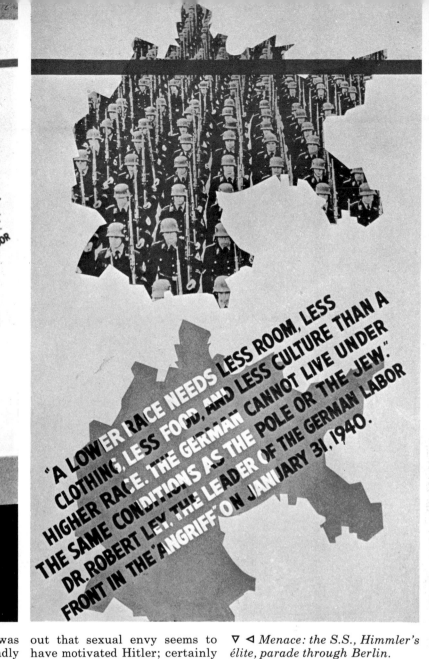

"A LOWER RACE NEEDS LESS ROOM, LESS CLOTHING, LESS FOOD, AND LESS CULTURE THAN A HIGHER RACE. THE GERMAN CANNOT LIVE UNDER THE SAME CONDITIONS AS THE POLE OR THE JEW." DR. ROBERT LEY, THE LEADER OF THE GERMAN LABOR FRONT IN THE 'ANGRIFF' ON JANUARY 31, 1940.

Mein Kampf was the Nazi bible and enshrined Hitler's anti-Semitic fetish. He wallowed in it. When he told of his fastidious reactions to pre-1914 Vienna he really plumbed the depths: "Was there any form of filth or profligacy, particularly in cultural life," he shrieked in *Mein Kampf*, "without at least one Jew involved in it? If you cut even cautiously into such an abscess, you found, like a maggot in a rotting body, often dazzled by the sudden light – a yid!"

"Gradually," Hitler solemnly went on, "I began to hate them." The tragedy was that he was not alone, that the hate-ridden tripe of *Mein Kampf* was retailed to the German public with consummate ease. The sales of *Mein Kampf* made Hitler a millionaire. The book was second only to the Bible in the number of copies sold in Nazi Germany. The book was ostentatiously displayed in the homes of the prudent and was solemnly presented to the happy couple at weddings.

What made matters worse was that *Mein Kampf* is such a badly written book that few people – let alone Germans – managed to read it thoroughly. For it conceals nothing of Hitler's long-term plans for Germany and the German-dominated world to which he aspired. It was the blueprint for the "Final Solution", the total eradication of Jewry which was the only logical goal of the Nazi creed. *Mein Kampf* was published for the first time in the autumn of 1925 – but as early as that Hitler was laying down that argument that the spaces of eastern Europe – and Russia – were the only areas into which Germany could and must expand.

One of the most unpleasant aspects of the Nazi brand of Jew-baiting was its obsession with sexual corruption. Here again Hitler took the lead in *Mein Kampf,* accusing the Jews of being at the heart of the white slave traffic and of corrupting the German race with vile seductions. It has often been pointed out that sexual envy seems to have motivated Hitler; certainly the Führer's enigmatic private life was a real puzzle for everyone but the Nazi propagandists, who held it up to the nation as a splendid example of selfless and blameless living.

With Julius Streicher, Nazi Jew-baiting hit rock bottom. A brute of a man, a sadist and pervert who loved to strut the streets of Nuremberg carrying a whip, Streicher peddled anti-Semitic filth to the nation in *Der Stürmer.* Its pages constantly featured warning cartoon strips of innocent blond German girls falling into the clutches of Jewish schoolteachers or doctors. The victims were invariably paragons of teutonic beauty, with blonde hair and blue eyes; the villains fat, swarthy, reeking of garlic, with thick lips, and a monstrous nose.

It was crude to the point of childishness – but the German people consistently looked the other way.

▽ ◁ *Menace: the S.S., Himmler's élite, parade through Berlin. It was one of Himmler's deputies, Hans Frank, who told his men that "I could not eliminate all lice and Jews in only one year. But in the course of time, and if you help me, this end will be attained."*
△ *Reply: the obvious counter-blast to the Nazi anti-Semitic programme. It was a simple truth, stated simply. But it could never aspire to the murderous glamour of the Nazi line.*

Depressing the "D-day dodgers"

△ *Death on the beach-head: a theme much used in Axis propaganda after the landings at Salerno. The American forces were given a rough time at Salerno, but ultimately the Allied landings were always successful.*

The campaign in Italy produced a splendid crop of propaganda. Once again it was the Germans who took the initiative, and their favourite topic was the slow crawl of the Allied advance.

The 8th Army–or the "D-Day dodgers", as they became known after ill-advised criticism back at home–found themselves on the receiving end of a series of telling propaganda leaflets. Some of these were parodies of tourist literature, extolling the natural beauties of Italy on one side and showing death waiting for all on the other. Axis propagandists developed a number of different approaches, most of which made the most out of local setbacks and defeats suffered by the Allies.

Then there was "Axis Sally", who broadcast to the front-line troops. Unlike the chilling conviction of the "black" broadcasts of *Soldatensender Calais,* the "Axis Sally" broadcasts

failed. They had too high an entertainment value. After playing a record of dance music "to cheer up you poor boys in your cold trenches", "Sally" would then commiserate with the uncomfortable time they were having. She used a sultry, caressing tone which completely failed to achieve the desired effect; it sounded like a bad impersonation of Mae West and Marlene Dietrich combined, and the result was frankly comic.

Against heavy-handed blandishments of this kind, 8th Army morale held up well. The 8th Army had, by the time of the Italian campaign, evolved its own image. This was typified by the cartoonist Jon and his "Two Types" – hardened veteran officers from the days of the desert war, with desert boots, elaborately sloppy turn-out, and formidable R.A.F. handlebar moustaches.

As for the Americans in Italy, they had cartoon heroes of their own. These were the sloppy G.I.s "Willie and Joe", the creation of Bill Mauldin, which appeared in the American forces newspaper *Stars and Stripes.* Willie and Joe summed up the lot of the weary infantryman to whom no discomfort came as a real surprise. "I can't get no lower, Willie, my buttons is in the way"–or, sourly regarding a shot-torn village: "Let B Company go in first. They ain't been kissed yet."

The propaganda war in Italy therefore had its highlights, but little practical effect on either side. Despite the many setbacks encountered between Salerno and the final German surrender in the north, the Allies knew that they were winning the war. For their part, the Germans resisted every effort of the Allied propagandists. Kesselring's troops fought on undaunted to the end.

INDIA ARISE!

Encouraged by India's pre-war record of civil disobedience and demands for independence, the Japanese made many attempts to sabotage the war effort of British India by inducing the population to expel the British, and some very strong leaflets appeared. The Indian politician Subhas Chandra Bose became the figurehead of this movement abroad, first in Germany and then in Japan. He headed a skeletal Indian government-in-exile under Axis patronage and formed the "Indian National Army", recruited from Indian deserters and intended to fight beside the Japanese on the Burma front.

Although the Indian Congress refused to identify itself with the British warfare, and despite several disturbances within the country, India's response to the war was magnificent. Bose's "Indian National Army" only attracted a trickle of volunteers and never became a force to be reckoned with. Despite the strenuous efforts of the Japanese propagandists, India fought for the Imperialist cause. In fact the country contributed the largest voluntary recruitment ever recorded in history: over two million by 1945. Even more important than the manpower contribution was India's economic aid, which made the country militarily self-sufficient and enabled her to supply the imperial armies in Africa and the Middle East. India emerged from the war as a creditor nation, ripe for independence. Her most serious problem was her internal differences–not the Imperialism played on by Japanese propaganda.

▷ △ and ▷ *Attempts to canalise the independence movement and shake off British control.*

Pleas for Co-Prosperity

There was always a note of naïveté about Japanese propaganda. It was reflected in the cosy title which the Japanese gave to their conquests in South-East Asia and the Pacific: the "South-East Asia Co-Prosperity Sphere", suggestive of a giant co-operative friendly society. It did not fit in with the brutal reality of Japanese military occupation. The trouble was that the reason for the sudden expansion of the Japanese Empire was painfully obvious: exploitation.

During the battle for the Philippines in 1941-42, the Japanese issued a crude, line-drawn leaflet showing a genial Japanese soldier giving a cigarette to a battered-looking Filipino soldier. In the background American troops can be seen running away, carrying a

▽ *A pathetic attempt to justify Japan's "Runaway Victory" in the eyes of her victims. Even the Nazi boast of the "New Order in Europe" carried more conviction.*

ripped and tattered American flag. "You are our pals," announced the legend. Our enemies are the Americans." Simple efforts such as this, and rhyming tags like the example below (more appropriate to a nursery school wall than an international propaganda campaign) had little chance. They certainly did not prevent the Filipino resistance movement from becoming one of the most powerful subversive elements in the entire "Co-Prosperity Sphere".

Primary education pamphlets were issued in Tokyo in series with titles like "The Schools Weekly, Primer Edition", and "The A.B.C. Weekly". A typical, run of the mill example read as follows:

"We have a new *Ministry*. It is the *Greater East Asia Ministry*.

"Mr. Kazuo Aoki is the *Minister* of the new Ministry."

Then, accompanying a photograph of prisoners from the "Doolittle Raid" on Tokyo: "Here you see some American *airmen*.

"They are the crew of the American planes which *raided* Japan on April 18.

"They have been *punished with heavy penalties.*

"The crew of any aircraft raiding Japan will be punished *with death.*"

An Anglo-Japanese translation key follows.

In general, Japan's propaganda efforts always retained the amateur look of a back-streets printer. They never made the most out of the formidable achievements born of the months of victory, or whipped up any effective anti-British feeling.

Let us join hands!
Don't lose your lovely native lands
Trust not the sly Americans.
Come, join hands and help us build
A true home of our God sent East.

必勝

KEKOEATAN ASIA

LIHATLAH IN KEKOEATAN

HIMPOENLAH KERTAS APIAPI NO.75

HIMPOENLAH KERTAS APIAPI NO.111

◁ and ▽ Match-box label propaganda was widely used by the Japanese. Colourfully printed, extolling Japanese military might, and ridiculing the British, Americans, and Chinese, they were sold "over the counter" and were often solemnly dropped on Allied airfields as well.

TENTOE DAPAT KEMENANGAN

HIMPOENLAH KERTAS APIAPI NO. 3

TENTOE DAPAT KEMENANGAN

必勝

HIMPOENLAH KERTAS APIAPI NO. 20

NISTJAJALAH, TENTARA NIPPON MENDAPAT KEMENANGAN

日軍必勝

HIMPOENLAH KERTAS APIAPI NO.

TENTOE DAPAT KEMENANGAN

必勝

HIMPOENLAH KERTAS APIAPI NO. 61

TENTOE DAPAT KEMENANGAN

必勝

HIMPOENLAH KERTAS APIAPI NO.101

A POSTMARK BETRAYED THIS H.Q...

USE THE **ARMY POST OFFICE**

Just how effective was the propaganda of World War II?

Webster's International Dictionary defines "propaganda" as "any systematic, widespread dissemination or promotion of particular ideas, doctrines, practices, etc., to further one's own cause or to damage an opposing one". And as far as war-time propaganda is concerned certain generalisations have to be considered.

First, propaganda of any kind has singularly little effect on the enemy when he happens to be winning. But this obvious fact is compounded by other factors. The Japanese were a case in point. The loyalty of their rank and file was proverbial; surrender or capture spelled unthinkable disgrace. Nothing proved this more clearly than the jungle fugitives on Guam in the Marianas islands who refused to accept that Japan had surrendered and held out against the day when the Japanese Army would return. These men continued to be rounded up long after 1945, one of them holding out until 1972. They belonged to an army which had been told that only torture and death awaited them at the hands of the Americans; but far more effective was the Japanese soldier's instinctive, unshakeable loyalty to his Emperor.

Similarly, German S.S. troops were also generally impervious to Allied propaganda, but this was not unique to the S.S. The best example was to be found in the Luftwaffe airborne units, which proved themselves tough and determined fighters from their early triumphs, right through the North African and Italian campaigns, with a fighting tradition and pride in their unit second to none.

The records show that only 59 British P.O.W.s responded to the call of the "Crusade Against Bolshevism" and enlisted in the *Waffen*-S.S. German recruiting propaganda had much greater success on the Eastern Front— but there the situation was different because of the wider array of minority nationalities: Latvians, Ukrainians, Cossacks, etc. In fact, one of the last actions of the war in Europe was a cavalry attack by a Cossack unit fighting with the Germans in northern Italy.

Awareness of victory, then, plus nationalist pride and military tradition, created a formidable shell for propaganda to crack. But – paradoxically – World War II produced plenty of cases where the reverse did not hold true in defeat. The population of besieged Warsaw in September 1939; the Finns during the "Winter War" of 1939-40; the British under the shadow of invasion and the perils of the Blitz in 1940; the endurance of the Leningraders during their 30-month siege: all were apparently hopeless situations in which propaganda appeals by the enemy had little or no effect.

The same applied to the fighting men. The British Guards held out at "Knightsbridge" in the Battle of Gazala—because they were the Guards. Four months later the Italo-German *Panzerarmee* and *Afrika Korps* fought on long after any reasonable hope of victory had evaporated. Similarly, the stand of the German paratroops at Cassino was later mirrored by that of the British 1st Airborne Division at Arnhem. And the hopeless defence of Iwo Jima in 1945 by General Kuribayashi's Japanese surpassed all these examples. While radio contact with Japan remained, Kuribayashi's messages reflected nothing but regret at having let the Americans establish themselves on Imperial Japanese territory.

It has often been claimed that the French collapse in 1940 was largely the result of months of eroding propaganda. There was certainly an intense propaganda campaign during the "Phoney War" while the French and German armies watched each other across the No-Man's Land between the Maginot and Siegfried Lines. Huge loudspeakers hurled messages backwards and forwards and leaflets were scattered lavishly. But on at least one occasion German attempts to sap the morale of the Maginot Line garrisons broke down in farce. A huge German placard appeared one morning, informing the French "Soldiers of the North" that their wives and girl friends were being unfaithful back home. The French troops at whom this was aimed riposted with a placard of their own: "We don't give a damn—we're from the south!" The truth of the matter is that the propaganda which did the most damage to French morale before the catastrophe of 1940 was not German, but Communist; Communist subversion and agitation had been rife in France long before the signing of the Nazi-Soviet Non-Aggression Pact of August 1939.

When all is said and done, propaganda aims at the mind; and war-time propaganda could be described as a form of mental tear gas to prevent the enemy from doing his job as effectively as he might otherwise have done. In war-time conditions, propaganda aimed at one's own population tends to pall after a while— people get tired of being exhorted. But it is nevertheless essential, for morale; a good parallel is the anti-aircraft barrage during the London Blitz. The damage done by the A.A. guns to the German bombers was negligible; but the Londoners found that air raids were far more bearable when they knew that their own guns were replying to the thunder of enemy bombs.

Conversely, the German people proved that even when the news is uniformly bad and official propaganda manifestly untrue, the general reaction is one of cynical humour, never of confusion and despair.

◁ ◁ *Familiar images used to ram home a principle of war-time security precautions.*

▽ *Simple, cartoon treatment— and an easy-to-remember rhyming slogan.*

TITTLE TATTLE LOST THE BATTLE

Like Napoleon, Hitler was a master of the big lie; and one of the biggest lies produced by the propaganda machine of the Third Reich was the "crusade against Bolshevism for the New Europe" line. Unfortunately this took some little time to emerge. Until 1940 Goebbels and his copywriters concentrated their efforts against individual victims—the Czechs, the Poles, the French, the British. Not until the invasion of Russia did the "crusade against Bolshevism" take shape. Once established, however, it remained—particularly when the Eastern Front began to be beaten back towards the Reich.

Joachim Peiper, the *Waffen-S.S.* commander who narrowly escaped hanging for his responsibility for the deliberate murder of American prisoners during the Battle of the Bulge in December 1944, was one among thousands who believed in the "New Europe" dream. Seven years after the end of the war, he wrote to his former comrades: "Don't forget that it was in the ranks of the S.S. that the first European died."

Here, for a certainty, Nazi propaganda had won a lasting victory . . .

▷ *An ever-recurring theme in German propaganda: the German soldier as the champion of European freedom.*

▽ *To win over Russians to the side of their German "liberators"—the horrors of Bolshevism compared with the brave new world for which the Third Reich was fighting the war.*

EUROPAS FREIHEIT

БОЛЬШЕВИЗМ

НОВАЯ ЕВРОПА

CHAPTER 119
Assault from the East

In 1944 the Soviet summer offensive was to move forward successively over all sectors of the front from the Arctic tundra to the mouth of the Dniestr on the Black Sea. It can thus be compared in extent to Hitler's Operation "Barbarossa" begun three years before. Now the situation was reversed.

In addition to the will to destroy the armed forces of Germany and her satellites, the U.S.S.R. also had territorial and political ambitions: to impose a dictated peace on Finland; to bring Estonia, Latvia, and Lithuania back under Soviet rule; to install a puppet government in Poland; and to prepare to take over Rumania, Bulgaria, Hungary, and Yugoslavia.

Stalin, the head of the Soviet Government and Secretary General of the Soviet Communist Party, was not only taking as axiomatic, Clausewitz's view of war as subordinate to politics; but he was also going further, along the principles laid down by Lenin: "War is essentially a political fact . . . war is one part of a whole: that whole is politics", and by Frunze, the creator of the Red Army:

▽ *Red Army infantry advance over somewhat meagre German barbed wire defences. With ever-improving co-operation between Soviet infantry, armour, and aircraft, the Red Army was more than a match for the German Army, for all its skill in defensive fighting.*

"Questions of military strategy and political and economic strategy are closely inter-related and form a coherent whole."

This is clearly opposed to the American military doctrine which Eisenhower obeyed in early April 1945 when he stopped his 12th Army Group on the Elbe at Magdeburg, since Berlin no longer had any importance militarily. There have, it is true, been many cases in which military operations have been gravely compromised by political interference.

Stavka's resources

In view of the failing strength of the Wehrmacht, Stalin could well afford to plan boldly, using the Red Army's material superiority in pursuit of long-term goals. Early in the summer of 1944 Stavka had 500 infantry and 40 artillery divisions, and 300 armoured or mechanised brigades with over 9,000 tanks, supported by 16,600 fighters, fighter-bombers, and twin-engined bombers, whilst behind the front the effort put into training, organisation, and industrial production in 1943 was kept up at the same rate in 1944. It should also be emphasised that the Red

Army's conduct of operations was now more relaxed. A judicious series of promotions had brought to the top of the major units many exceptionally able commanders. Stalin and *Stavka* allowed them an easier rein than in the past, whereas their enemy was being deprived of all initiative by the despot of Berchtesgaden.

First offensive: Finland

The first blows of the Soviet summer offensive fell on Finland. As we have seen, thanks to the Swedish Government's action as an intermediary, negotiations were on the point of being concluded between Helsinki and Moscow in the late winter, and the Finns were no longer insisting on the return to the *status quo* of March 1940. The talks fell through, however, because Moscow demanded from this small unhappy country an indemnity of 600 million dollars' worth of raw materials and goods, spread over the next five years.

When spring came, the situation of Finland and her valiant army could hardly give rise to optimism. The defeat

of Field-Marshal von Küchler and the German Army Group "North", driven from the banks of the Neva to those of the Narva, deprived Marshal Mannerheim of any hope of German help in the event of a Soviet offensive.

Mannerheim had therefore divided the bulk of his forces in two: in the isthmus between the Gulf of Finland and Lake Ladoga he had put six divisions, including his 1st Armoured Division, and two brigades, all under III and IV Corps; on the front of the river Svir', which runs from Lake Onega to Lake Ladoga, he had nine divisions and three brigades. This was a lot, to be sure but, Mannerheim wrote:

"A reduction of the troops in East Karelia would, however, constitute a surrender of this strategically valuable area and be a good bargaining-point for the attainment of peace. The disposition of the troops was also based on the not unreasonable hope that the fortifications of the Isthmus would compensate for the weakness of man-power."

The Finnish III and IV Corps could in fact count on three successive lines of fortifications, the first two from 44 to 50 miles long and the third 75 miles.

This was small stuff against the powerful forces massed by the Russians, especially in artillery, for the Leningrad Front, still under the command of General L. A. Govorov. Finnish Intelligence sources revealed that the Russians put some 20 infantry divisions on the Finnish front, together with four armoured brigades, five or six tank regiments, and four regiments of assault guns, that is some 450 armoured vehicles in all, and about 1,000 aircraft. For their part the official Soviet sources give no figures, so that we are inclined to believe the Finns. Silence implies consent.

Karelia overrun

On June 9 the Leningrad Front went over to the attack, with an artillery barrage of up to 250 guns per mile. Lieutenant-General D. N. Gussev and his 21st Army had been given the main task and this developed over a ten-mile front along the coastal sector, which allowed the Red Navy's Baltic Fleet to take part under the command of Admiral V. F. Tributs.

Mannerheim wrote: "June 10th may

△ ◁ *Russian 122-mm howitzers in action. The 122-mm howitzer, an excellent weapon, was introduced in 1938, and could fire a 48-lb shell up to 12,900 yards. At a weight of only 2.2 tons, the weapon was easy to move, clearly a factor of considerable importance in the swift Russian advances in the second half of the war.*
◁ ◁ *Improvised observation post in the forests of Karelia.*
△ *The standard but effective Russian pattern of assault: tanks and infantry.*
◁ *A Soviet mortar crew provides front line punch.*

The Russian Yakovlev Yak-1 fighter and fighter-bomber

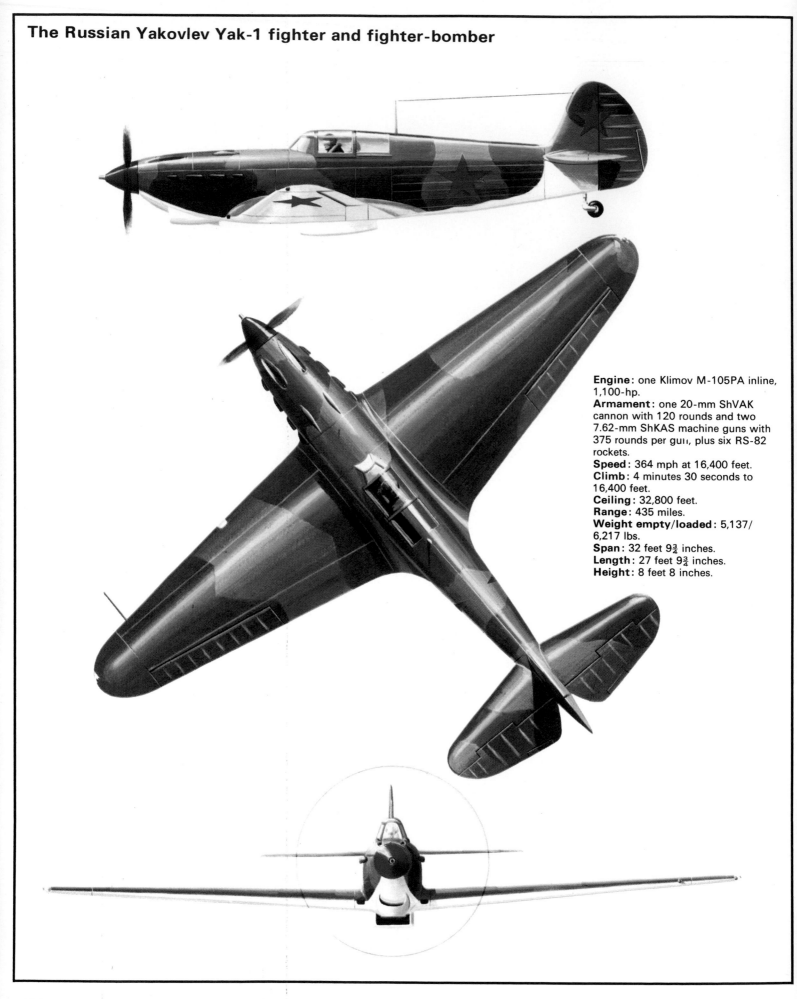

Engine: one Klimov M-105PA inline, 1,100-hp.
Armament: one 20-mm ShVAK cannon with 120 rounds and two 7.62-mm ShKAS machine guns with 375 rounds per gun, plus six RS-82 rockets.
Speed: 364 mph at 16,400 feet.
Climb: 4 minutes 30 seconds to 16,400 feet.
Ceiling: 32,800 feet.
Range: 435 miles.
Weight empty/loaded: 5,137/6,217 lbs.
Span: 32 feet 9¾ inches.
Length: 27 feet 9¾ inches.
Height: 8 feet 8 inches.

The Russian Petlyakov Pe-8 heavy bomber

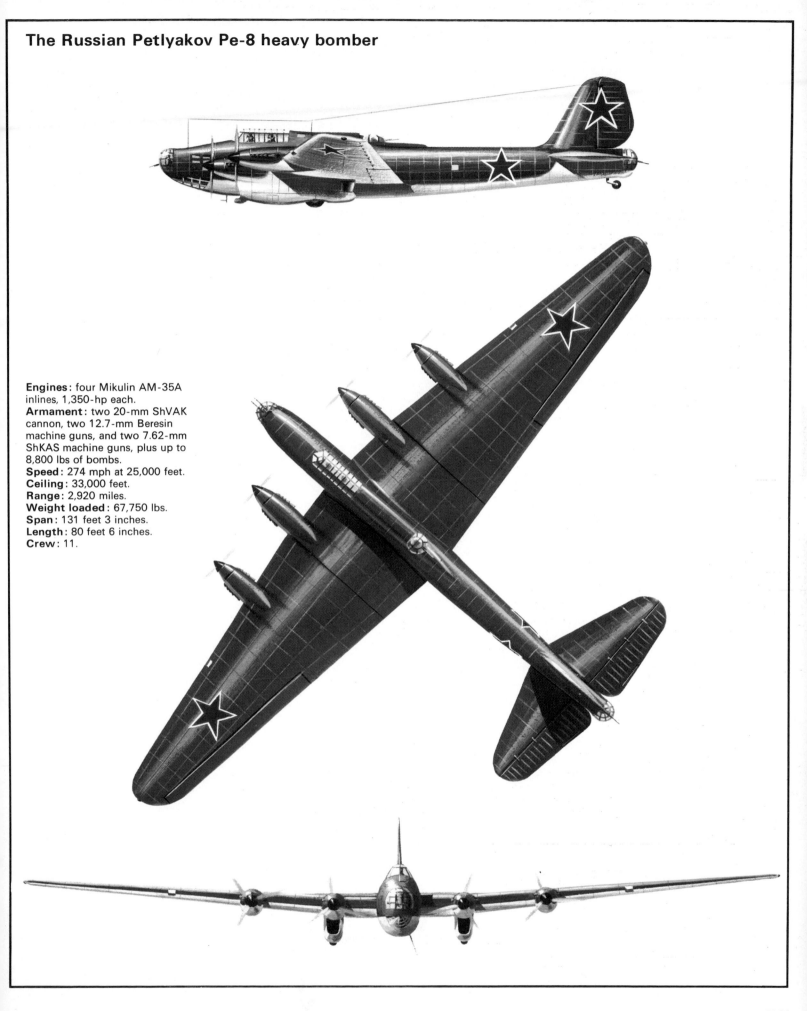

Engines: four Mikulin AM-35A inlines, 1,350-hp each.
Armament: two 20-mm ShVAK cannon, two 12.7-mm Beresin machine guns, and two 7.62-mm ShKAS machine guns, plus up to 8,800 lbs of bombs.
Speed: 274 mph at 25,000 feet.
Ceiling: 33,000 feet.
Range: 2,920 miles.
Weight loaded: 67,750 lbs.
Span: 131 feet 3 inches.
Length: 80 feet 6 inches.
Crew: 11.

▷ *Safe from the prying eyes of Axis aircraft: a Russian tank turret dug in as a strongpoint on the Karelian front.*

△ *Women of Petrosavodsk on the Karelian front greet Major-General Kupryanon with light refreshments.*

with reason be described as the black day of our war history. The infantry assault, carried out by three divisions of the Guards against a single Finnish regiment, broke the defence and forced the front in the coastal sector back about six miles. Furious fighting raged at a number of holding lines, but the on-storming massed armour broke their resistance.

"Because of the enemy's rapid advance, the 10th Division fighting on the coast sector lost most of its artillery. On June 11th, its cut-up units were withdrawn behind the V.T. (Vammelsuu-Taipale) position to be brought up to strength."

But hardly had the defenders of the isthmus taken up their positions than they were driven back by an attack which broke through north of the Leningrad–Viipuri (Vyborg) railway. The 1st Armoured Division counter-attacked, but

to no avail. Faced with this rapidly deteriorating situation, Mannerheim left the defence of the isthmus to General Oesch and ordered the evacuation of Karelia. This enabled him to pull out four divisions. Before there could be any reployment in force in the threatened sector, the Russian 21st Army made a fresh breakthrough and seized Viipuri on June 20.

What would have happened to the defence if the armies of the Karelian Front (General K. A. Meretskov) had come into battle on the same day as the Leningrad Front and had trapped the Finnish V and VI Corps between Lakes Ladoga and Onega? For unknown reasons the Russians only started their attack five or six days after Mannerheim had ordered the defenders to break off contact.

The Russian offensive in eastern Karelia took the form of a pincer movement. One army crossed the Svir' and pushed northwards to meet the other which, having forced the Masselskaya defile, exploited this success southwards. But the pincers closed on a vacuum and at the beginning of July the Finns, though reduced to four divisions, had nevertheless succeeded in re-establishing their positions on a pre-arranged line from Lake Ladoga on their right to Lake Loymola on their left, some 45 miles from the present Soviet-Finnish frontier.

Between Lake Ladoga and the Gulf of Finland, Govorov had a few more successes, in particular establishing a bridgehead on the north bank of the Vuoksa, along which ran the third defen-

sive position between Viipuri and Taipale. But finally everything quietened down and about July 15 General Oesch was able to state that the enemy forces opposite him were considerably thinner on the ground.

It would certainly be absurd to deny that the Red Army had won. The Finns had been driven back to their last line of defence and had lost the Karelia area, which they had intended to use as a counter in the forthcoming peace negotiations. The Soviet Union had also got the use of the Leningrad–Murmansk railway and canal which the Finns had begun in 1941.

In spite of the defeat, however, the fighting spirit of the Finnish Army lived on. It counter-attacked incessantly and in the whole campaign very few Finns were taken prisoners. On balance Moscow seems to have realised that to wipe out the Finnish Army would have cost more than the literal submission of Helsinki to the March 1940 conditions was worth.

Time to get out

As we can see, Mannerheim had played the cards of dissuasion well. But, like his government, he agreed that the time had come for Finland to get out of the war. During the battle, instead of the six divisions for which he had asked O.K.H., he had got only one, the 129th, and a brigade of 80 assault guns. All the assurances, intermingled with threats,

proffered by Ribbentrop to President Ryti could not make up the difference. The day after Viipuri fell, and with it Finland's hopes, the Wehrmacht was suffering in Russia one of the bloodiest defeats in the history of the German Army, including Jena and Stalingrad.

On June 28, when he rejoined the German 20th Army fighting north of the Arctic Circle, Colonel-General Rendulic wrote of the impression Mannerheim made on him at their first meeting: "In spite of the prudence which he continually showed in official declarations, his words had an unmistakably pessimistic ring." This goes to show that the 76-year old Marshal saw further than Rendulic.

△ *Russian troops in "liberated" Viipuri.*

▽ *Soviet troops move up towards the front through Viipuri. Note the large number of anti-tank rifles in evidence.*

Second offensive: Polotsk and the Pripet

On June 22, 1944, as if to celebrate the third anniversary of the German aggression, Stalin opened his last great summer offensive between the Polotsk area and the north bank of the Pripet. This brought into action Bagramyan's 1st Baltic Front, Chernyakhovsky's 3rd Belorussian Front, Zakharov's 2nd Belorussian Front, and Rokossovsky's 1st Belorussian Front.

According to the *Great Patriotic War,* which we quote in Alexander Werth's version, the following were engaged in this offensive, including reserves: 166 infantry divisions, 31,000 guns and mortars, 5,200 tanks and self-propelled guns, and 6,000 aircraft. The Red Army had never before achieved such a concentration of force or had such huge quantities of supporting *matériel,* which included 25,000 two-ton lorries.

Michel Garder gives a lively account of the atmosphere of the Soviet summer offensive in his book *A War Unlike The Others.* He says:

"The patient work of the Red Army's general staff, which had prepared in great detail the grand plan of *Stavka,* resulted in this fantastic cavalcade. This was the true revenge for the summer of 1941! In the burning-hot July sky the Red Air Force was unopposed. White with dust the T-34's drove on westwards, breaking through the hedges, crushing down thickets, spitting out flame . . . with clusters of infantry clinging on to their rear platforms, adventure-bound. Swarms of men on motor-cycles . . . shouting cavalry . . . infantry in lorries . . . rocket-artillery cluttering up the road . . . the tracks . . . the paths . . . mowing down everything in their way.

"This was a long way from the stereotyped image of 'dejected troops herded to slaughter by Jewish political commissars'."

Marshal Vasilevsky had been sent to

Marshal Ivan Danielovich Chernyakhovsky was born in 1908 in the Ukraine, and entered the army via the Artillery Military School. In 1940 he was a captain in an armoured division, and distinguished himself at Yelna and Voronezh. As a brigadier he took Kursk in February 1943 and then held it during *"Zitadelle"*. With further promotion he took Ternopol' in spring 1944 and then received command of the 3rd Belorussian Front. He was killed on February 28, 1945.

Bagramyan and Chernyakhovsky as *Stavka*'s representative to co-ordinate their operations. Zhukov performed the same function with Zakharov and Rokossovsky.

The objective of the Soviet offensive was the destruction of Army Group "Centre", then commanded by Field-Marshal Busch, who in the early days of 1944 had taken over from Kluge at the latter's H.Q. at Minsk. Busch had four armies deployed from north to south as follows:

1. 3rd *Panzerarmee* (Colonel-General Reinhardt)
2. 4th Army (General von Tippelskirch)
3. 9th Army (General Jordan)
4. 2nd Army (Colonel-General Weiss)

By the end of the winter the withdrawals forced upon Army Groups "North" and "South" by the Soviet winter offensives had left Army Group "Centre" in a salient: the fortified area of Vitebsk on the Dvina was two-thirds encircled, whereas south of the Pripet Marshes Rokossovsky had got as far as the approaches to Kovel'. To counteract the threat to Field-Marshal Model's left at the end of March, Busch had been asked to send him eight divisions, including two Panzer.

Russian superiority in tanks and aircraft

When the Soviet summer offensive started, Army Group "Centre" was thus reduced to 37 divisions. On June 22 the 2nd Army was not attacked, and so the initial clash in the battle for Belorussia was between 166 Soviet and 28 German divisions, on a front extending over 435 miles. The Russian divisions each had 10,000 men. Those of Generals Jordan, Tippelskirch, and Reinhardt were very much under-strength, as can be seen in the account given by Major-General Heidkämper, chief-of-staff of the 3rd *Panzerarmee*. He showed that the Vitebsk salient was being held by LIII Corps along a front of 55 miles with the 206th, 4th and 6th Luftwaffe, and 246th Divisions, with 8,123 rifles (about 150 rifles per mile). Reserves consisted of a battalion of heavy artillery, two heavy anti-tank companies, and one Luftwaffe special service battalion.

Colonel-General Reinhardt's VI and IX Corps were no better off, nor were the 4th and 9th Armies. German dispositions between the Pripet and the Dvina were thus as thin as a spider's web.

The mobile reserves which were to slow down then stop the onslaught of 4,500 Soviet tanks consisted of only the 20th Panzer and the 18th, 25th, and 60th *Panzergrenadier* Divisions with 400 tracked vehicles between them. For good measure add the same number of assault guns, and it will be seen that in armour the Germans were outnumbered by 5.6 to 1.

It was the same in the air: *Luftflotte* VI could get only an insignificant number of planes off the ground.

"Fortified areas"

The situation of Army Group "Centre" was such that if the enemy unleashed against it an attack of any strength it

◁ *German artillerymen prepare to reload their gun. Despite all their efforts, however, the out-numbered Germans could not stem the Russian advance.* △ *The proof: German dead in the wake of the 2nd Belorussian Front's triumphant progress.*

could not expect to hold it. Again Hitler was to intervene and make Stalin's task easier. Firstly he laid down, in an order dated March 8, 1944, the building on the Eastern Front of a number of "fortified areas" to take over the rôles of the former fortresses. "Their task," his *Führerbefehl* of that day ordered, "is to prevent the enemy from seizing centres of decisive strategic importance. They are to allow themselves to be encircled so as to engage as many of the enemy as possible. They are to create opportunities for fruitful counter-attacks."

Controlled by an army group or army, the strongpoint garrison had instructions to hold out to the last man and no one except the Führer, acting on information from the army group commander, had the right to order withdrawal.

In the Army Group "Centre" sector nine towns were to be made fortified areas. These included Bobruysk on the Berezina, Mogilev and Orsha on the Dniepr, and Vitebsk on the Dvina. The troops manning these new areas were to be taken from the armies in the field, which their commanders regarded as a heresy.

Reinhardt made repeated objections to Hitler's orders, transmitted to him through Field-Marshal Busch, to shut away LIII

Corps (General Gollwitzer) and three divisions in the so-called "fortified area" of Vitebsk. In the event of an attack in this sector the absence of these units would open up a breach which could not possibly be stopped, and enemy armour would thus pour through. Reinhardt even went to Minsk to state his case and was told sharply on April 21:

"Vitebsk's value is as a fortified area and the Führer will not change this point of view at any price. His opinion is that Vitebsk can engage between 30 and 40 enemy divisions which would otherwise be free to attack west and south west," then: "It is also a matter of prestige. Vitebsk is the only place on the Eastern Front whose loss would resound throughout the world."

Reinhardt was dismissed in these terms; neither Tippelskirch nor Jordan were any better received by Busch. Jordan, who on the following May 20 proposed to Hitler that if it were to appear likely that the Soviets would launch an offensive in Belorussia, the Germans should withdraw to the Dniepr and the Berezina, thus shortening their line from 435 to 280 miles, was summarily dismissed with: "Another of those generals perpetually looking backwards".

△ *The promise that was wearing thin: the German Army staving off the Red flood from Poland's agricultural areas.*
◁ *Albert Speer, wearing an* Organisation *"Todt" brassard, in conversation with Major Dr. Kupfer. Upon Speer's department fell most of the work involved in throwing up Germany's eastern ramparts.*
Overleaf:
Left *How Kukryniksy saw Nazi militarism: surveying its options from a mound of skulls.*
Top right *Russian infantry double over a pontoon bridge across the River Bug, another major river barrier overcome.*
Centre right *Germans struggle to extricate a sidecar combination during the retreat from Vitebsk.*
Bottom right *The same problem for horsed transport.*

Hitler misunderstands Soviet intentions

It is true that the Führer did not consider that Army Group "Centre" would be the immediate objective of the offensive which, he admitted, the enemy would launch as soon as the ground was sufficiently hard again. In all evidence it was Army Groups "North Ukraine" and "South Ukraine" which were threatened, as Stalin clearly had his eyes fixed on the Rumanian capital and the Ploieşti oil-fields, then the Balkan peninsula and the Turkish narrows, the age-old goal of Imperial Russia, not to mention Budapest and the rich Hungarian plains.

From early June onwards reports from the front, based on direct information, on aerial reconnaissance by the Luftwaffe, on the interception and analysis of radio messages, and on the interrogation of prisoners and deserters, all seemed to indicate the progressive build-up of a powerful assault force between the Pripet and the Dvina. In particular the Red Air Force was growing steadily in numbers every day. When Major-General Gehlen, head of Section East of O.K.H. Intelligence, told Hitler about all this, the Führer retorted that it was merely a clumsy decoy movement. Stalin wanted the Germans to bring over from Moldavia to Belorussia the forces they were holding opposite the true centre of gravity of Russian strategy, but Hitler was not going to fall into that trap.

This opinion was so fixed in his mind that during the night of June 24–25 he obstinately refused to yield to the despair of his closest collaborators, who entreated him to agree to the measures which had become necessary consequent upon the collapse of the 3rd *Panzerarmee* in the Vitebsk sector, whilst at the confluence

of the Dniepr and the Berezina the 9th Army had reached the limits of endurance under ever increasing attacks. There was an eye-witness to these events.

Colonel-General Dr. Lothar Rendulic was at the Berghof that evening, having been summoned there urgently to be given command of the German 20th Army (Lappland) after the accidental death of Colonel-General Dietl. In his memoirs Rendulic says:

"Hitler thought that the main Soviet effort was developing in the south and considered that these Russian attacks east of Warsaw were mere demonstrations. It was a notable miscalculation, as events were to show. He forbade any reserves to be taken from the south and moved to Warsaw. I can say here that when I came out of the conference I asked Colonel-General Jodl how he could let this appreciation of the situation go unchallenged. He replied: 'We fought the Führer for two whole days, then when he ran out of arguments he said: "Leave me. I am relying on my intuition." What can you do in a situation like that?'"

The offensive begins

During the night of June 19–20 the 240,000 partisans who controlled the forests in Belorussia cut the lines of communication of Army Group "Centre" in more than 10,000 places as far west as

▷ *A nurse examines a wounded Russian soldier somewhere in the 2nd Belorussian Front's sector.*
▽ *The Russian advance rolls on.*

Minsk. At dawn on the 22nd the forces of the 1st Baltic and the 3rd Belorussian Fronts went over to the attack on both sides of Vitebsk. The 1st Belorussian Front went into action on the following day. Generals Bagramyan and Chernyakhovsky had been given as their first objective the capture of Vitebsk by a pincer movement, which would give their comrade Rokossovsky the time to pierce the German 9th Army's positions in the area of Bobruysk. When both these results had been achieved the two Belorussian Fronts would let loose their armoured formations, which would converge in the direction of Minsk. A second pincer would thus be formed and this would crush Army Group "Centre". Bagramyan and Chernyakhovsky took just 48 hours to overpower the resistance of the 3rd *Panzerarmee* north-west and south-east of Vitebsk. During this brief spell the German commander also used up his meagre reserves as well as the 14th Division, sent to him by Busch as a reinforcement. Busch could ill afford the loss. In particular the German right wing, which consisted of VI Corps (General Pfeiffer, killed in this action), collapsed completely under the impact of the Soviet 5th Army and four armoured brigades, whose attack was preceded and supported by V Artillery Corps (520

◁ *The inhabitants of the Minsk area left behind by the Germans greet the liberating Russian forces.*
▽ *Ground crew at work on Lavochkin fighters on a forward airfield. Note the Russian-built "Dakota" landing. By 1944 the Red Air Force's disasters of 1941 and 1942 were no more than evil memories. Its squadrons now had good equipment and enjoyed total superiority over the Luftwaffe.*

heavy guns) and tactical air formations acting with a strength, a spirit, and an accuracy hitherto unknown on the Eastern Front.

No retreat from Vitebsk

At 1520 hours on June 24 Zeitzler called Reinhardt from the Berghof to ask if he considered the mission assigned to him at the fortified area of Vitebsk to be vital. The army commander, according to his chief-of-staff, replied candidly that "LIII Corps was surrounded, though still only

ВСТРЕЧАЙ
самолеты врага
ЛИВНЕМ ОГНЯ С ЗЕМЛИ!

weakly; that this was the moment to order him to try to break out; that every quarter of an hour the Russian ring to the west of Vitebsk was thickening."

When Zeitzler remarked that the Führer feared heavy losses in supplies of all kinds if the fortified area were to be abandoned hastily, Reinhardt burst out: "If the ring closes we shall lose not only supplies and ammunition, but the whole of LIII Corps with its five divisions." As usual nothing came of these remonstrations, for at 1528 hours Zeitzler came back from seeing Hitler and informed Reinhardt: "The Führer has decided that Vitebsk will be held." According to Major-General Heidkämper, Reinhardt stood "petrified" at the news.

At 1830 hours, however, the incompetent despot agreed to some relaxation of this grotesque order and signalled 3rd *Panzerarmee:* "LIII Corps will leave one division to garrison Vitebsk and break out westwards to rejoin our lines. Report name of commander of this division. Swear him in by radio as new commander of 'Vitebsk fortified area'. Make him confirm his oath."

This order was no less absurd than the one which went before it. The 206th Division (Lieutenant-General Hitter) was nominated. To this unit alone was entrusted the defence of positions prepared for four divisions. And it was too late. LIII Corps was intercepted and crushed during its retreat and when its commander, General Gollwitzer, surrendered to the

Russians on June 27 he had only 200 of his men with him and of these 180 were wounded. The worst had happened: the destruction of Vitebsk opened a breach in the German line more than 28 miles wide. Reinhardt was now reduced to three worn-out divisions and 70 guns. Nothing and nobody could now stop the thrustful Chernyakhovsky from driving on along the Lepel'–Minsk axis with the 5th Guards Army under Marshal of Armoured Forces Pavel A. Rotmistrov.

Rokossovsky takes Bobruysk

Further south on the Belorussian front, the same causes could only produce the same effects and General Jordan, C.-in-C. 9th Army, was no luckier than Reinhardt; XXXV Corps, defending the fortified area of Bobruysk with four divisions, suffered the same fate as LIII Corps. When he opened his offensive on June 24, General Rokossovsky had taken good care not to launch his 1st Belorussian Front forces against the German fortified areas, but to push them into gaps north and south of the River Berezina. Three days of hard fighting brought him victory. South of Bobruysk he overcame XLI Panzer Corps (Lieutenant-General Hoffmeister) and cut off the retreating XXXV Corps (Lieutenant-General von Lützow), leaving

it trapped in the fortified area.

On June 29 16,000 Germans emerged from the pocket and gave themselves up, leaving behind them the bodies of 18,000 of their comrades. By now the mounted, motorised, mechanised, and armoured forces of General Pliev, one of the most brilliant cavalry commanders of the war, had reached Ossipovichi, some eight miles south-east of Minsk, and were rumbling forward to meet the 5th Guards Tank Army, which had passed Lepel' and was now in Borisov.

The situation of the German 4th Army, now at grips with greatly superior forces on the 2nd Belorussian Front, was scarcely any better. Faced with disasters on his right and left, General von Tippelskirch, now in command *vice* Colonel-General Heinrici, had to use all his initiative to get his army out of its positions along the River Proina and back to the Dniepr. The fortified areas of Mogilev and Orsha on the Dniepr, however, were soon overcome by Zakharov and Chernyakhovsky, and became the graveyards respectively of the 6th (Lieutenant-General Henie) and the 12th (Lieutenant-General Wagner) Divisions.

Tippelskirch thus had to continue his retreat westwards across rough forest land infested with marches and, particularly, thick with partisans. It is no wonder that, as planned by *Stavka,* Rotmistrov and Pliev got to Minsk before him on July 3, joining forces behind his back and condemning his XII and XXVII

The German Messerschmitt Bf 109G-6 fighter

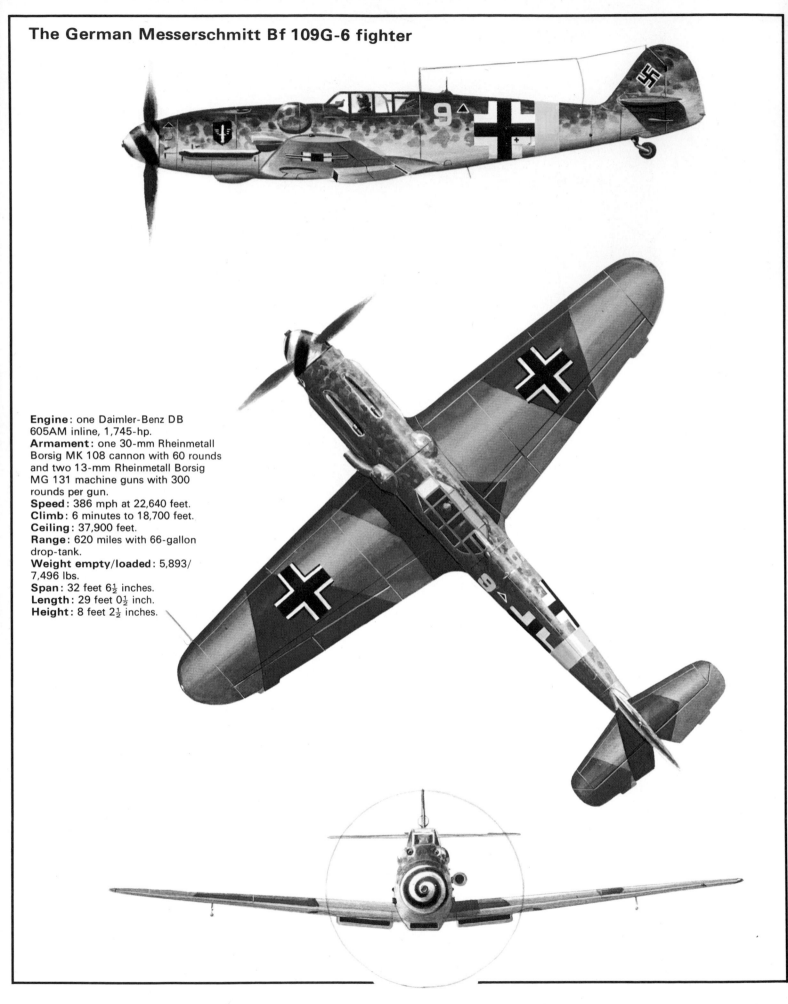

Engine: one Daimler-Benz DB 605AM inline, 1,745-hp.
Armament: one 30-mm Rheinmetall Borsig MK 108 cannon with 60 rounds and two 13-mm Rheinmetall Borsig MG 131 machine guns with 300 rounds per gun.
Speed: 386 mph at 22,640 feet.
Climb: 6 minutes to 18,700 feet.
Ceiling: 37,900 feet.
Range: 620 miles with 66-gallon drop-tank.
Weight empty/loaded: 5,893/ 7,496 lbs.
Span: 32 feet 6½ inches.
Length: 29 feet 0½ inch.
Height: 8 feet 2½ inches.

The Russian Yakovlev Yak-9D fighter

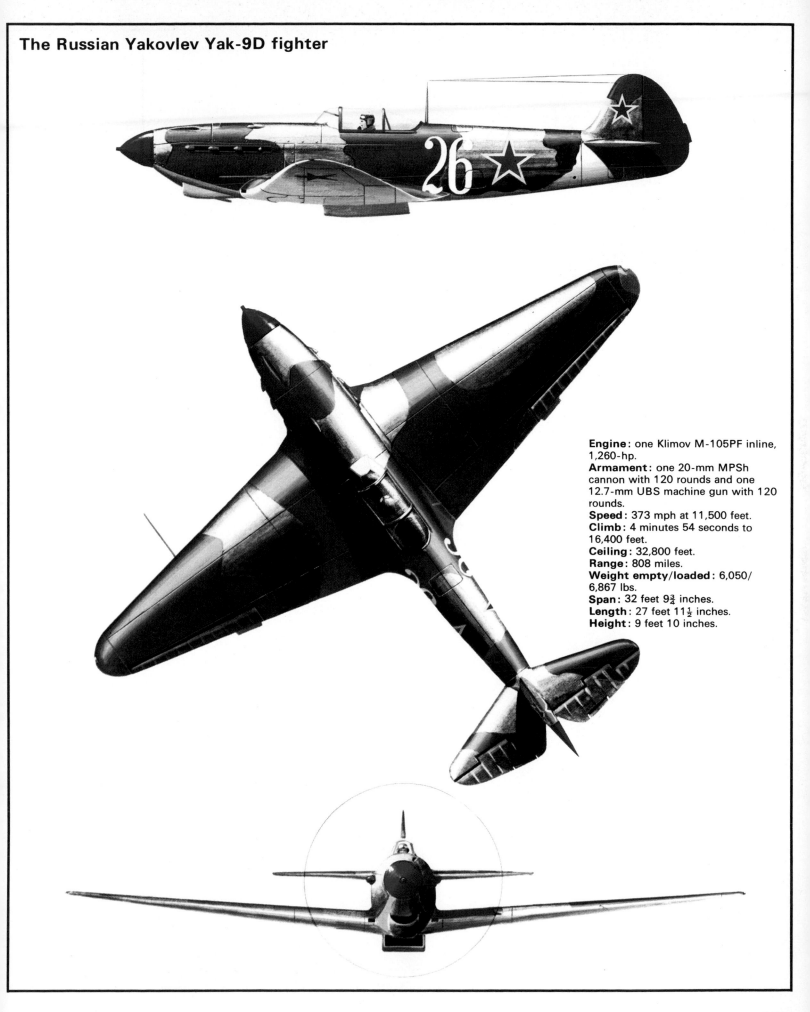

Engine: one Klimov M-105PF inline, 1,260-hp.
Armament: one 20-mm MPSh cannon with 120 rounds and one 12.7-mm UBS machine gun with 120 rounds.
Speed: 373 mph at 11,500 feet.
Climb: 4 minutes 54 seconds to 16,400 feet.
Ceiling: 32,800 feet.
Range: 808 miles.
Weight empty/loaded: 6,050/6,867 lbs.
Span: 32 feet 9¾ inches.
Length: 27 feet 11½ inches.
Height: 9 feet 10 inches.

△ *German self-propelled guns,
guarded by Panzers, prepares to
meet the next Russian thrust.*

▽ *The Russian assault moves
into a German-held village.*

Corps and XXXIX Panzer Corps (respectively under Generals Vincenz Müller, Voelkers, Martinek) to the sad fate of "moving pockets".

A defeat worse than Stalingrad

It was June 28 before Hitler finally admitted that the Belorussian offensive was something more than a diversion. On that day he sacked General Busch, who had obeyed his directives unquestioningly, and replaced him by Field-Marshal Model, who strove to limit the extent of the disaster. Army Group "North", though now uncovered on its right flank by the defeat of the 3rd *Panzerarmee,* was required to give up three divisions. Ten more, including four Panzer, were taken from Army Group "North Ukraine". These units were sent to the Belorussian front in the hope of an attack on the flank of Rokossovsky, who was now exploiting his victory along the line Minsk – Baranovichi – Brest-Litovsk. The breach now open between the Pripet and the Dvina was some 185 miles wide and, according to the O.K.H., this was swallowing up 126 infantry divisions and no fewer than 62 armoured or

△ *The inevitable victims: a German armoured column destroyed by Russian artillery and aircraft.*

▷ *German prisoners walk back to a collection point in the rear, past a less fortunate compatriot.*
▽ *A German soldier lies by an abandoned* leichte Feldhaubitze *18/40 of 10.5-cm calibre.*
△▷ *Civilians freed from a Nazi camp near Minsk begin their journey home.*
▽▷ *Some of the 57,600 German prisoners taken by the Belorussian Fronts wait to be paraded through Moscow.*

mechanised brigades with at least 2,500 tanks. On July 8 the last "moving pocket" surrendered behind the Russian lines with 17,000 men, having run out of ammunition. Out of 37 divisions in Army Group "Centre" on the previous June 22, 28 had been badly mauled, if not actually cut to pieces, and an enormous mass of *matériel,* including 215 tanks and more than 1,300 guns, had been captured.

According to statistics from Moscow, which appear reliable, the Germans lost between these two dates some 285,000 dead and prisoners, including 19 corps and divisional commanders. The Belorussian disaster was thus worse than Stalingrad and all the more so since, when Paulus resigned himself to the inevitable, the "Second Front" was still only a distant threat to the Third Reich.

Stalin celebrated in true Roman style by marching seemingly endless columns of 57,600 prisoners-of-war through the streets of Moscow with their generals at the head. Alexander Werth, the *Sunday Times* correspondent, was there and he described the behaviour of the Russian crowd as the men passed by:

"Youngsters booed and whistled, and even threw things at the Germans, only to be immediately restrained by the adults; men looked on grimly and in silence; but many women, especially elderly women, were full of commiseration (some even had tears in their eyes) as they looked at these bedraggled 'Fritzes'. I remember one old woman murmuring 'just like our poor boys . . . tozhe pognali ne voinu (also driven into war)'."

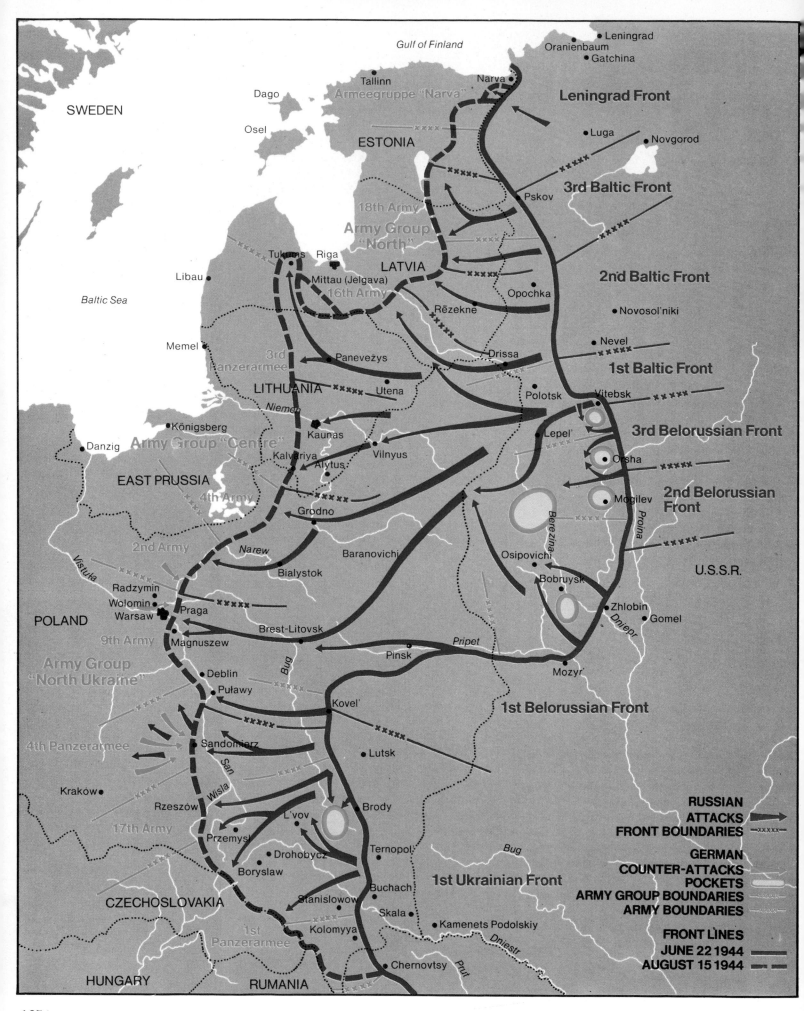

SWEDEN

Gulf of Finland

Leningrad
Oranienbaum
Gatchina

Dago

Tallinn

Narva

Leningrad Front

Osel

Armeegruppe "Narva"

ESTONIA

Luga

Novgorod

Pskov

3rd Baltic Front

18th Army

Army Group
"North"

Tukums

Riga

LATVIA

2nd Baltic Front

Libau

Mittau (Jelgava)

16th Army

Rēzekne

Opochka

Novosol'niki

Baltic Sea

Drissa

Nevel

1st Baltic Front

Memel

3rd
Panzerarmee

Panevežys

Polotsk

Vitebsk

Lithuania

Utena

Lepel'

3rd Belorussian Front

Königsberg

Army Group "Centre"

Kaunas

Orsha

Danzig

Vilnyus

Mogilev

**2nd Belorussian
Front**

EAST PRUSSIA

Kalvariya

Alytus

4th Army

Berezina

Proina

Grodno

Osipovichi

2nd Army

Narew

Baranovichi

U.S.S.R.

Vistula

Bialystok

Bobruysk

Radzymin

Wolomin
Warsaw

Praga

Zhlobin

Gomel

POLAND

9th Army

Brest-Litovsk

Dniepr

Magnuszew

Pripet

Pinsk

Army Group
"North Ukraine"

Deblin

Bug

Mozyr'

Puławy

1st Belorussian Front

Kovel'

4th Panzerarmee

Sandomierz

Lutsk

San

Kraków

Brody

Wisła

Rzeszów

L'vov

17th Army

Przemysl

Ternopol

Bug

Drohobycz

Buchach

1st Ukrainian Front

Boryslaw

CZECHOSLOVAKIA

Stanislowow

Skala

Kamenets Podolskiy

Kolomyya

Dniestr

1st
Panzerarmee

Prut

HUNGARY

RUMANIA

Chernovtsy

**RUSSIAN
ATTACKS** ——→
FRONT BOUNDARIES --xxxxx--

**GERMAN
COUNTER-ATTACKS**
POCKETS
ARMY GROUP BOUNDARIES
ARMY BOUNDARIES

**FRONT LINES
JUNE 22 1944** ——
AUGUST 15 1944 – – –

CHAPTER 120
On to the Vistula

Stalin gave Bagramyan, Chernyakhovsky, Zakharov, and Rokossovsky the job of exploiting as deeply and as fast as possible the victory at Minsk, the extent of which, thanks to Hitler, seems to have exceeded even *Stavka*'s highest hopes.

Under the terms of the new directives, the forces of the 1st Baltic Front were given as their objective the Gulf of Riga, whilst the three Belorussian Fronts would move first on to the line Kaunas–Grodno–Brest-Litovsk, then force their way across the Niemen and the Bug, as they had done over the Dniepr and the Berezina. Colonel-General Chernyakhovsky would then take on the defences of eastern Prussia, whilst Zakharov and Rokossovsky (the latter just having been promoted Marshal of the U.S.S.R.) would invade Poland.

For three weeks the victors of Minsk covered their ten to fifteen miles a day, by-passing without much difficulty at first the units which Field-Marshal Model, like General Weygand after June 11, 1940, threw in piecemeal to stop the gaps. Model, the new C.-in-C. Army Group "Centre", now had the job of holding back the enemy long enough for O.K.H. to regroup its forces and to reform the

indispensable continuous front. He was more highly regarded by Hitler than his unfortunate predecessor, and was thus able to obtain in time permission to evacuate a whole series of so-called "fortified areas" which otherwise would have become so many death-traps for the army's divisions. This meant, of course, considerable sacrifices of territory:

July 13: Chernyakhovsky takes Vilnyus;
July 14: Rokossovsky envelops Pinsk, on the Pripet;
July 15: Chernyakhovsky forces the Niemen at Alytus, while Zakharov takes Grodno;
July 18: Rokossovsky crosses the Russo-Polish frontier fixed at Teheran;
July 23: Rokossovsky's advance guard enters Lublin;
July 27: Zakharov breaks through the defences of Białystok;
July 28: Rokossovsky takes Brest-Litovsk;
July 31: Rokossovsky enters Praga, across the Vistula from Warsaw;
August 1: Chernyakhovsky reaches Kalvariya, 15 miles from the Prussian frontier; and
August 2: Chernyakhovsky takes Kaunas.

On Chernyakhovsky's right, General Bagramyan and the armies of the 1st

▽ *A wounded German officer awaits transport at a dressing station on the Eastern Front. The label gives details of the wound and treatment he has received. The war in Russia had drained Germany of many of its older experienced soldiers, and they were now being replaced by new recruits unversed in battle craft and the skills of survival.*

△ *Soviet troops in position with a 45-mm anti-tank gun.*
▷ *In liberated Vilnyus Russian officers pass a rather more potent tank killer: an 8.8-cm Flak gun and a Volkswagen* Kübelwagen *captured from the Germans.*

▽ *A Russian junior lieutenant with his sergeant check their map during a reconnaissance in a forward position.*

Baltic Front poured through the breaches in the inner flanks of Army Groups "North" and "Centre" caused by the Vitebsk catastrophe. Whilst the means were lacking to stop the enemy's advance towards Riga, was it advisable to keep the German 16th and 18th Armies on the Polotsk–Pskov–Lake Peipus line, which they had been holding since their painful retreat of the preceding winter? Colonel-General Lindemann, C.-in-C. Army Group "North", concluded that it was not and advised the withdrawal of his forces on the left bank of the Dvina. He was also being asked to transfer certain of his units to Army Group "Centre", which strengthened his point of view.

But to abandon Estonia might risk the "defection" of Finland, as O.K.W. put it. And so on July 2 Hitler relieved Lindemann of his command and handed it over to General Friessner, who in February 1944 had distinguished himself as commander of *Armeegruppe* "Narva". This change of personnel did nothing to improve the strategic situation.

On July 11 Bagramyan crossed the Dvina at Drissa and further to the left his advance guard reached Utena in Lithuania. On the following day the 2nd Baltic Front (General A. I. Eremenko) came into the battle and, breaking out from the area of Novosol'niki, drove deep into the positions of the German 16th Army (General Loch).

Caught up in front by Eremenko and behind by Bagramyan, the latter threatening his communications, Friessner, who had had to give up 12 divisions to Model, could only come to the same conclusions on July 12 as his predecessor had done. But, faced with the same refusal from Hitler to meet the situation with common sense, he did not hesitate, at the end of his letter dated that day, to stake his command:

"If, *mein Führer,*" he wrote, "you are not prepared to accept my idea and give me the liberty of action necessary to carry out the measures proposed above, I shall be compelled to ask you to relieve me of the responsibilities I have assumed so far." Summoned by return of post to Rastenburg, Friessner upheld his view in the presence of the Führer, who reproached him for having used threats and for having shown an unmilitary attitude throughout. Reminding Hitler that he was responsible for some 700,000 men, and that he was fighting at the relative strength of one to eight, according to the account he has left of this interview he went so far as to say:

"I am not trying to hang on to my job. You can relieve me of it. You can even have me shot if you want to. But to ask me, *in full knowledge of the facts and against the dictates of my conscience*, to lead the men entrusted to me *to certain destruction*–that you can never do."

Hitler, with tears in his eyes, is thereupon supposed to have seized General Friessner's hand and promised him every support. But the facts are that each one stuck to his own position. And so Colonel-General Schörner, C.-in-C. Army Group "South Ukraine", was ordered on July 23 to change places immediately with Friessner, C.-in-C. Army Group "North", who was himself promoted to Colonel-General.

Army Group "North" cut off

Amongst the general officers of the Wehrmacht, Schörner was one of the few who was unswerving in his loyalty to the Führer. However great his National Socialist zeal, however, it was not in his power to satisfy Hitler, for the 3rd Baltic Front (General Maslennikov) now went over to the offensive and extended the battle further northwards. This was followed on July 25 by an attack by the Leningrad Front (Marshal of the U.S.S.R. L. A. Govorov). In all a dozen armies totalling at least 80 divisions took part in this concentric offensive.

▽ *Soviet 76-mm guns on the 2nd Belorussian Front. With a range of over 12,000 yards these guns were the backbone of Soviet field artillery. The heavy losses suffered at the beginning of "Barbarossa" allowed the Russians to start from scratch with the reorganisation and standardisation of their artillery, some of which dated back to before World War I.*

Whilst Govorov was breaking through the Narva defile and Maslennikov, after liberating Pskov on July 21, was also driving on into Estonia, on July 26 Eremenko, anchoring his left flank on the Dvina, captured the towns of Rēzekne (Rositten) and Dvinsk (Daugav'pils) in Latvia. Bagramyan, who was using what Hitler called the "hole in the Wehrmacht", or the still gaping breach between the right and left of Army Groups "North" and "Centre", changed direction from west to north-west and, driving through Panevežys, Jelgava (Mittau), and Tukums, reached the Gulf of Riga to the west of the great Latvian port in the evening of August 1. As Generals Lindemann and Friessner had never ceased to predict, Army Group "North", with some 30 divisions, was cut off in Estonia and northern Latvia. More fortunate than Paulus at Stalingrad, however, Schörner could confidently rely on the Baltic for supplies and evacuation, since the Gulf of Finland was blocked right across so that Soviet submarines could not operate in the open sea. In the Gulf of Riga his right flank was efficiently supported by the guns of the German fleet - by the very warships which Hitler had wanted to scrap in 1943.

Konev attacks

On the German side of the immense front line stretching from the Baltic to the Carpathians, the second fortnight in July brought defeat to Army Group "North Ukraine". This added further disaster to the crushing of Army Group "Centre", the last consequences of which were still far from being played out. The tension was such that, taking also into account the American breakthrough in Normandy, it might have been thought that the last hour had struck for the Wehrmacht and for Greater Germany's Third Reich. This was how Marshal Rokossovsky saw events when he stated to a correspondent of the British *Exchange Telegraph* on July 26:

"It is no longer important to capture such and such a position. The essential thing is to give the enemy no respite. The Germans are running to their deaths . . . Their troops have lost all contact with their command."

On the following day a spokesman of *Stavka* spoke in the same terms at a press conference: "The Führer's G.H.Q. will no more be able to hold the line of the Vistula than it did those of the Bug and the San. The German Army is irremediably beaten and breaking up."

Also on July 13 Marshal Konev and the forces of the 1st Ukrainian Front had come into the battle, extending the action of the three Belorussian Fronts from the area of Kovel' to the left bank of the Dniestr. According to the Soviet military historian Boris S. Telpukhovsky, whose account we have no reason to doubt, Konev had been given by *Stavka* all the necessary men and *matériel* to secure an easy victory over Army Group "North Ukraine", which was still, together with Army Group "Centre", under the command of Model. For this assault Konev had 16,213 guns and rocket-launchers, 1,573 tanks, 463 assault guns, 3,240 aircraft, and no fewer than seven armies, including the 1st and 3rd Guards Tank Armies and the 4th Tank Army, commanded respectively by Generals M. E. Katukov, P. S. Rybalko, and D. D. Lelyushenko, all three very experienced tank commanders.

On the German side, Army Group "North Ukraine" had had to give up to Army Group "Centre" four Panzer and three infantry divisions since June 22 and was reduced to 43 divisions (of which five were Panzer and one *Panzergrenadier*) and two mountain brigades. Assuming that between April and June the German armoured divisions had been brought up to their normal strength of 160 fighting and command tanks which, knowing the aberrations of Adolf Hitler, seems highly unlikely, the Russians outnumbered them by two to one. In the air Russian superiority was of the order of five to one. Hence the disaster which befell 8th Panzer Division on July 14. Disregarding orders, it took the main road to Brody to speed up its counter-attack. Major-General von Mellenthin writes:

"Eighth Panzer was caught on the move by Russian aircraft and suffered devastating losses. Long columns of tanks and lorries went up in flames, and all hope of counterattack disappeared."

Marshal Konev had forces so powerful and so numerous at his command that he could give his offensive two centres of gravity. On the right, in the area southwest of Lutsk, a first group containing notably the 1st Guards Tank Army, was to break up the 4th *Panzerarmee* (General Harpe) then exploit its victory in a general south-west direction. On the

◄ ◄ *The crew of a 15-cm gun proceeds with routine maintenance while their comrades lend a hand with the ploughing.*
△ *Rokossovsky: "It is no longer important to capture such and such a position. The essential thing is to give the enemy no respite. The Germans are running to their deaths . . ."*

△ *Schörner, one of Hitler's most fanatically loyal generals – he, too, was given the impossible task of plugging the vast breaches torn open in the German front.*

△ *Illusion. "The Führer is saved!" "Then the secret weapon's failed." (From* Götenborg Hand Tidning).

△ Detroit Star's *cartoonist Burch neatly sums up Hitler's unenviable position: "Between two fires".*

▽ *From Moscow's* Krokodil. *The "Hitlerite hordes" dash themselves to ruin against the rock of the Red Army.*

left a second group, containing the 3rd Guards Tank Army and the 4th Tank Army, had concentrated in the area of Ternopol': attacking due west it was to engage the 1st *Panzerarmee* (Colonel-General Raus) and form a pincer with the first group.

Model retreats

By evening on D-day the German defences in the two sectors were already seriously damaged. On the following day Colonel-General Raus put the 1st and 8th Panzer Divisions under XLVIII Panzer Corps for an eventual counter-attack, but this failed as a result of the circumstances described above by Mellenthin. Twenty-four hours later not only had the Russians broken through at the points previously designated by Konev, but the pincers had closed on General Hauffe's XIII Corps between L'vov and Brody.

And so a new "moving pocket" was formed, from which several thousand men managed to escape during a night-attack of hand-to-hand fighting. On July 23, however, General Hauffe had been taken prisoner together with 17,000 men of his corps and the victors counted 30,000 German corpses on the battlefield.

In the German sectors facing Rokossovsky and Konev, it was Model's intention to re-establish his line along the Bug. This evidently over-optimistic plan came to nothing in view of the weakness of Army Group "Centre" and the recent defeat of Army Group "North Ukraine". Worse still, the breach between the right flank of the 4th *Panzerarmee* and the left flank of the 1st was now wide open and there was the great danger that the latter's communications with Kraków would be cut and that the army would be driven back against the Carpathians. Hence, in full agreement with Colonel-General Guderian, who had succeeded Zeitzler as Chief-of-Staff at O.K.H. after the attempt on Hitler's life on July 20, Model drew back to the line of the Vistula and its extension the San above Deblin.

Even if the Germans, after their defeats of June 22 and July 13, had managed to establish a front line behind these ditches, this last-minute attempt could not have saved the Polish oilwells at Drogobycz and Boryslaw which became a heavy and irreparable loss to the military economy of the Third Reich. The situation between the Narew and the Carpathians was now deteriorating so rapidly that O.K.H. had to draw on the strength of Army Group "South Ukraine" and send four Panzer and seven infantry divisions from Molda via to Galicia.

The Russians reach the Vistula

Before these reinforcements could be put to use, Marshals Rokossovsky and Konev had reached the Vistula and the San at Blitzkrieg speed, mopping up German columns retreating on foot or in horse-drawn vehicles. Between July 28 and 31, tanks of the 1st Belorussian Front covered the 120 miles between Brest-Litovsk and the suburbs of Warsaw. They also crossed the Vistula at Magnuszew and Pulawy, upstream from the capital. Rokossovsky's optimistic view of events quoted above seems to have been justified. The 1st Ukrainian Front had similar quick successes, covering 125 miles on a front some 250 miles wide on July 27. On that same day its formations on the right got beyond Przemysl on the west bank of the San and cleaned up L'vov on the way, whilst on the left, having crossed the Dniestr, it captured Stanislawow and threw back to the Carpathians the Hungarian 1st and 2nd Armies, which had formed the right flank of Army Group "North Ukraine" since the end of the winter. The situation now looked very dangerous.

A few days later Konev got a bridgehead over 30 miles deep over the Vistula in the area of Sandomierz, drove on beyond the San as far as Rzeszów, more than 90 miles beyond L'vov, and on August 7 occupied the oil wells at Drogobycz and Boryslaw.

Massive losses

A Moscow communiqué dated July 25 put the German losses since the start of the summer offensive at some 60 divisions, or 380,000 killed and more than 150,000 prisoners. The figures seem acceptable. On the other hand, the figure of 2,700 tanks destroyed or captured, as the complement of 17 fully-equipped Panzer divisions, seems unlikely.

The retreat halts

From the Dvina at Vitebsk to the Niemen at Kaunas is 250 miles as the crow flies and from the Dniepr at Orsha to the Vistula at Warsaw 400; the bridgehead at Sandomierz reached by Konev's advance guard was over 180 miles from the area of Lutsk. The 1944 Russian summer offensive, carried out on the old cavalry principle of "to the last breath of the last horse and the last horseman" had therefore reached its strategic limit.

Between the Carpathians and the Narew, O.K.H.'s reinforcements, though desperate and improvised, were beginning to take effect. The 17th Army (General Schulz) filled the gap between the 1st and 4th *Panzerarmee* and the 9th Army (General von Vormann) occupied the left flank of the 4th *Panzerarmee* between the Sandomierz bridgehead and a point downstream of Warsaw. There also came into the battle from the interior or from Moldavia a good half-dozen armoured divisions, including the "Hermann Göring", the S.S. 3rd *"Totenkopf"* and 5th *"Wiking"* Panzer, and the excellent *"Grossdeutschland" Panzergrenadier*. Volume IV of the *Great Patriotic War* gives a good account of this change in the situation of the two sides:

"At the end of July . . . the tempo of the

offensive had greatly slowed down. The German High Command had by this time thrown very strong reserves against the main sectors of our advance. German resistance was strong and stubborn. It should also be considered that our rifle divisions and tank corps had suffered heavy losses in previous battles; and the artillery and the supply bases were lagging behind, and that the troops were short of both petrol and munitions.

"Infantry and tanks were not receiving nearly enough artillery support. During the delays in re-basing our air force on new airfields, this was much less active than before. At the beginning of the Belorussian Campaign, we had complete control of the air. At the beginning of

△ △ *A 76-mm gun of the 1st Ukrainian Front in action as an anti-tank weapon.*
△ *A Panther tank and a column of trucks overtake bicycle riding infantrymen during the German retreat through Galicia. The bicycle featured throughout the war as a cheap and efficient mode of transport which did not need convoys of petrol tankers. Even towards the end of the war, British airborne troops used a handy collapsible version.*

August our superiority was temporarily lost. In the 1st Belorussian sector between August 1 and 13 our planes carried out 3,170 sorties and the enemy planes 3,316."

The situation reviewed

Doubtless, and for reasons which we shall see shortly, these statements by the Soviet writers are not completely impartial. Nevertheless by August 16, soon after Model had been given the job of repairing the situation, the position on the Eastern Front can be said to have stabilised temporarily between Kalvariya and the Carpathians. In particular the 4th *Panzerarmee* and the 9th Army had managed to reduce the bridgeheads at Sandomierz (Baranow), Pulawy, and Magnuszew, but not to eliminate them completely. On the right bank of the Vistula the Soviet 2nd Tank Army suffered a defeat at Wolomin and Radzymin, a few

miles from Warsaw, which cost 3,000 killed and 6,000 prisoners together with a considerable amount of *matériel*.

This pause gives us an opportunity to put forward some conclusions on these six weeks of operations on the Eastern Front:

1. Warsaw may be 400 miles from Orsha, but it is only 350 from Berlin. So a repetition of the German mistakes which led to this victory by the Red Army would land the Russians in the heart of the Third Reich.

2. Between June 1 and August 30, 1944, Germany's land forces lost on the Eastern Front alone 916,860 in killed, wounded, and prisoners. The human resources of the Third Reich were therefore rapidly running out and would not be made up by the expedient of "people's grenadier" (*Volksgrenadier*) divisions.

3. French émigrés returning to their country after the fall of Napoleon were said to have learned nothing and forgotten nothing. Hitler's example shows that one can do worse: he learned nothing and forgot everything. The failure of the attempt on his life on July 20 would therefore allow him to indulge his despotism and incompetence to the full.

4. The fourth and last conclusion comes in the form of a question. The *Great Patriotic War* says that the forces of

◁▽ *A Wespe self-propelled howitzer. Armed with the standard 10.5-cm gun of the German artillery, the Wespe was one of the best known self-propelled guns of the war.*
▽ *Russian gunners using captured German 10.5-cm guns to supplement the fire of their 76-mm guns in a shoot in the Carpathians. Both sides used captured equipment, from tanks and artillery to boots and small arms.*

the 1st Belorussian Front arrived exhausted on the banks of the Vistula, which explains the halt in their advance: but could not *Stavka* have made up its strength with units and *matériel* already earmarked for campaigns in Rumania and Hungary so as to maintain the drive westwards?

As we are aware that a theatre of operations can only absorb as many men and as much *matériel* as can be supplied by its means of communication, we leave the last question unanswered.

Warsaw – betrayed?

We are thus brought to the controversy which arose between the West and the Soviets over the behaviour of Stalin, *Stavka*, and the Red Army towards the Warsaw rising started at 1700 hours on August 1 by General Bor-Komorowski, C.-in-C. of the Polish Home Army. We cannot imitate Telpukhovsky, who maintains a prudent silence on this subject but nevertheless devotes a page and a half of his extensive work to the liberation of the little Polish village of Guerasimowichy on July 26, 1944. In his memoirs, Winston Churchill, reporting the return to Praga of Rokossovsky about September 15, made no bones about the reasons for the tragic episode as he saw them:

"The Russians occupied the Praga suburb, but went no further. They wished to have the non-Communist Poles destroyed to the full, but also to keep alive the idea that they were going to their rescue.

"Such was their liberation of Poland, where they now rule. But this cannot be the end of the story."

Churchill was doubtless writing under the influence of the exchange of telegraph messages he had had with Stalin on the subject of Warsaw, and was remembering the help he had wanted to give by air to the stricken city and its heroic defenders. He did not know then as well as we do now about the operations in the suburbs of the Polish capital between August 1 and 4. Michel Garder, writing in 1961 after carefully researching Soviet material published after 1953, agrees in broad essentials with Churchill. "With Rokossovsky within 32 miles of Warsaw," he writes, "it seemed to General Bor-Komorowski that the arrival of the Russian troops could only be a matter of

a few days. It was the duty of the Poles to welcome the Soviets as allies and not as 'liberator-occupiers'. This was just what Stalin did not want.

"In the eyes of the Kremlin, the Polish Home Army was merely a tool of the 'reactionary Polish clique' in London whose leaders, in addition to their 'enslavement to capitalism' and their 'bourgeois chauvinism' had had the effrontery to state that the Katyn massacres were the work of the N.K.V.D.

"Having suddenly run out of steam, the irresistible 1st Belorussian Front offensive had found itself facing the German bridgehead in front of Warsaw. To get so far had, it is true, cost Rokossovsky's armies a great effort. Their lines of communication were stretched. They needed a few days' respite and probably considerable reinforcements in men and *matériel* to bring them back up to strength. But nothing, other than political considerations by the Kremlin, could justify the semi-inertia of the Soviet troops in September when they reached the suburbs of Praga."

Werth is less certain than Churchill or Garder. He seems to give credence to the pessimistic figures for the 1st Belo-

△ *German prisoners in Maidanek concentration camp march past stacks of unrecognisable human remains. The Russians showed the camp to their own soldiers and to Western journalists. Alexander Werth reported that "the Germans went through the camp, at first at an ordinary pace, and then faster and faster, till they ran in a frantic panicky stampede, and they were green with terror, and their hands shook and their teeth chattered."*

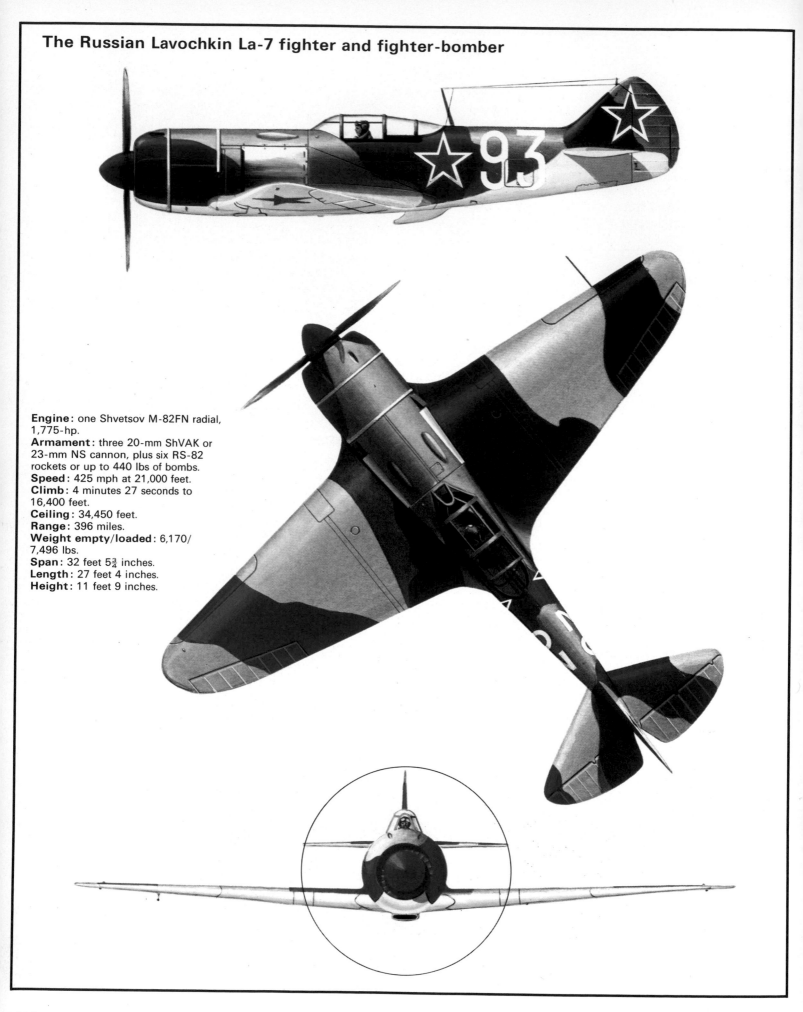

The Russian Lavochkin La-7 fighter and fighter-bomber

Engine: one Shvetsov M-82FN radial, 1,775-hp.
Armament: three 20-mm ShVAK or 23-mm NS cannon, plus six RS-82 rockets or up to 440 lbs of bombs.
Speed: 425 mph at 21,000 feet.
Climb: 4 minutes 27 seconds to 16,400 feet.
Ceiling: 34,450 feet.
Range: 396 miles.
Weight empty/loaded: 6,170/ 7,496 lbs.
Span: 32 feet 5¾ inches.
Length: 27 feet 4 inches.
Height: 11 feet 9 inches.

russian Front on August 1 quoted above from the *Great Patriotic War*. On the other hand, he does not omit the passage which refers to the defeat of the Soviet 2nd Tank Army before Praga, where it was attacked on its left flank by five German divisions, including four Panzer. It is interesting to see that he was personally involved on one occasion. Received in Lublin by Rokossovsky he recorded the following on the spot:

"'I can't go into any details. But I'll tell you just this. After several weeks' heavy fighting in Belorussia and eastern Poland we finally reached the outskirts of Praga about the 1st of August. The Germans, at this point, threw in four armoured divisions, and we were driven back.'

'How far back?'

'I can't tell you exactly, but let's say nearly 100 kilometres (sixty-five miles).'

'Are you still retreating?'

'No—we are now advancing—but slowly.'

'Did you think on August 1 (as was suggested by the *Pravda* correspondent that day) that you could take Warsaw within a very few days?'

'If the Germans had not thrown in all that armour, we could have taken Warsaw, though not in a frontal attack; but it was never more than a 50-50 chance. A German counter-attack at Praga was not to be excluded, though we now know that before these armoured divisions arrived, the Germans inside Warsaw were in a panic, and were packing up in a great hurry.'

'Wasn't the Warsaw Rising justified in the circumstances?'

'No it was a bad mistake. The insurgents started it off their own bat, without consulting us.'

'There was a broadcast from Moscow calling on them to rise.'

'That was routine stuff *(sic)*. There were similar calls to rise from *Swit* radio [Home Army], and also from the Polish service of the BBC—so I'm told, though I didn't hear it myself. Let's be serious. An armed insurrection in a place like Warsaw could only have succeeded if it had been carefully co-ordinated with the Red Army. The question of timing was of the utmost importance. The Warsaw insurgents were badly armed, and the rising would have made sense only if we were already on the point of *entering Warsaw. That point had not been reached*

△ *Soviet sub-machine gunners ford the west Bug river in the Ukraine.*

▽ *A KV-85 roars past the shattered remains of a 3.7-cm anti-tank gun during the fighting before Warsaw.*

1665

▲ Russian prisoners digging an anti-tank trench near Warsaw. Aware of the threat that the large numbers of people in Warsaw posed to their rear areas, the Germans had plans to evacuate the population of the city.

at any stage, and I'll admit that some Soviet correspondents were much too optimistic on the 1st of August. We were pushed back. We couldn't have got Warsaw before the middle of August, even in the best of circumstances. But circumstances were not good, but bad. Such things do happen in war. It happened at Kharkov in March 1943 and at Zhitomir last winter.'

'What prospect is there of your getting back to Praga within the next few weeks?'

'I can't go into that. All I can say is that we shall try to capture both Praga and Warsaw, but it won't be easy.'

'But you have bridgeheads south of Warsaw.'

'Yes, but the Germans are doing their damnedest to reduce them. We're having much difficulty in holding them, and we are losing a lot of men. Mind you, we have fought non-stop for over two months now.'"

Whilst accepting the good faith and accuracy of Werth's report, it would seem that it should be interpreted as follows: Rokossovsky and, behind him, the Soviet high command, had well and

truly got over their elation of July 26, and at a distance now of 30 days were claiming never to have felt it. However, at 2015 hours on July 15 Radio Moscow broadcast a stirring appeal to the population of Warsaw and a few hours later the Union of Polish Patriots station, which followed the Soviet line, took up the call:

"The Polish Army now entering Polish territory had been trained in the U.S.S.R. It unites with the People's Army to form the body of the Polish Armed Forces, the backbone of our nation in her struggle for independence. The sons of Warsaw will rally to its ranks tomorrow. Together with the allied army they will drive out the enemy to the west, expel Hitler's vermin from Poland and deal a mortal blow to the remains of Prussian imperialism. For Warsaw which did not yield, but fought on, the hour has struck."

And, as it was to be expected that the enemy, now cornered, would retreat into the capital, the appeal for an uprising continued: "This is why . . . by energetic hand-to-hand fighting in the streets of Warsaw, in the houses, the factories, the warehouses, not only shall we hasten the coming of our final liberation, but we shall safeguard our national heritage and the lives of our brothers."

Stalin stands aloof

On August 5 Churchill sent Stalin a request to intervene on behalf of the insurrectionists, but he was answered by scepticism: Stalin doubted, if not the reality, at least the importance of the uprising.

On August 16, when Churchill repeated his demands, Stalin expressed his conviction that "the Warsaw operation is a horrible and senseless venture which is costing the lives of a great many of the population. This would not have arisen if the Soviet Command had been informed beforehand and if the Poles had kept in constant touch with us."

However, it was not Mikołajczyk's Polish Government-in-Exile which had broken off relations with the Kremlin. Must one therefore assume that Stalin supposed that the Home Army would be deaf to the call to arms given on July 29? Surely not. Be that as it may, this led Stalin to the following conclusion: "From the situation thus created, the Soviet Command deduces that it must dissociate itself from the Warsaw adventure, as it has no responsibility, either direct or indirect, in the operation."

Stalin was not content, however, merely with dissociating himself from the insurrectionists (whom he called on August 22 a "handful of criminals who, in order to seize power, have unleashed the Warsaw venture") but also obstinately refused to allow Anglo-American aircraft to land on Soviet territory in order to refuel from their operations over Warsaw. He knew that this would severely restrict the Allies, who were attempting to fly in supplies to the defenders of the unhappy city.

No help from Roosevelt

Would Stalin eventually have given in to Churchill if Roosevelt had thrown in the weight of his authority? We do not know. What we do know, however, is that on August 26, taking into account the "general perspectives of the war", the American President refused to join forces with the British Prime Minister in a new approach to Stalin. He was doubtless influenced by Hopkins and Morgenthau. On September 2, James V. Forrestal, who had succeeded Frank Knox (who died on April 28, 1944) as Secretary of the Navy, noted in his diary:

"I find that whenever any American suggests that we act in accordance with the needs of our own security he is apt to be called a god-damned fascist or imperialist, while if Uncle Joe suggests that he needs the Baltic Provinces, half Poland, all Bessarabia and access to the Mediterranean, all hands agree that he is a fine frank, candid and generally delightful fellow who is very easy to deal with because he is so explicit in what he wants."

Warsaw's epic fight

The rest is history. The defenders of Warsaw met their fate with the most sublime heroism. Having driven the Russians back over 30 miles from the right bank of the Vistula, the Germans calmly set about the reconquest of the Polish capital with large numbers of Tiger tanks, assault guns, and little

△ *Soviet soldiers move cautiously through a state room of Razdravanu Castle, during the fighting for Iaşi.*

▽ *Know your enemy: German soldiers examine a captured T-34, taken during the fighting near the Warsaw suburb of Praga.*

Goliath tanks, a kind of remote-controlled bomb on tracks. The heaviest weapons the defenders had were of 20-mm calibre.

They fought from barricade to barricade, from house to house, from storey to storey and even in the sewers. The area occupied by the defenders gradually shrank, so that the meagre supplies dropped by Anglo-American aircraft fell increasingly into enemy hands. The repression of the uprising was entrusted to Himmler. He appointed *Waffen*-S.S. General von dem Bach-Zalewski and gave him, amongst others, S.S. police units, a brigade of Russian ex-prisoners, and a brigade of ex-convicts, all of whom had committed such excesses that Guderian had persuaded Hitler to remove them from the front.

In the second fortnight of September the Russians reoccupied Praga but remained virtually passive opposite the capital. Under these conditions Bor-Komorowski, who had had 22,000 killed, missing, or seriously wounded out of his 40,000 fighters, resigned himself to surrender on October 2, obtaining from von dem Bach-Zalewski an assurance that his men would without exception be treated under the Geneva Convention of August 27, 1929 governing prisoners-of-war.

Stalin's responsibility

From this brief summary of the essential facts it is possible to conclude:

1. The Warsaw "venture", which aroused the ire and indignation of Stalin, was sparked off by a radio broadcast from Moscow, but without criminal intent.
2. Since the Russians played down as much as possible the defeat of Rokossovsky at Praga, the will to let the Polish Home Army be massacred was imputed to an inertia which arose to a great extent from impotence.
3. Under these conditions it cannot be proved that Anglo-American aircraft taking off from Foggia could have saved the Home Army if Stalin had allowed them to land on Soviet territory.
4. But it can be stated that, by refusing them this permission, Stalin left no alternative to the insurrectionists of August 1 but death or captivity and that he did so knowingly and willingly.

The Poles will never forget.

THE
WARSAW
RISING

1. *A patrol dashes across a street in the opening stages of the Warsaw Rising. As the fighting developed they captured uniforms and equipment and began to look like a regular army.*
2. *A German vehicle captured in the early days.*
3. *After nearly a month of fighting the Home Army stormed the "Pasta" Telephone Exchange, one of the German strongpoints. Here prisoners taken on August 20 emerge from the battered building.*

"Soldiers of the capital! I have today issued the order which you desire, for open warfare against Poland's age-old enemy, the German invader. After nearly five years of ceaseless and determined struggle, carried on in secret, you stand today openly with arms in hand, to restore freedom to our country, and to mete out fitting punishment to the German criminals for the terror and crimes committed by them on Polish soil."

With these words General Bor-Komorowski, Commander-in-Chief of the Polish Home Army, proclaimed the Warsaw Rising of August 1, 1944. With the guns of the Red Army already audible on the eastern bank of the Vistula, it seemed indeed that the long-awaited moment had come to rid the Polish capital of its German overlords.

"With arms in hand"–that was the rub, for there were precious few of them. Aid from outside was essential, but at the outset it was considered inevitable. The insurgents counted on aid from the Red Army–and from the long air arm of the Western Allies. But international power politics intervened, and the men and women of Warsaw were left on their own.

No account of the Warsaw Rising, no matter how objective, can ignore this fact. In telling the story for later generations one returns, time and again, to the unmitigated heroism of an army which fought, like the French at Waterloo, "without fear and without hope".

Hope, certainly, was not lacking in the first week of the Rising.

But by August 8 an inevitable note of anxiety, of perplexity, was beginning to infuse the despatches from the stricken city:

"**August 2.** We have inflicted very heavy and bloody losses in men and motorised equipment on the enemy; we have taken prisoners. We are afraid of nothing except a shortage of ammunition . . .

"**August 3.** The initiative is in our hands. German morale has been greatly undermined . . .

"**August 5.** At present our offensive weakens in proportion to our expenditure of ammunition . . . Since yesterday morning there has been complete silence on the other side of the Vistula.

"**August 6.** I have to state that in her present struggle Warsaw is getting no aid from the Allies, just as Poland got no aid in 1939

1671

4. *General Bor-Komorowski, C.-in-C. of the Polish Home Army.*

5. *General Tadeusz Pełczyński or "Grzegorz", Bor's deputy and chief-of-staff.*

6. *A captured German half-track personnel carrier, clearly marked with a Polish eagle.*

7. *Polish soldiers receive a lecture in the field on reloading the 7.62 DP light machine gun.*

8. *A patrol of the Polish Kosciuszko Division in the fighting on the outskirts of the city. When elements of this unit, which was attached to the Red Army, penetrated the suburbs, they were heavily attacked by the Germans.*

1673

YOUR HELP IS URGENTLY NEEDED

WARSAW

fights for freedom

CHWAŁA WYZWOLICIELOM

1·VIII·1944

DO TU BRONI

W SZEREGACH A.K.

Warsaw's fight aroused the admiration of the world but inspired far too little in the way of practical aid.

9. *A typical example—an English poster which was of as much effective use as the placards of 1938 urging the British to "Stand by the Czechs".*

10. *"To Arms!"—poster calling the Warsaw Home Army forces to begin the Rising.*

11. *Moscow's myth: Warsaw's prison bars, shattered by the joint efforts of the Red Army and the Polish units fighting under its aegis.*

. . . *but even if the situation were to become critical, none the less we should go on fighting* . . .

"**August 8.** We have almost completely lost any possibility of aggressive action, owing to our remaining ammunition being used up . . .

"**August 10.** A German leaflet entitled 'ultimatum' calls on the population to leave the city in a westerly direction. From the Soviet side—silence . . . You must positively bomb us today and tomorrow and under cover of it drop maximum supplies at the points indicated . . .

"**August 12.** Today again no supplies although the night was fine; we are exasperated; we are exasperated; we demand a greater effort . . .

"**August 15.** Our possession of the town hall makes it impossible for the enemy to use the route through Theatre Square . . . Your Air Force's effort has made it possible for us to continue the struggle. Fighting Warsaw sends the heroic airmen words of grati-tude and appreciation. We bow our heads before the fallen . . .

"**August 19.** In the Old Town from morning until 1900 hrs. this was our worst day in regard to air bombing, artillery, and mortar bombardment . . .

"**August 21.** A company from the S.S. Cadet School in Poznan called up in the early days of August is taking part in the fight. The enemy's crushing technical superiority has severely tested the resistance of our soldiers and the people . . .

12. *The exhilaration of the early days. Volunteers of the Home Army swear the oath of loyalty.*
13. *In a devoutly religious nation the Church played an important part in the Rising. A priest conducts Mass on August 15, the "Day of the Soldier" commemorating the Battle of the Vistula.*

14. *Altar boys, now messengers in the Home Army, attending Mass at a school in Powiśle.*

14

15. *A horse slaughtered for food* **16**
*is dragged away to be cut up
by members of the Home Army.
As conditions grew worse
rationing was introduced in the
city.*

16. *A medical team lift a
wounded soldier onto a
stretcher. Though there were
qualified doctors and staff, the
Poles suffered from a shortage
of supplies and equipment.*

17. *Colonel Antoni Chrusciel
("Monter"), commander of the
Warsaw city district.*

August 4 1944

AREA HELD BY HOME ARMY
"DISPUTED AREA"
FORMER GHETTO
GERMAN COUNTERATTACK

MARYMONT
ŻOLIBORZ
CITADEL
OLD TOWN
PRAGA
GRZYBÓW
WOLA
SIELCE
MOKOTÓW
Vistula

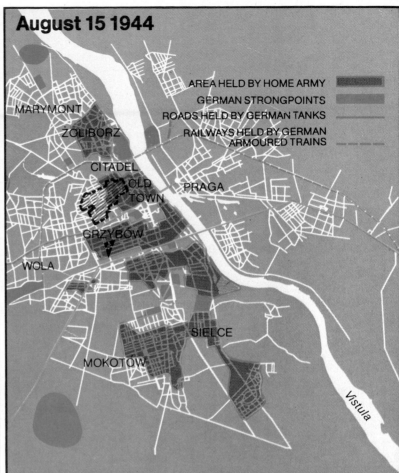

August 15 1944

AREA HELD BY HOME ARMY
GERMAN STRONGPOINTS
ROADS HELD BY GERMAN TANKS
RAILWAYS HELD BY GERMAN ARMOURED TRAINS

MARYMONT
ŻOLIBORZ
CITADEL
OLD TOWN
PRAGA
GRZYBÓW
WOLA
SIELCE
MOKOTÓW
Vistula

"**August 28.** We are now fighting for the 28th day in Warsaw. Our situation in the Old Town is difficult. We are stubbornly holding on . . .

"**August 30.** OLD TOWN: Gradual and steady loss of terrain together with the shortage of food, to some extent of water, and the desperate sanitary conditions is causing a more and more serious condition . . .

"**September 3.** Organised detachments coming to the relief of Warsaw were disarmed by Soviet forces on 28.8.44. Please intervene . . .

"**September 5.** We have again changed the seat of our headquarters. Since yesterday there has been no water or electricity in any part of the city . . .

"**September 9.** A hopeless situation. We are losing extensive terrain, we are being compressed into smaller and smaller islands . . . The receipt of powerful and immediate help by bombing and dropping of supplies will prolong our defence. Without that we must capitulate . . .

"**September 15.** During the night of 14th/15th supplies were dropped and received: a few automatic pistols and six mortars . . . after occupying Marymont the enemy rounded up the civil population and shot them . . .

"**September 20.** Wireless liaison with the Soviet Army of Rokossovsky in Praga has been established. On the western side of the Vistula a Soviet force of one battalion has landed on the bank. Contact effected.

"**September 26.** The food situation for both forces and civilians is catastrophic . . . the Rising is breaking down for lack of food . . .

"**September 30.** Our struggle is in its last agony. Today we need mainly food and equipment. Only an immediate blow by the Soviets against Warsaw can save us . . ."

"**October 1.** Warsaw has no longer any chance of defence. I have decided to enter into negotiations for surrender with full combatant rights, which the Germans fully recognise. Negotiations tomorrow . . .

"**October 4.** I report that in fulfilment of the capitulation agreement, which I concluded on 2nd inst., the troops fighting in Warsaw will lay down their arms today and tomorrow . . .

"The conduct of our troops is irreproachable. It arouses the admiration of the enemy. Tadeusz Komorowski, Lieutenant-General."

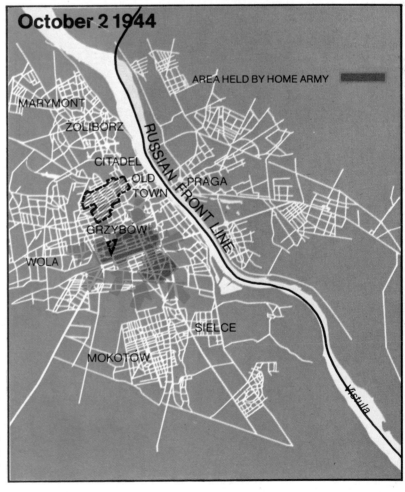

October 2 1944

AREA HELD BY HOME ARMY

MARYMONT
ŻOLIBORZ
CITADEL
OLD TOWN
PRAGA
RUSSIAN FRONT LINE
GRZYBÓW
WOLA
SIELCE
MOKOTÓW
Vistula

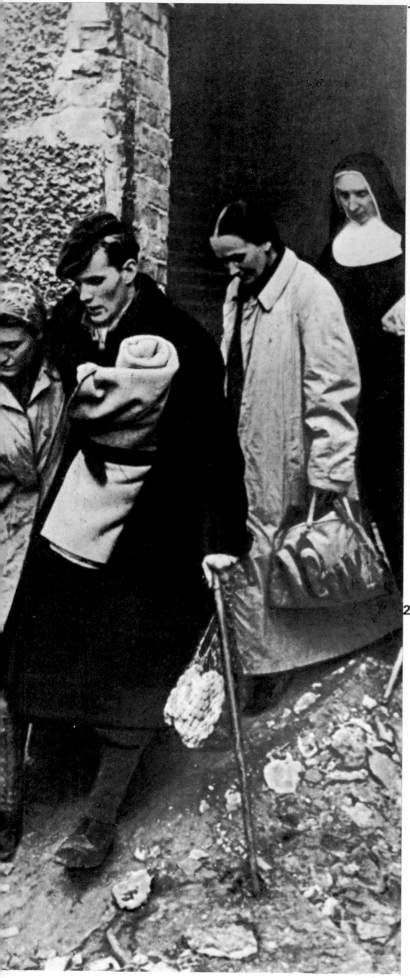

18. *With faces displaying the strain of the intense fighting, a group of civilians emerges from a ruined building.*
19. *Soldiers of the Home Army with P.I.A.T. anti-tank weapons dropped to them by the R.A.F.*
20. *Parachutes stream from weapons containers in a daylight drop by the U.S. Air Force. Near the end of the fighting the Americans made the biggest supply drop of the battle but, tragically, by then it was too late.*
21. *Barricades and shell-damaged buildings in Kredytowa Street. The Germans used tanks, demolition vehicles, and aircraft in their attacks on Polish strongpoints.*
22. *Exhausted and wounded: a group of soldiers captured in October.*

23. *As General Bor-Komorowski prepares to enter a car, his Chief of Intelligence, Colonel Iranek-Osmecki shakes hands with General von dem Bach. The Germans permitted the officers to retain their swords after the surrender.*

24. *A salute is fired over the graves of members of the Home Army.*

25. *Defeated, but not broken, the surviving members of the Army march proudly out of Warsaw with their colours flying and wearing their national armbands.*